Anonymous

Christian Songs

for the Sunday school

Anonymous

Christian Songs
for the Sunday school

ISBN/EAN: 9783337850975

Printed in Europe, USA, Canada, Australia, Japan

Cover: Foto ©Lupo / pixelio.de

More available books at **www.hansebooks.com**

CHRISTIAN SONGS

FOR THE SUNDAY SCHOOL.

Entered according to Act of Congress, in the year 1872, by BIGLOW & MAIN, in the Office of the Librarian of Congress at Washington.

To the Friends of Sunday Schools:

In accordance with what we believe to be a growing sentiment, and hoping in some degree at least, to meet the oft-repeated and earnest demand for a better class of Hymns and a higher grade of Music in our Sunday Schools, these CHRISTIAN SONGS are presented to those engaged in the good work. How far we have succeeded in supplying the want thus expressed, we leave to the judgment of others.

There seemed to be no good reason for discarding old friends and throwing aside Hymns and Tunes which have been eminently useful in years gone by, and which are dearly loved to-day. Many of these (and we have tried to select the most desirable) will be found in these pages. There will also be found in CHRISTIAN SONGS more than one hundred of the old *Standard Hymns* which have been, and to the end of time will continue to be, sources of help and comfort to the Christian soul in its longings after a brighter hope and a stronger faith. We have indicated for these hymns the tunes most widely used in connection with them.

If some of the music in this work should at first seem a little difficult of execution, we earnestly recommend perseverance in its study, feeling confident that it will abundantly repay all the time and trouble thus bestowed upon it.

CHRISTIAN SONGS are intended for the PRAYER MEETING, as well as for the Sunday School, and we hope and trust, that *there* too they will prove valuable in kindling the fires of true devotion, and bringing the soul into more loving communion with GOD.

We desire to acknowledge our obligations to Messrs. LASAR, HOLBROOK, CAMP, SHERWIN, and others, for valuable suggestions and compositions.

And now we send out our CHRISTIAN SONGS, praying that GOD may so bless their use that they shall be Christian Helpers to both old and young.

NEW YORK, *January 1st, 1872.*

THE COMPILERS.

☞ Nearly all the Pieces in the body of this work, both WORDS and MUSIC, are Copyright Property, and persons re-printing them without permission, will be held to strict accountability by the Publishers.

KEEP THOU MY WAY, O LORD.

F. J. CROSBY.

Andante, with expression.

HUBERT P. MAIN.
From "Bright Jewels," by per.

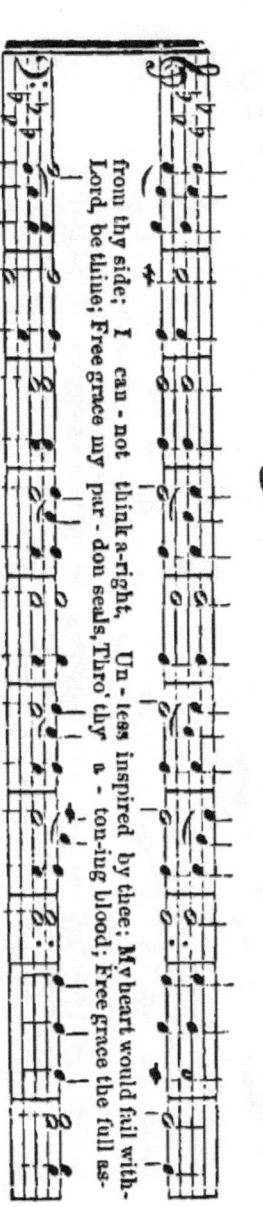

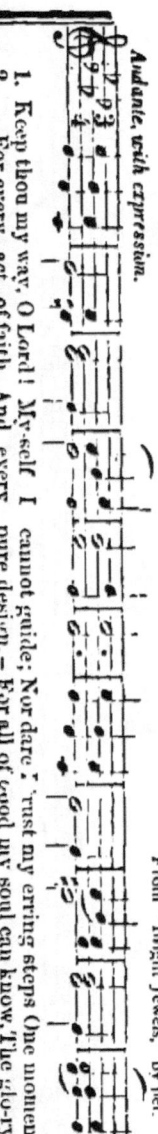

1. Keep thou my way, O Lord! My-self I can-not guide; Nor dare I trust my erring steps One moment from thy side; I can - not think a-right, Un - less inspired by thee; My heart would fail with-out thy aid, Choose thou my thoughts for me.

2. For every act of faith, And every pure design,—For all of good my soul can know,'The glo-ry, Lord, be thine; Free grace my par-don seals, Thro' thy a - ton-ing blood; Free grace the full as-sur-ance brings, Of peace with thee, my God.

3 O speak, and I will hear;
    Command, and I obey;
My willing feet with joy shall haste
    To run the heavenly way;
Keep thou my wand'ring heart,
    And bid it cease to roam;
O bear me safe o'er death's cold wave
    To heaven, my blissful home.

MY SABBATH HOME

Words by Dr. C. R. BLACKALL.
W. H. DOANE.
From "Pure Gold," by per.

"It shall be a Sabbath of rest unto you." — Lev. 16:31.

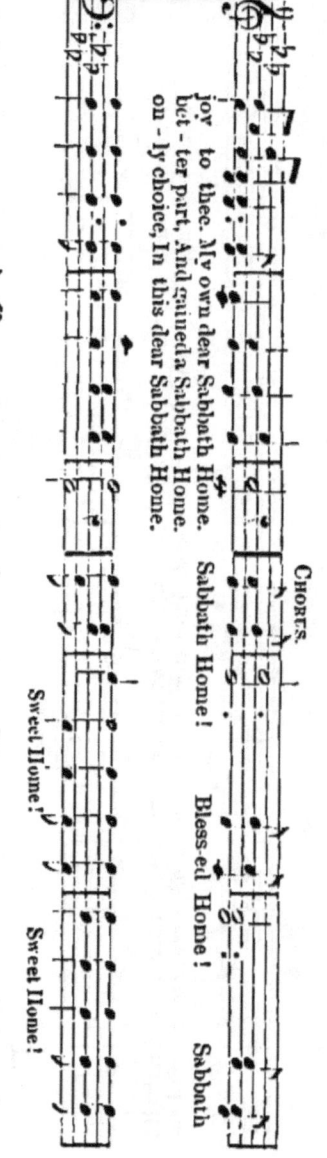

1. Sweet Sabbath School! more dear to me Than fair-est pa-lace dome, My heart e'er turns with joy to thee, My own dear Sabbath Home.
2. Here first my wil-ful, wand'ring heart, The way of life was shown; Here first I sought the bet-ter part, And gained a Sabbath Home.
3. Here Je-sus stood with lov-ing voice, En-treat-ing me to come, And make of Him my on-ly choice, In this dear Sabbath Home.

CHORUS.

Sweet Home! Sweet Home! Bless-ed Home! My heart e'er turns with joy to thee, My own dear Sabbath Home.

Sweet Home! Sweet Home! Bless-ed Home! Sabbath Home!

HOW CAN I KEEP FROM SINGING.

Rev. R. LOWRY.
From "Bright Jewels," by per.

1. My life flows on in end-less song; A-bove Earth's la-men-ta-tion, I catch the sweet, tho'
2. What tho' my joys and comfort die? The Lord my Sav-iour liv-eth; What tho' the dark-ness
3. I lift my eyes; the cloud grows thin; I see the blue a-bove it; And day by day this

far-off hymn That hails a new cre-a-tion; Through all the tu-mult and the strife, I
gath-er round? Songs in the night He giv-eth; No storm can shake my in-most calm, While
pathway smooths, Since first I learned to love it; The peace of Christ makes fresh my heart, A

hear the mu-sic ring-ing; It finds an e-cho in my soul—How can I keep from sing-ing?
to that re-fuge cling-ing; Since Christ is Lord of heaven and earth, How can I keep from sing-ing?
fountain ev-er spring-ing; All things are mine since I am His—How can I keep from sing-ing?

NEVER BE AFRAID.

WM. B. BRADBURY
From "Golden Censer," by per.

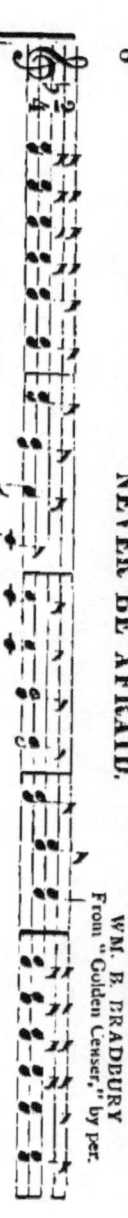

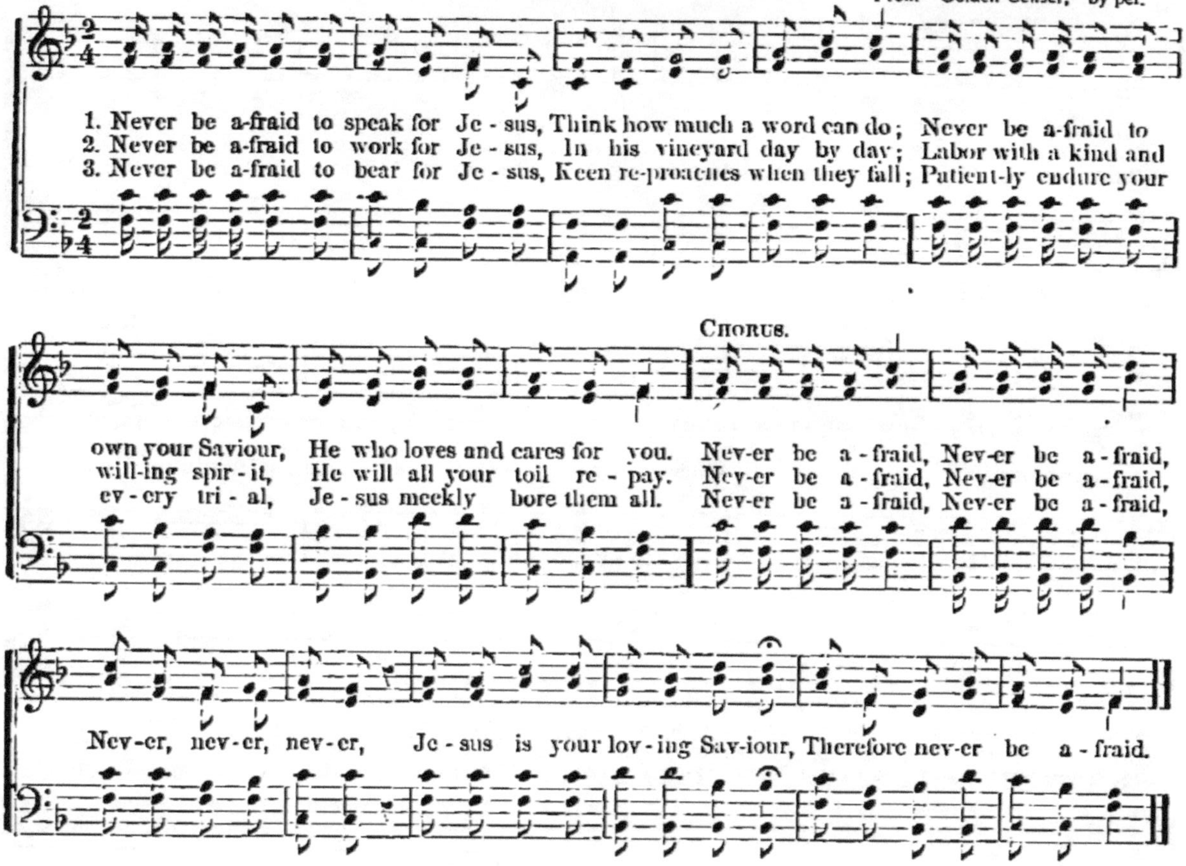

NEVER BE AFRAID. Concluded.

4 Never be afraid to live for Jesus,
  If you on his care depend
  Safely shall you pass through every trial,
  He will bring you to the end
  Never be afraid, &c.

5 Never be afraid to die for Jesus;
  He the life, the truth, the way,
  Gently in his arms of love will bear you
  To the realms of endless day.
  Never be afraid, &c.

MT. BLANC.

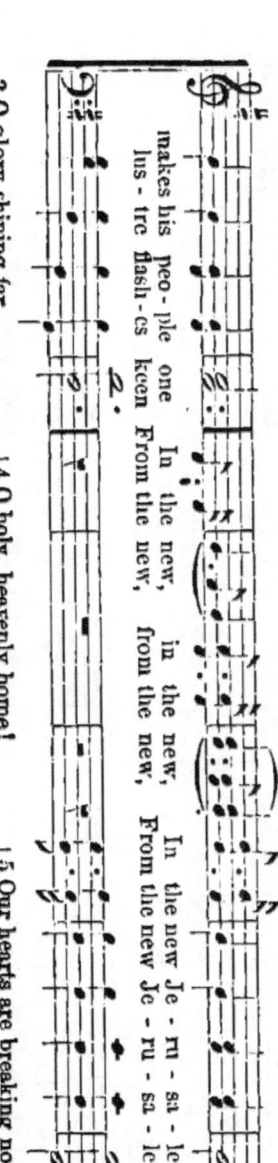

1. We are on our journey home, Where Christ our Lord is gone; We shall meet around his throne, When he makes his peo-ple one In the new, in the new, In the new Je - ru - sa - lem.
2. We can see that dis-tant home, Tho' clouds run dark be-tween; Faith views the radiant dome, And a lus - tre flash-es keen From the new, from the new, From the new Je - ru - sa - lem.

3 O glory shining far
  From the never-setting sun!
  O trembling morning star!
  Our journey's almost done
  To the new Jerusalem.

4 O holy, heavenly home!
  O, rest eternal there!
  When shall the exiles come,
  Where they cease from earthly [care,]
  In the new Jerusalem.

5 Our hearts are breaking now,
  Those mansions fair to see;
  O Lord! thy heavens bow,
  And raise us up with thee
  To the new Jerusalem.

HE SHALL REIGN FOREVER. Concluded.

Blessed Saviour, King of glory, praise to thee.

1. We will bear his glorious banner nobly till we die,
We are pressing boldly onward where our treasures lie,
He has promised His protection and His promise cannot fail,
Our hope is in His mercy, and we must prevail.—*Cho.*

2. Walking still beneath the shadow of His mighty wings,
We shall reach the golden city of the King of kings;
Oh! the pleasures that await us on that bright celestial shore,
We'll join the noble army who have gone before.—*Cho.*

11

SOMETHING FOR JESUS.

"Lord, what wilt thou have me do?" Acts 9: 6.

Words by Rev. S. D. PHELPS.

Rev. R. LOWRY.
From "Pure Gold," by per.

1. Saviour! Thy dy-ing love Thou gav-est me, Nor should I aught withhold, Dear Lord, from Thee;
2. At the blest mer-cy-seat, Plead-ing for me, My fee-ble faith looks up, Je - sus, to Thee;
3. Give me a faithful heart—Like-ness to Thee—That each de-parting day Henceforth may see
4. All that I am and have—Thy gifts so free—In joy, in grief, through life, Dear Lord, for Thee!

In love my soul would bow, My heart fulfill its vow, Some offering bring Thee now, Something for Thee.
Help me the cross to bear, Thy wondrous love declare, Some song to raise, or prayer, Something for Thee.
Some work of love begun, Some deed of kindness done, Some wanderer sought and won, Something for Thee.
And when Thy face I see, My ransomed soul shall be, Through all e - ter - ni - ty, Something for Thee.

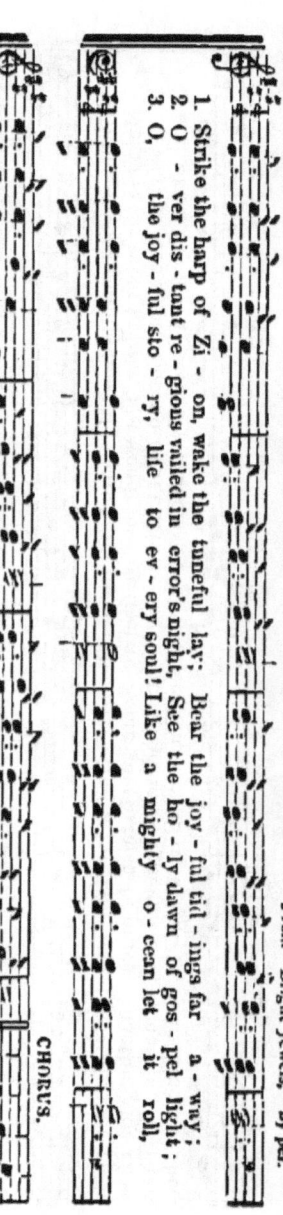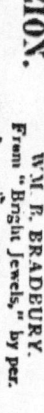

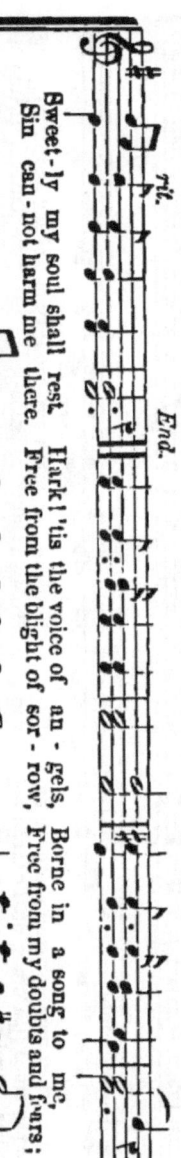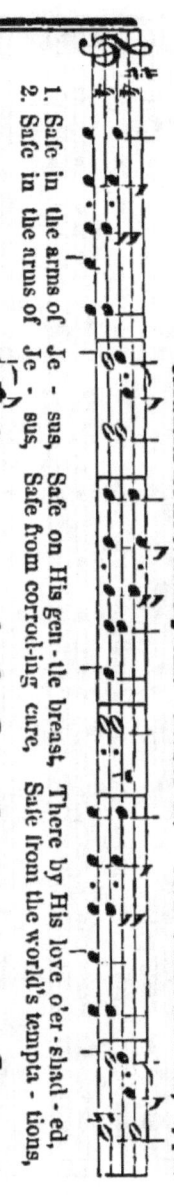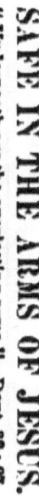

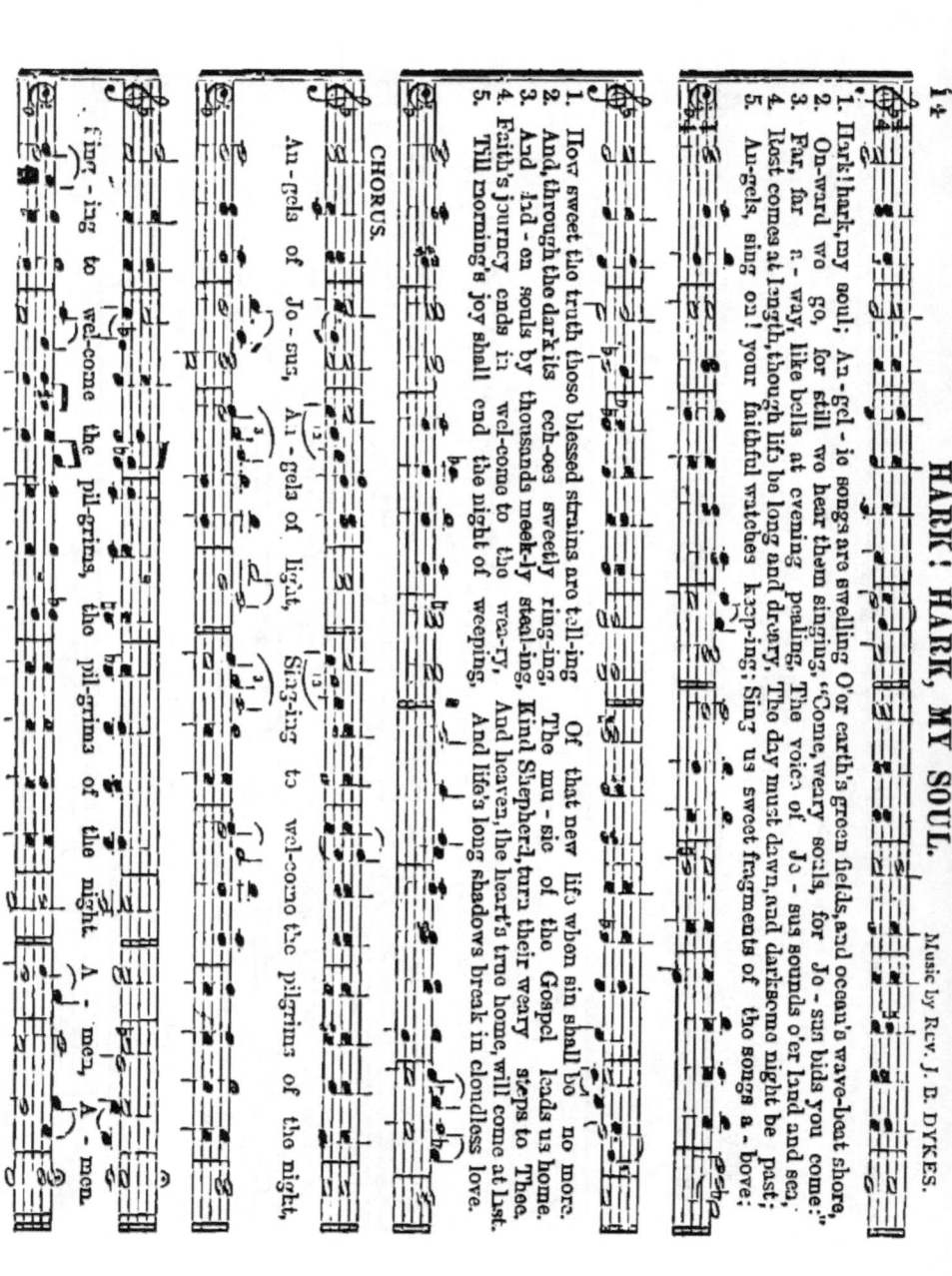

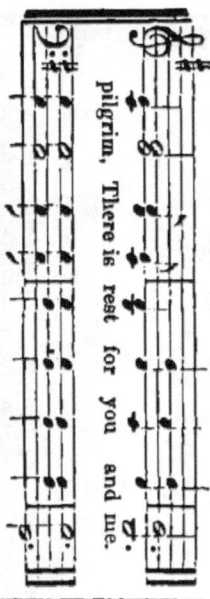

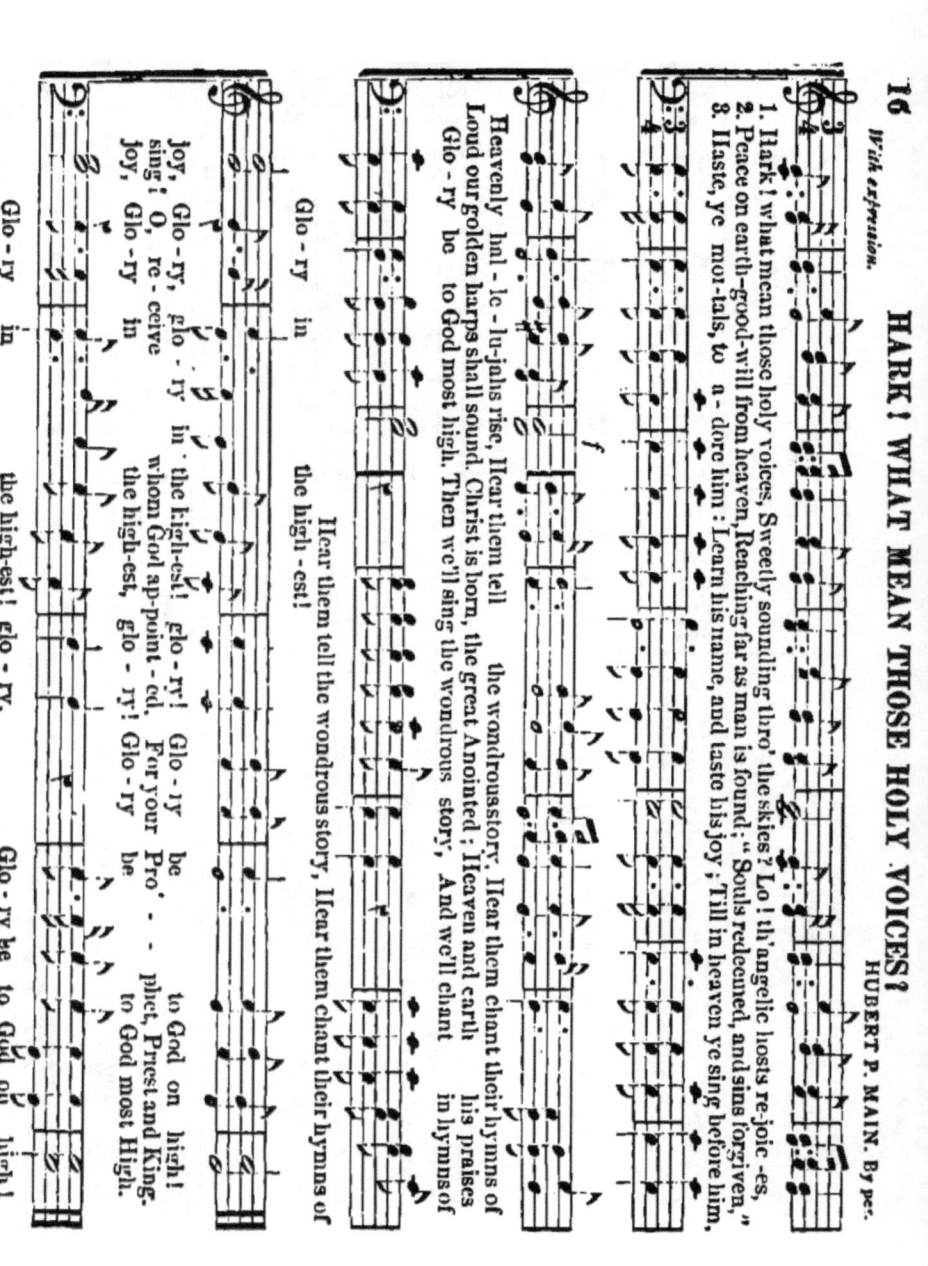

16 OUR SAVIOUR IS RISEN.

R. W. Raymond. Music by Rev. R. LOWRY. By permission.

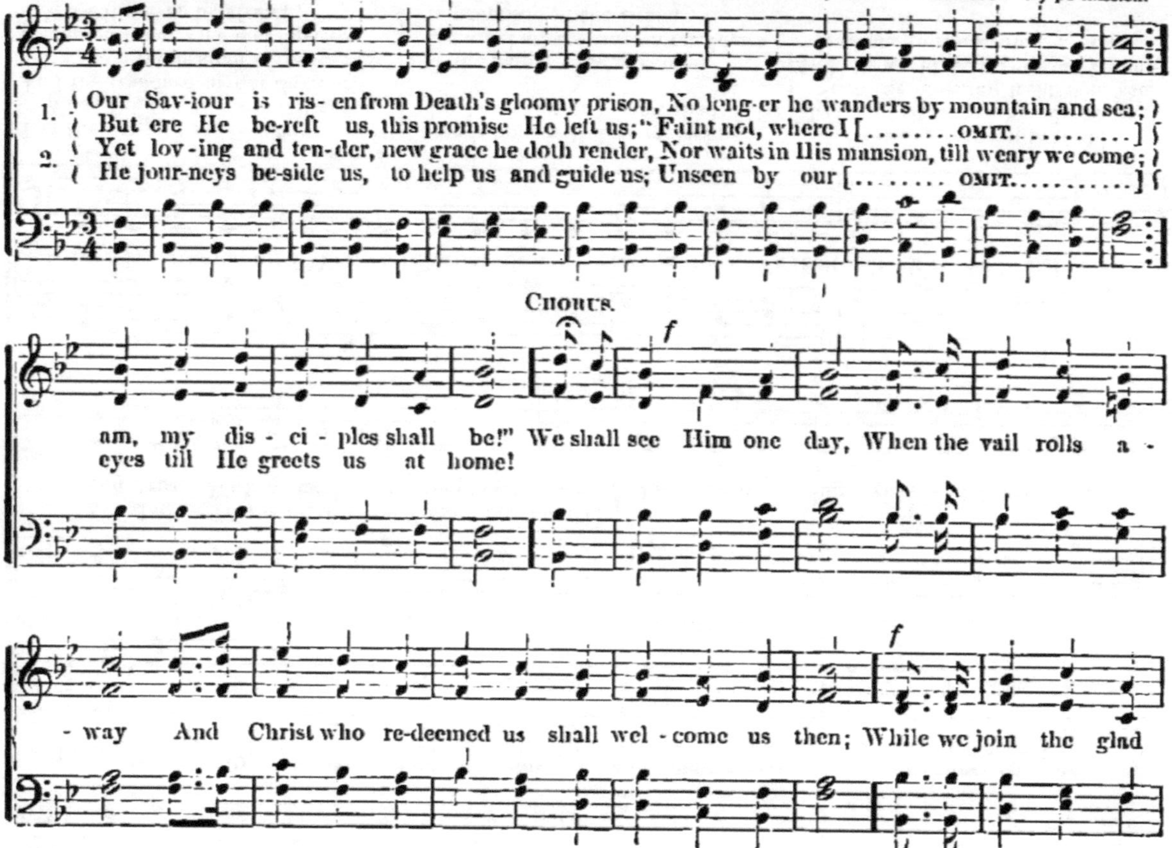

1. Our Saviour is risen from Death's gloomy prison, No longer he wanders by mountain and sea; But ere He bereft us, this promise He left us; "Faint not, where I [........ OMIT.........]
2. Yet loving and tender, new grace he doth render, Nor waits in His mansion, till weary we come; He journeys beside us, to help us and guide us; Unseen by our [........ OMIT.........]

Chorus.

am, my disciples shall be!" We shall see Him one day, When the vail rolls a-
eyes till He greets us at home!

-way And Christ who redeemed us shall welcome us then; While we join the glad

OUR SAVIOUR IS RISEN. Concluded.

throng, singing are the new song, And shout Hal-le-lu-jah! Hal-le-lu-jah! A-men!

3. Our boat often veering obeys not our steering;
'Tis Jesus' strong arm over ours at the helm!
He knows the hid dangers, to which we are strangers,
And He'll bring us safe to His beautiful realm!
We shall see him one day, &c.

4. Then while the swift river flows onward forever,
That bears us upon its dark tide to the sea,
We view without sighing the banks swiftly flying,
And joyfully haste with our Master to be!
We shall see Him one day, &c.

LORD, ABIDE WITH ME.

Words by FANNY CROSBY. S. MAIN. By permission.

1. Je-sus, Saviour! hear my call, Sin-ful tho' my heart may be; Thou, my life, my hope, my all, Lord, abide with me.
2. Lonely in a stranger land, Cast me not a-way from thee; Lead me by thy gentle hand, Lord, abide with me.

3. Thou hast died the lost to save,
Died to set the captive free;
Thou didst triumph o'er the grave,
Lord, abide with me.

4. Fill me with thy love divine,
Consecrate my life to thee;
Bend my stubborn will to thine,
Lord, abide with me.

5. When the shades of death pre'vail,
Father, let me cling to thee;
When I pass the gloomy vail,
Lord, abide with me.

6. Then, oh! then, my raptured soul
Heaven's eternal rest shall see;
There, while endless ages roll,
Live and reign with me.

BEAUTIFUL RIVER.

Rev. R. LOWRY.
From "Bright Jewels," by per.

"And he showed me a pure River of Water of Life, clear as crystal, proceeding out of the Throne of God and of the Lamb."—Rev. xxii. 1.

Cheerful.

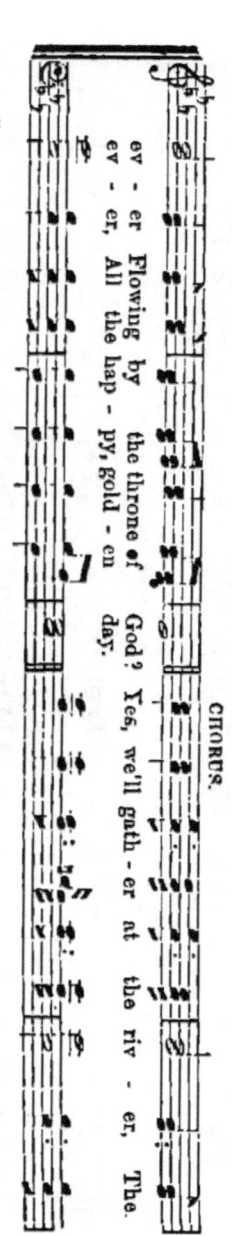

1. Shall we gath - er at the riv - er Where bright angel feet have trod; With its crys - tal tide for -
2. On the mar - gin of the riv - er, Washing up its sil - ver spray, We will walk and worship

CHORUS.

ev - er Flowing by the throne of God? Yes, we'll gath - er at the riv - er, The
ev - er, All the hap - py, gold - en day.

beauti-ful, the beau-ti-ful riv - er—Gather with the saints at the river That flows by the throne of God.

3. On the bosom of the river,
Where the Saviour-king we own,
We shall meet, and sorrow never
'Neath the glory of the throne. *Cho.*

4. Ere we reach the shining river,
Lay we every burden down;
Grace our spirits will deliver,
And provide a robe and crown. *Cho.*

5. At the smiling of the river,
Rippling with the Saviour's face,
Saints, whom death will never sever,
Lift their songs of saving grace. *Cho.*

6. Soon we'll reach the shining river,
Soon our pilgrimage will cease,
Soon our happy hearts will quiver
With the melody of peace. *Cho.*

THE BRIGHT FOREVER.

Words by FANNY CROSBY.

HUBERT P. MAIN.
From "Pure Gold," by per.

"At thy right hand there are pleasures for evermore."—Psalms 16: 11.

1. Breaking thro' the clouds that gather O'er the christian's natal skies, Distant beams, like floods of glory,
2. Yet a lit - tle while we lin-ger, Ere we reach our journey's end; Yet a lit - tle while to la - bor,
3. O the bliss of life e - ter-nal! O the long unbroken rest! In the gold-en fields of pleasure,

Fill the soul with glad surprise; And we al - most hear the e - cho Of the pure and ho-ly throng,
Ere the evening shades descend; Then we'll lay us down to slumber, But the night will soon be o'er;
In the re - gion of the blest But, to see our dear Redeem-er, And be - fore His throne to fall,

CHORUS.

In the bright, the bright for-ev - er, In the summer-land of song. On the banks beyond the riv-er,
In the bright, the bright for - ev - er, We shall wake, to sleep no more.
There to bear His gracious welcome—Will be sweeter far than all.

ritard.

We shall meet, no more to sev-er; In the bright, the bright forever, In the summer-land of song.

THE GOOD OLD WAY. Concluded.

God; 'Tis the on-ly path to the realms of day; We are go-ing home in the Good Old Way.

REVIVE US AGAIN.

"O Lord, revive thy work."—Hab. 3: 2.

1. We praise Thee, O God! for the Son of Thy love, For Je-sus, who died, and is now gone a-bove.
2. We praise Thee, O God! for Thy Spir-it of light, Who has shown us our Saviour, and scattered our night.
3. All glo-ry and praise to the Lamb that was slain, Who has borne all our sins, and has cleansed every stain.
4. All glo-ry and praise to the God of all grace, Who has bought us, and sought us, and guided our ways.
5. Re-vive us a-gain; fill each heart with Thy love; May each soul be rekindled with fire from a-bove.

Chorus.

{ Hal - le - lu - jah! Thine the glo - ry, Hal - le - lu - jah! A - men.
{ Hal - le - lu - jah! Thine the glo - ry, [Omit.............] } Re - vive us a - gain.

23

THE BRIDEGROOM COMES!

J. BAPTISTE CALKIN.

1. The Bridegroom comes! Bride of the Lamb, awake! The midnight cry is heard; Thy sleep forsake.
2. Shake off earth's dust, And wash thy weary feet; Arise, make haste, go forth, The Bridegroom greet.

Lift up thy head, The marriage day has come; Put on thy bridal robe, The feast is spread.
Sing the new song! Thy triumph has begun; Thy tears are wiped away, Thy night is done! Amen.

OH! HOW HAPPY ARE THEY.

[*Tune Rowley.*]

1. Oh! how happy are they
   Who the Saviour obey,
   And have laid up their treasure above;
   Oh! what tongue can express
   The sweet comfort and peace
   Of a soul in its earliest love!

2. It was heaven below
   My Redeemer to know,
   And the angels could do nothing more
   Than to fall at his feet,
   And the story repeat,
   And the Lover of sinners adore.

3. Jesus all the day long
   Was my joy and my song:
   O that all his salvation might **see**;
   He hath loved me, I cried,
   He hath suffer'd and died,
   To redeem even rebels like me.

HOSANNA TO THE LIVING LORD!

BISHOP REGINALD HEBER.
Rev. J. B. DYKES.

1. Ho-san-na to the Living Lord! Ho-san-na to th' Incarnate Word, To Christ, Cre-a-tor, Saviour, King, Let earth, let heav'n, Hosan-na sing, Ho-san-na in the high-est! A-men.

2. "Hosanna," Lord, Thine angels cry;
"Hosanna," Lord, Thy saints reply;
Above, beneath us, and around,
The dead and living swell the sound.
Hosanna in the highest!

3. O Saviour, with protecting care
Abide in this Thy house of prayer;
Assembled in Thy sacred name,
Here we Thy parting promise claim.
Hosanna in the highest!

4. But, chiefest, in our cleansèd breast
Eternal, bid Thy Spirit rest;
And make our secret soul to be
A temple pure, and worthy Thee.
Hosanna in the highest!

5. So, in the last and dreadful day,
When earth and heaven shall melt away,
Thy flock, redeemed from sinful stain,
Shall swell the sound of praise again.
Hosanna in the highest!

26

Mrs. H. B. STOWE.

STILL, STILL WITH THEE.

From MENDELSSOHN.

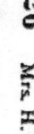

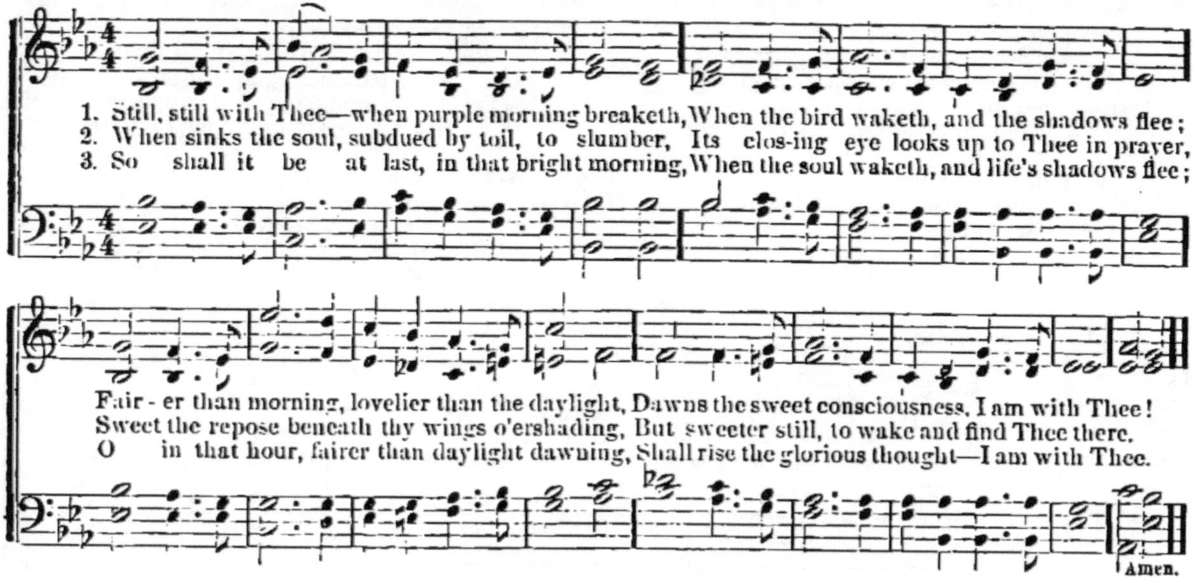

1. Still, still with Thee—when purple morning breaketh, When the bird waketh, and the shadows flee;
2. When sinks the soul, subdued by toil, to slumber, Its closing eye looks up to Thee in prayer;
3. So shall it be at last, in that bright morning, When the soul waketh, and life's shadows flee;

Fair-er than morning, lovelier than the daylight, Dawns the sweet consciousness, I am with Thee!
Sweet the repose beneath thy wings o'ershading, But sweeter still, to wake and find Thee there.
O in that hour, fairer than daylight dawning, Shall rise the glorious thought—I am with Thee.

Amen.

WE ARE BUT LITTLE CHILDREN WEAK.

C. E. WILLING.

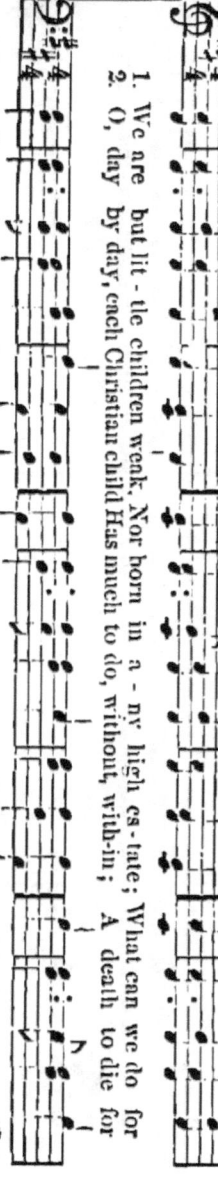

1. We are but lit-tle children weak, Nor born in a-ny high es-tate; What can we do for
2. O, day by day, each Christian child Has much to do, without, with-in; A death to die for

STRIKE! STRIKE FOR VICTORY.

Mrs. M. A KIDDER.

"Victory through our Lord Jesus Christ."—1 Cor. 15: 57.

W. H. DOANE.
From "Pure Gold," by per.

1. Strike! O strike for vict'ry, Soldiers of the Lord, Hop-ing in His mer-cy, Trusting in His word;
2. What though raging li-ons Meet us on the way! Zionward we're marching, Tow'rd the gates of day;
3. Strike! O strike for vict'ry, Heroes of the cross, Sac-ri-fic-ing pleasure, Glo-ry-ing in loss;
4. Hand to hand u-nit-ed, Heart to heart as one, Let us still keep marching Till our journey's done,

Lift the gos-pel banner High a-bove the world; Let its folds of beau-ty Ev-er be un-furled.
Ev-er pressing onward, Onward to the light, Till we reach the Jordan, With our home in sight.
Bind the helmet stronger, Tighter grasp the sword; Conquering and to conquer, Battle for the Lord.
Till we see the angels Come in glo-ry down, With the shining garments And the victor's crown.

CHORUS.

Strike! strike for Vic-t'ry, He-roes bold; Strike! till the vic-t'ry You be-hold;

STRIKE! STRIKE FOR VICTORY.

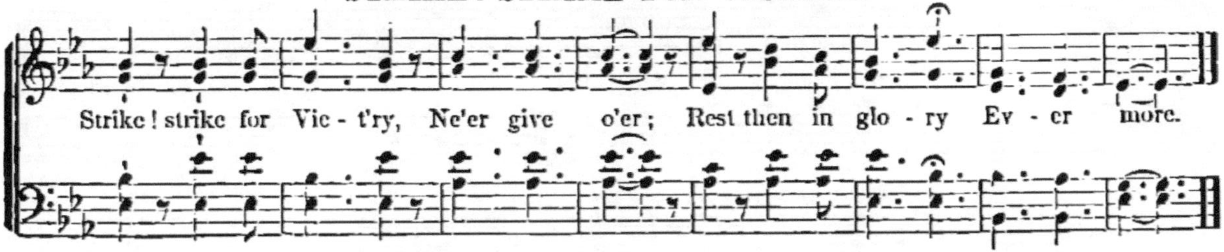

Strike! strike for Vic-t'ry, Ne'er give o'er; Rest then in glo-ry Ev-er more.

BRIGHTLY GLEAMS OUR BANNER.

JOS. P. HOLBROOK. By per

1. Brightly gleams our banner, Pointing to the sky, Wav-ing wand'rers onward To their home on high;
Cho.—*Brightly gleams our ban-ner, Point-ing to the sky, Wav-ing wand'rers on-ward To their home on high.*

Journeying o'er the desert, Glad-ly thus we pray, And with hearts united Take our heav'nward way.

2 Jesus, Lord and Master,
　At Thy sacred Feet,
Here with hearts rejoicing
　See Thy children meet;
Often have we left Thee,
　Often gone astray,
Keep us, mighty Saviour,
　In the narrow way.—*Cho.*

3 All our days direct us
　In the way we go,
Lead us on victorious
　Over every foe;
Bid Thine angels shield us
　When the storm-clouds lower,
Pardon Thou and save us
　In the last dread hour.—*Cho.*

4 Then with Saints and Angels
　May we join above,
Offering pray'rs and praises
　At Thy Throne of love;
When the toil is over,
　Then comes rest and peace,
Jesus, in His Beauty
　Songs that never cease.—*Cho.*

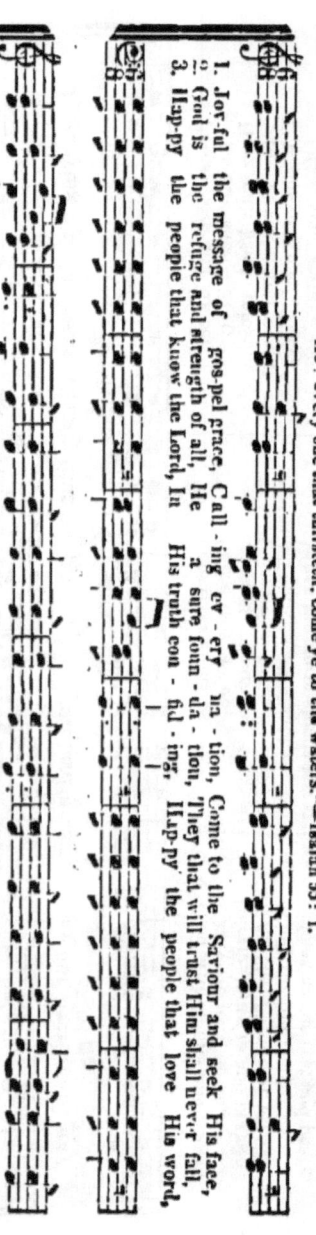

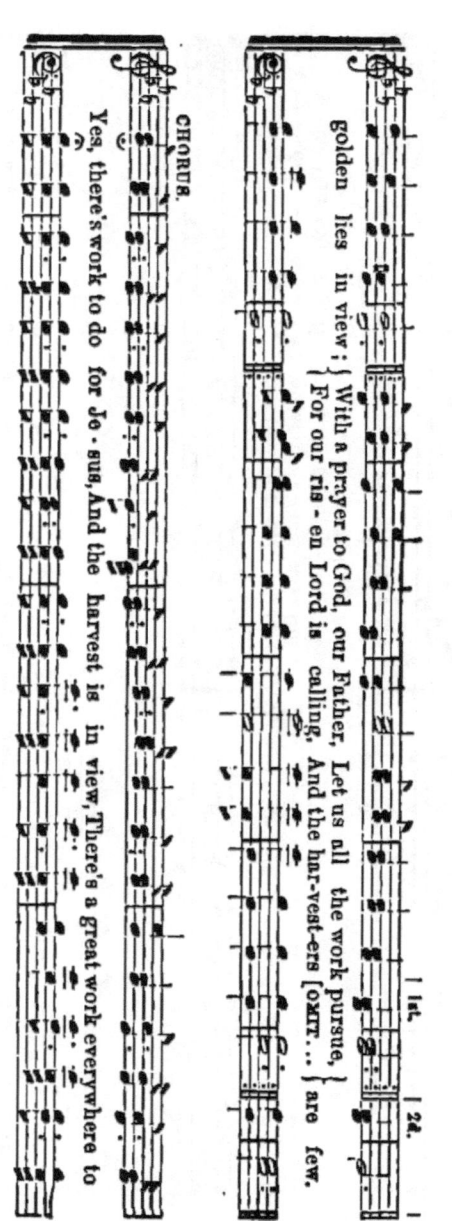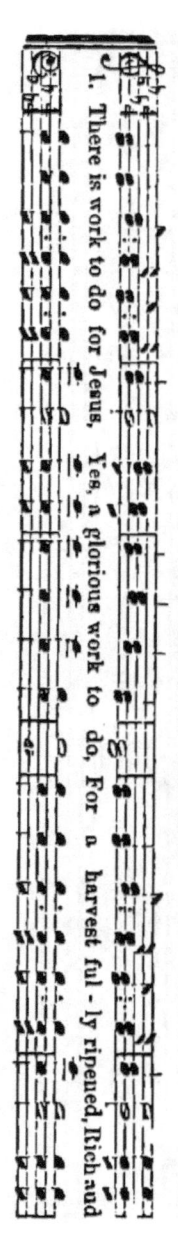

WORK TO DO FOR JESUS. Concluded.

2 There is work to do for Jesus,
And we hear the Saviour say,
"Why art standing here so idle,
At the noontide on the way?"
Even now I will accept thee;
With the rest, thy wages pay;
Go and labor in my vineyard
Till the closing of the day. *Cho.*

3 Yes, there's work to do for Jesus;
Who will answer to the call?
See! the vintage is abundant,
There is work to do for all;
God commands that we should labor,
Though the task our hearts appall;
For he claimeth our life service,
Till the shades of death shall fall. *Cho.*

CHILDREN'S PRAYER.

F. C. VAN ALSTYNE.   WM. F. SHERWIN.
From "Bright Jewels," by per.

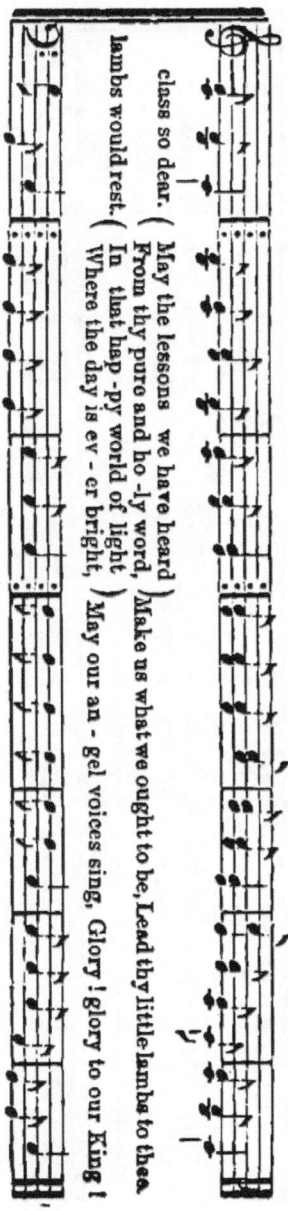

1. Gentle Saviour, God of love, Hear us from thy throne above, While we meet to praise thee here, In our Infant class so dear. (May the lessons we have heard) Make us what we ought to be, Lead thy little lambs to thee, From thy pure and ho-ly word,)
2. Jesus, thou wert once a child, Make us humble, meek, and mild. Kindly fold us on thy breast, There thy little lambs would rest. (In that hap-py world of light) May our an-gel voices sing, Glory! glory to our King! Where the day is ev-er bright,)

BEAUTIFUL EDEN. Concluded.

riv - ers, thy fountains how free! Beau-ti - ful E - den, my soul longs for the...

CHRISTMAS CAROL.

"Jesus was born in Bethlehem." Matt. 2: 1.

Rev. R. LOWRY.
From "Pure Gold," by per.

1. Let heaven with music ring, While joyous children sing Of Christ the Lord; The wond'rous story tell Of Him who loved us well, Who came on earth to dwell—The Son of God.
2. He came, a lit - tle child, Sin - less and un - de - filed. Our hearts to win; In manger low was laid That no - ble, king-ly head; The sac - ri - fice was made To van - quish sin.
3. Now, kneeling at His feet, The Christ-child humbly greet, His praise prolong; Well might that sweet birth-night With ra - diant stars grow bright, When Christ came down in light, With an - gels' song.

THE SWEETEST NAME.

"A name which is above every name."—Phil. 2 : 9.

Words by FANNY CROSBY.
CHESTER G. ALLEN.
From "Pure Gold," by per.

1. The sweet-est name in Heav'n a-bove, Child-ren sing, child-ren sing,; Our bless-ed Saviour
2. Sal - va - tion thro' His ho - ly name, Child-ren sing, child-ren sing ; His mer - cy to the
3. With those whose tri - als now are o'er, Child-ren sing; child-ren sing; With saints on yonder

crown'd with love, Children sing to - day; The Friend whose ev - er watchful care Will
world pro-claim, Children sing to - day; By Him re-deemed from death and sin, By
ra - diant shore, Children sing to - day; With mar-tyrs in the heavenly land, That

guard our feet from ev - ery snare, Who loves to hear our earn-est prayer, Children sing to - day.
Him redeemed and cleansed within, E - ter-nal life we all may win, Children sing to - day.
round His throne in glo-ry stand, With all the shin-ing an - gel band, Children sing to - day.

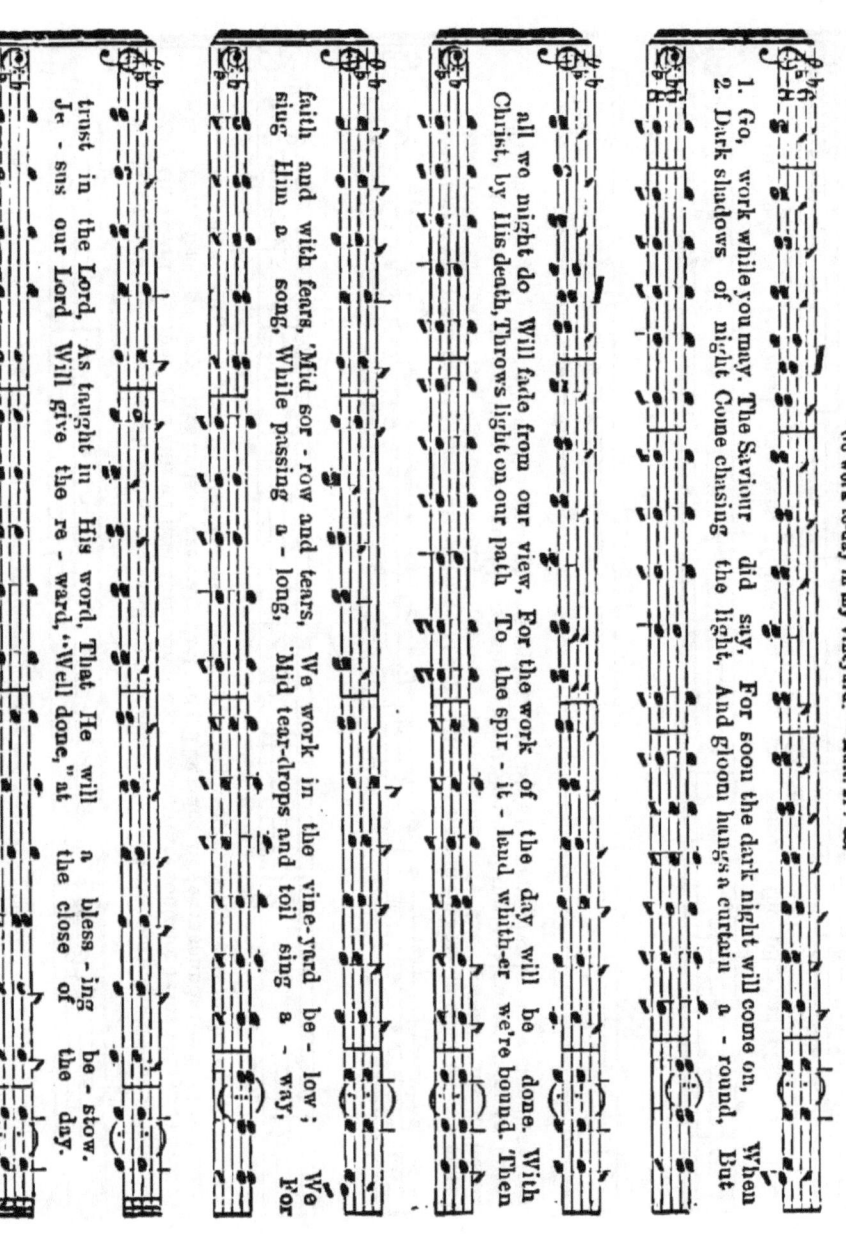

HARK! HARK! MY SOUL.

"A multitude of the heavenly host praising God."—Luke 2: 13.

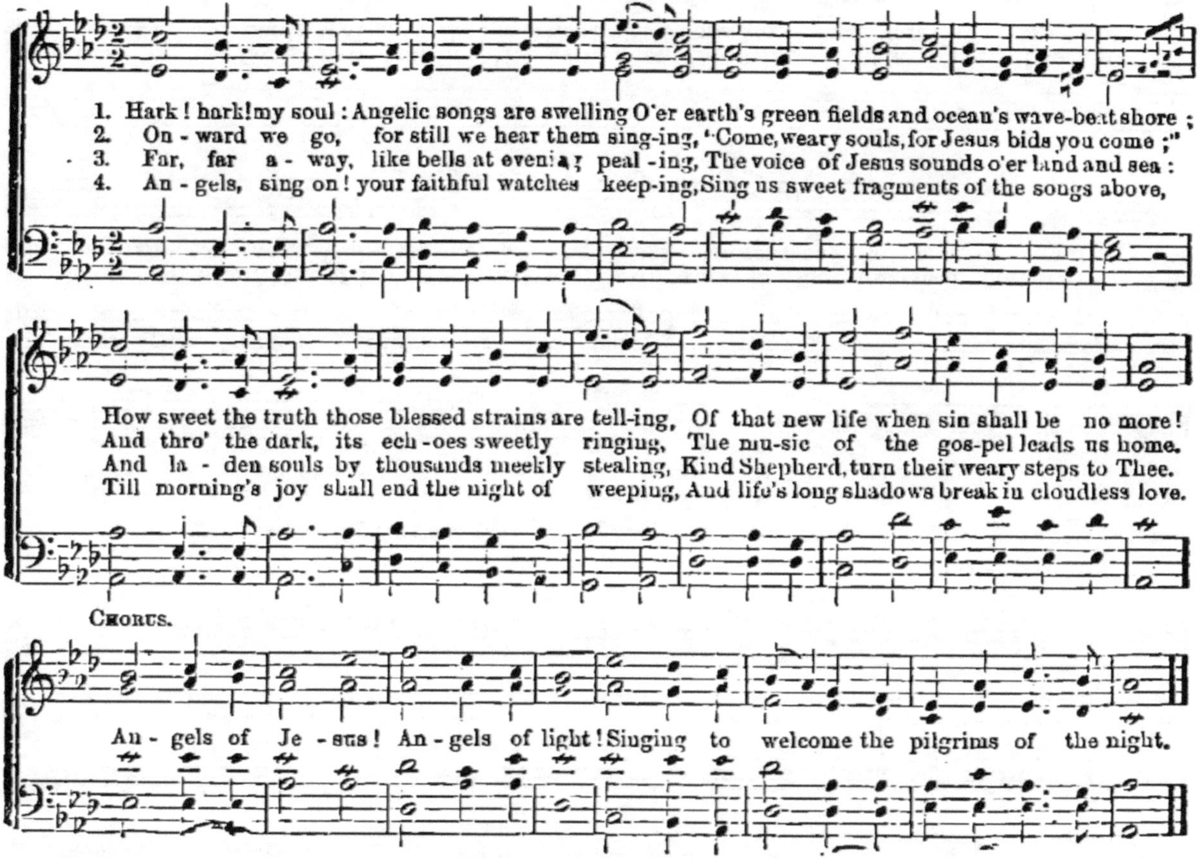

WM. F. SHERWIN, by per.

1. Hark! hark! my soul: Angelic songs are swelling O'er earth's green fields and ocean's wave-beat shore;
2. On - ward we go, for still we hear them sing-ing; "Come, weary souls, for Jesus bids you come;"
3. Far, far a - way, like bells at even-ing peal - ing, The voice of Jesus sounds o'er land and sea;
4. An - gels, sing on! your faithful watches keep-ing, Sing us sweet fragments of the songs above,

How sweet the truth those blessed strains are tell-ing, Of that new life when sin shall be no more!
And thro' the dark, its ech-oes sweetly ringing, The mu-sic of the gos-pel leads us home.
And la - den souls by thousands meekly stealing, Kind Shepherd, turn their weary steps to Thee.
Till morning's joy shall end the night of weeping, And life's long shadows break in cloudless love.

CHORUS.

An - gels of Je - sus! An - gels of light! Singing to welcome the pilgrims of the night.

SUNDAY SCHOOL VOLUNTEER SONG. Concluded.

2 We are marching on, our Captain ever near,
Will protect us still, His gentle voice we hear;
Let the foe advance, we'll never, never fear,
For we'll work till Jesus calls.
Then awake, awake, our happy, happy songs,
We will shout for joy, and gladly march along;
In the Lord of Hosts let every heart be strong,
While we work till Jesus calls.—*Cho*

3 We are marching on the straight and narrow way,
That will lead to life and everlasting day,
To the smiling fields that never will decay,
But we'll work till Jesus calls.
We are marching on and pressing toward the prize,
To a glorious crown beyond the glowing skies,
To the radiant fields where pleasure never dies,
And we'll work till Jesus calls.—*Cho*

MORE LOVE TO THEE, O CHRIST.

"Continue ye in my love." John 15: 9.

Words by MRS. E. PRENTISS.
W. H. DOANE.
From "Songs of Devotion," by per.

1. More love to Thee, O Christ! More love to Thee; Hear Thou the prayer I make On bend-ed knee;
   This is my earnest plea, More love, O Christ, to Thee, More love, O Christ, to Thee! More love to Thee!

2. Once earthly joy I craved, Sought peace and rest; Now Thee a-lone I seek, Give what is best;
   This all my prayer shall be, More love, O Christ, to Thee, More love, O Christ, to Thee! More love to Thee!

3. Let sorrow do its work, Send grief and pain; Sweet are Thy messengers, Sweet their re-frain,
   When they can sing with me,—More love, O Christ, to Thee, More love, O Christ, to Thee! More love to Thee!

4. Then shall my latest breath, Whisper Thy praise; This be the part-ing cry My heart shall raise;
   This still its prayer shall be: More love, O Christ, to Thee, More love, O Christ, to Thee! More love to Thee!

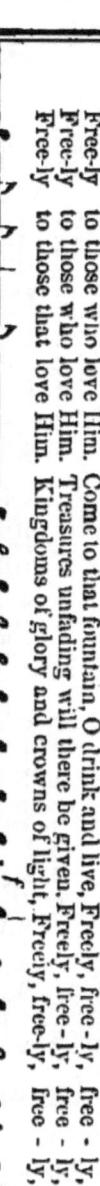

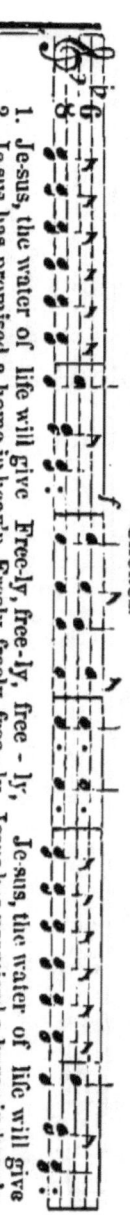

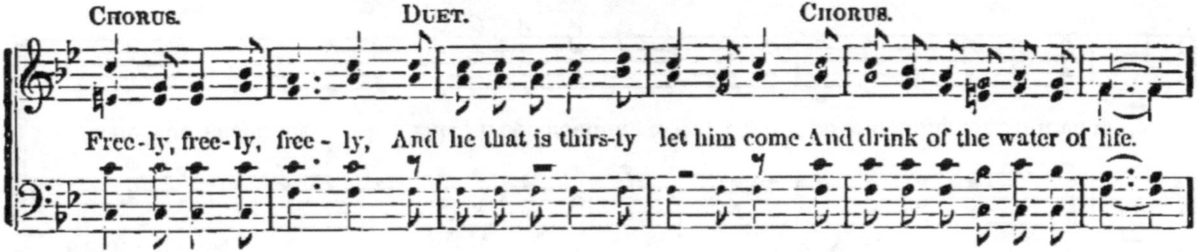

THE WATER OF LIFE. Concluded.

CHORUS.

DUET.

Free-ly, free-ly, free-ly, And he that is thirs-ty let him come And drink of the water of life.

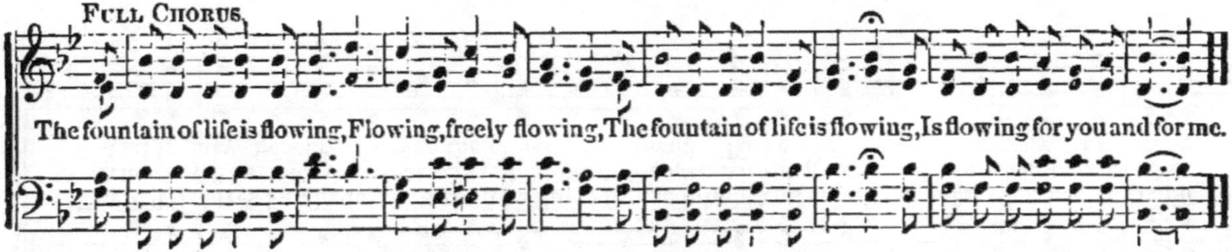

CHORUS.

FULL CHORUS.

The fountain of life is flowing, Flowing, freely flowing, The fountain of life is flowing, Is flowing for you and for me.

THE LITTLE WANDERER.

WM. B. BRADBURY.
From "Golden Censer," by per.

1. Jesus to thy dear arms I flee, I have no other help but thee; For thou dost suffer me to come, O take a little wand'rer home,

D. S. O take a lit-tle wand'rer home.

2. Jesus, I'll try my cross to bear,
I'll follow thee and never fear;
From thy dear fold I would not roam;
O take a little wanderer home,

3. Jesus, I cannot see thee here,
Yet still I know thou'rt very near;
O say my sins are all forgiven,
And I shall dwell with thee in heaven.

4. And now, dear Jesus, I am thine,
O be thou ever, ever mine,
And let me never, never roam
From thee, the little wanderer's home.

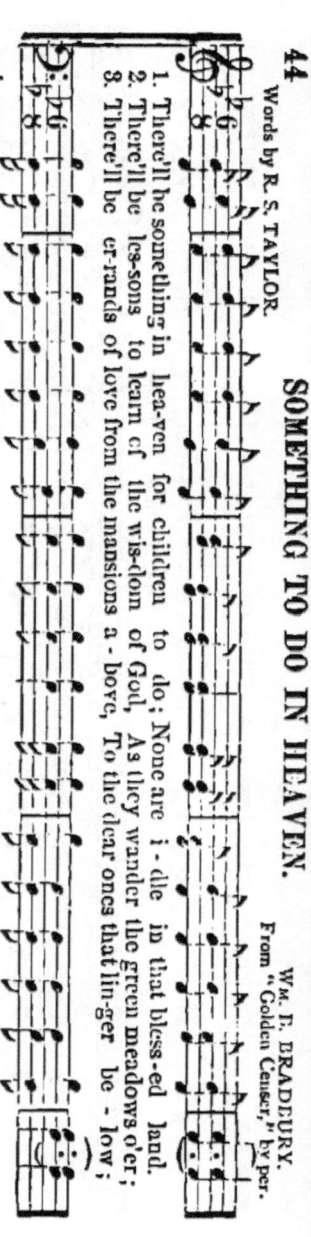

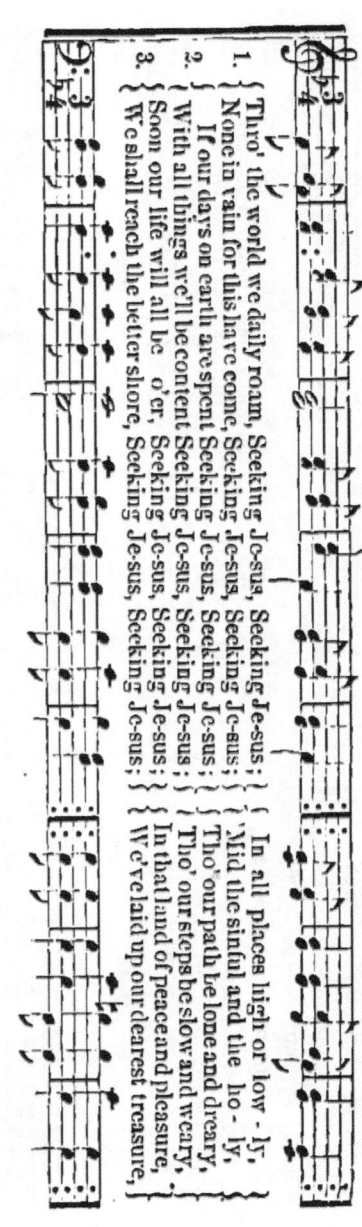

SOMETIMES A LIGHT SURPRISES.

JOHN HULLAH. 1867.

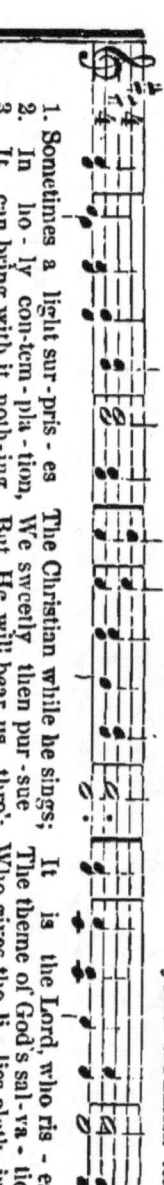
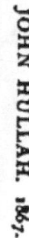

1. Sometimes a light sur-pris-es The Christian while he sings; It is the Lord, who ris-es
2. In ho-ly con-tem-pla-tion, We sweetly then pur-sue The theme of God's sal-va-tion,
3. It can bring with it noth-ing, But He will bear us thro'; Who gives the li-lies cloth-ing,

With heal-ings in His wings: When comforts are de-clin-ing, He grants the soul a-gain
And find it ev-er new: Set free from pre-sent sor-row, We cheerful-ly can say,
Will clothe His people too: Be-neath the spreading heav-ens, No crea-ture but is fed;

A season of clear shining, To cheer it af-ter rain. A-men.
Let the unknown to-morrow Bring with it what it may.
And He who feeds the ravens Will give His children bread.

4.

Though vine nor fig-tree neither,
Their wonted fruit should bear,
Though all the fields should wither,
Nor flocks nor herds be there;
Yet God the same abiding,
His praise shall tune my voice,
For while in Him confiding,
I cannot but rejoice. Amen.

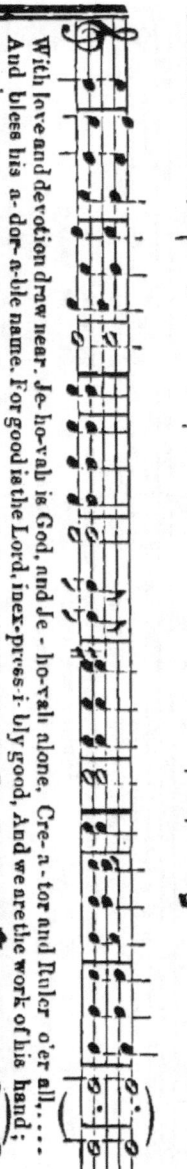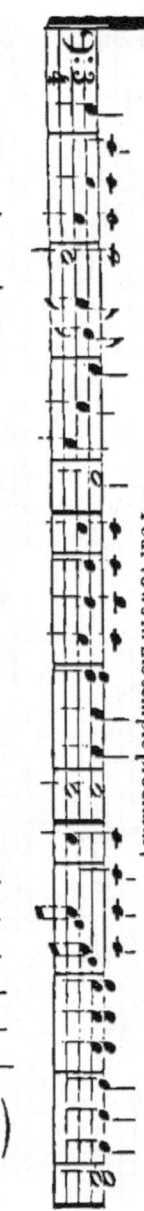

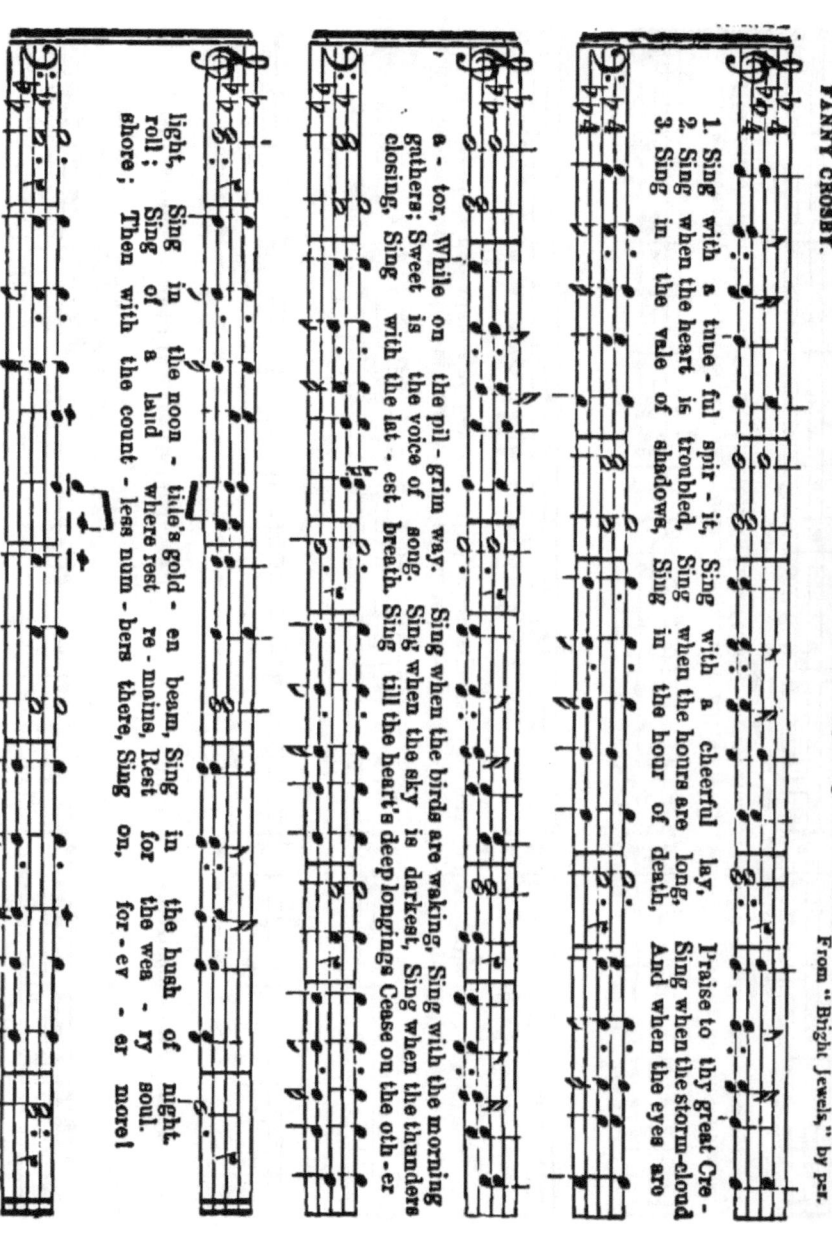

EVENTIDE.

Arr. by WM. H. MONK.

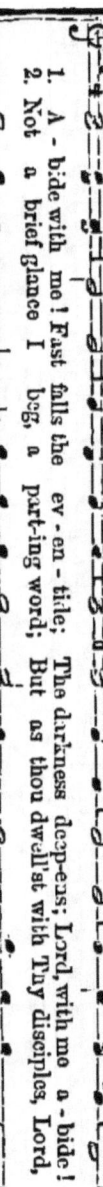

1. A-bide with me! Fast falls the ev-en-tide; The darkness deepens; Lord, with me a-bide!
2. Not a brief glance I beg, a part-ing word; But as thou dwell'st with Thy disciples, Lord,

When oth-er help-ers fail, and comforts flee, Help of the helpless, O a-bide with me! A-men.
Fa-mil-iar, con-des-cend-ing, patient, free, Come, not to sojourn, but a-bide with me!

3 Come not in terrors, as the King of kings,
But kind and good, with healing in Thy wings;
Tears for all woes, a heart for every plea:
Come, Friend of sinners, thus abide with me!

4 Thou on my head in early youth didst smile,
And, though rebellious and perverse meanwhile,
Thou hast not left me, oft as I left Thee:
On to the close, O Lord, abide with me!

5 I need Thy presence every passing hour;
What but Thy grace can foil the tempter's power?
Who like Thyself my guide and stay can be?
Through cloud and sunshine, O abide with me!

6 Hold Thou Thy cross before my closing eyes,
Shine through the gloom, and point me to the skies;
Heaven's morning breaks, and earth's vain shadows flee;
In life, in death, O Lord, abide with me! Amen.

THE BRIGHT CROWN. 52 Trio.

1 Ye valiant soldiers of the cross,
Ye happy praying band,
Tho' in this world you suffer loss,
You'll reach fair Canaan's land.

CHORUS.

Let us never mind the scoffs nor the frowns of the world,
For we've all got the cross to bear;
It will only make the crown the brighter to shine,
When we have the crown to wear.

2 All earthly pleasures we'll forsake,
For heaven appears in view,
In Jesus' strength we'll undertake
To light our passage through.—Cho.

3 O what a glorious shout there'll be,
When we arrive at home,
Our friends and Jesus we shall see,
And God shall say, "Well done."—Cho.

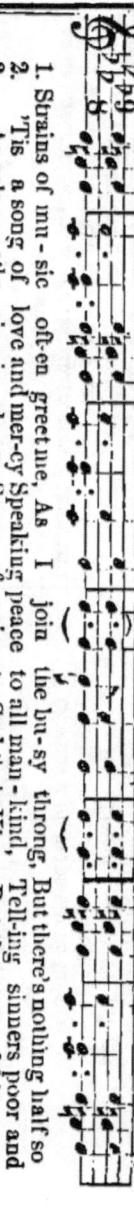

52. A LIGHT IN THE WINDOW. Song and Chorus.

Words by LUCIUS HART.

Wm. B. BRADBURY.

From "Golden Censer," by per.

1. There's a light in the win-dow for thee, broth-er, There's a light in the win-dow for thee;
2. There's a crown, and a robe, and a palm, broth-er, When from toil and from care you are free;

A dear one has moved to the man-sions a-bove, There's a light in the win-dow for thee.
The Sav-iour has gone to pre-pare you a home, With a light in the win-dow for thee.

CHORUS.

A mansion in heaven we see, And a light in the window for thee; A mansion in heaven we see,

And a light in the window for thee.

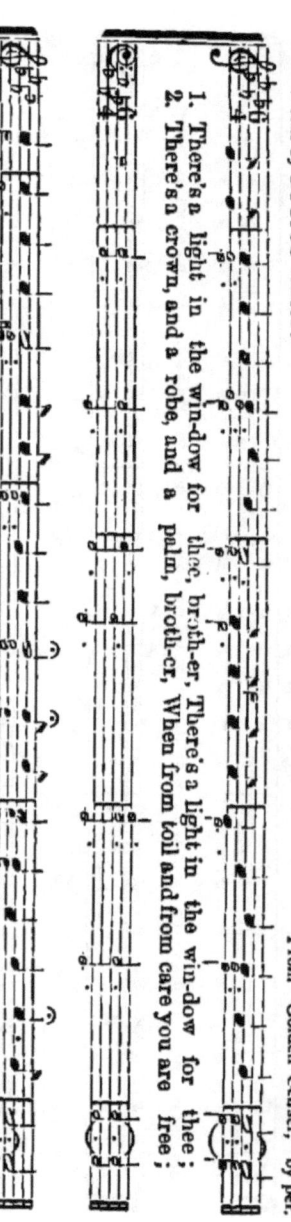

3 O watch, and be faithful, and pray, brother,
All your journey o'er life's troubled sea,
Though afflictions assail you, and storms beat severe,
There's a light in the window for thee.—Cho.

4 Then on, perseveringly on, brother,
Till from conflict and suffering free,
Bright angels now beckon you over the stream,
There's a light in the window for thee.—Cho.

SHALL WE ANCHOR.

Words by JOSEPHINE POLLARD.
W. H. DOANE.
From "Bright Jewels," by per.

1. Shall we anchor in the har-bor, When our journey's o'er; Shall we meet our blessed Sav-iour,
2. Shall we stem the surging billows, And the heaving tide; Shall we reach that peaceful ha-ven,

CHORUS.

On that hap-py gol-den shore? Yes, we'll anchor in the har-bor, When our tri-al days are
Where the ho-ly ones a-bide?

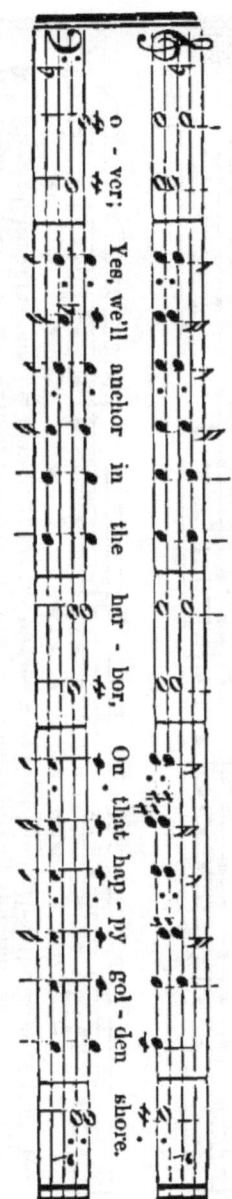

o - ver; Yes, we'll anchor in the har - bor, On that hap - py gol - den shore.

3 O, the skies are never clouded,
  In that happy land;
And a splendor gleams upon us,
  As we near the golden strand.—Cho.

4 We are sailing, we are sailing
  To that golden shore,
And we'll anchor in the harbor,
  Where we'll rest forever more.—Cho.

WHY WEEPEST THOU?

Mrs ANNIE S. HAWKS.

Rev. R LOWRY.
From "Bright Jewels," by per.

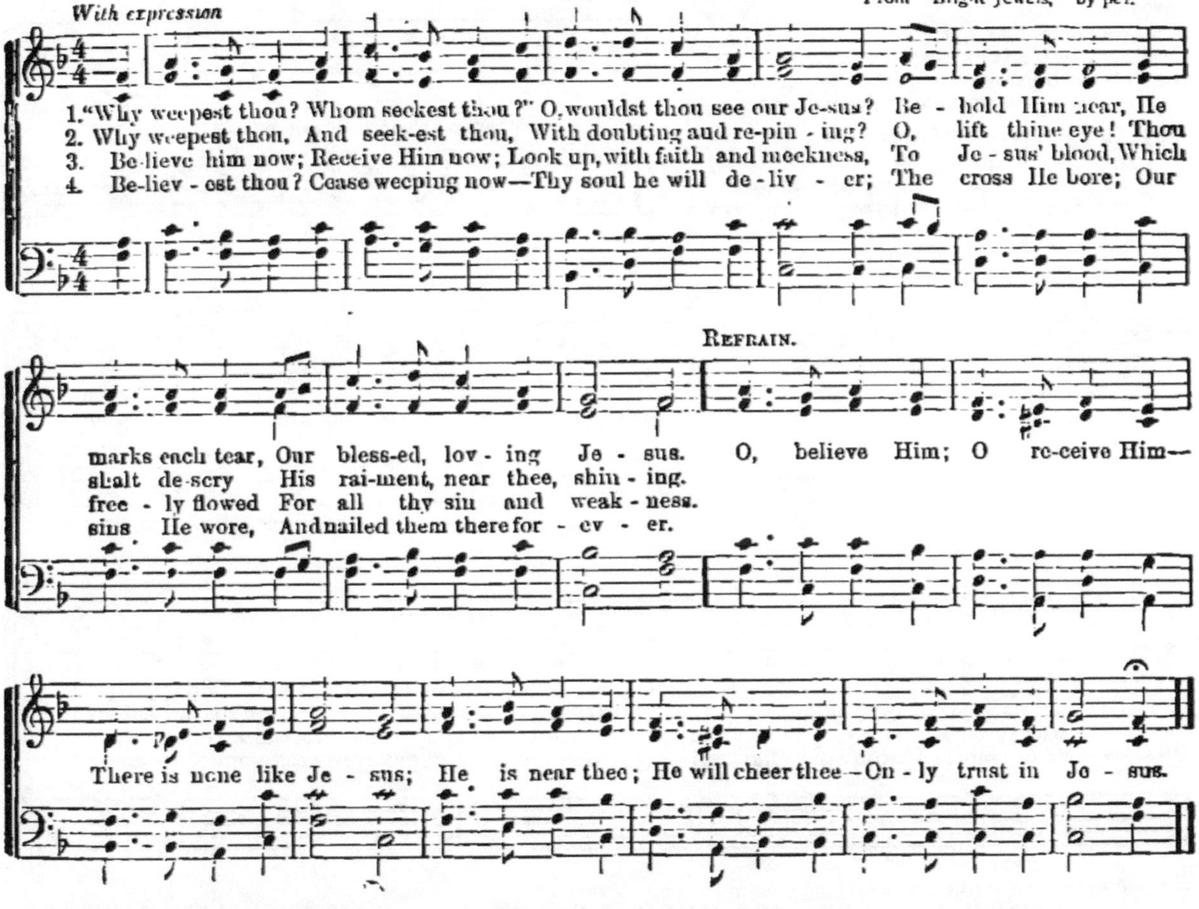

# 58. TO JESUS I WILL GO.

Words by FANNY VANALSTYNE.
W. H. DOANE.
From "Bright Jewels," by per.

1. There's a gentle voice within calls away, (calls away,) 'Tis a warning I have heard o'er and o'er; (o'er and o'er,)
But my heart is melted now, I o-bey; (I obey;) From my Saviour I will wander no [Our.............
2. He has promised all my sins to forgive, (to forgive,) If I ask in simple faith for his love; (for his love,)
In his holy word I learn how to live, (how to live,) And to labor for his kingdom a - [Our.............

|| Chorus.

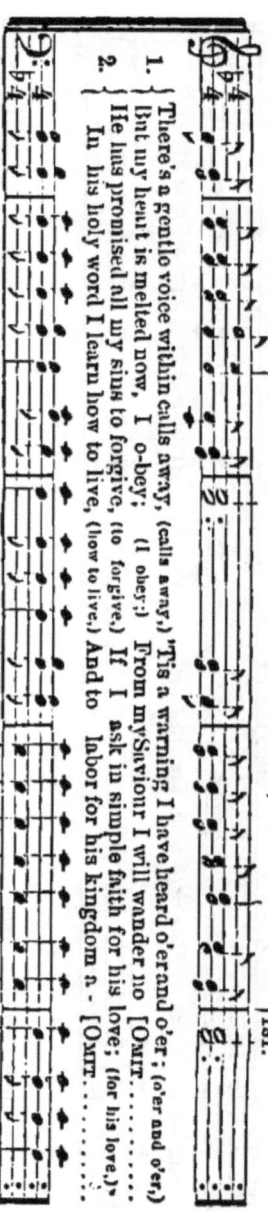

more.   Yes, I will go; yes, I will go; To Je-sus I will go and be saved;   Yes, I will go;
bove.

2d.

Yes, I will go; To Jesus I will go and be saved.

3 I will try to bear the cross in my youth,
  And be faithful to its cause till I die;
  If with cheerful step I walk in the truth,
  I shall wear a starry crown by and by.—*Cho.*

4 Still the gentle voice within calls away,
  And its warning I have heard o'er and o'er;
  But my heart is melted now, I obey;
  From my Saviour I will wander no more.
  —*Cho.*

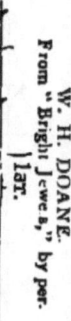

JESUS, HOLY, UNDEFILED.

Rev. J. B. DYKES.

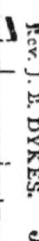

1. Je-sus, ho-ly, un-de-filed, Lis-ten to a lit-tle child, Thou hast sent the glorious light, Chasing far the
2. Thou hast sent the sun to shine, O'er this glorious world of Thine, Warmth to give, and pleasant glow, On each tender
3. Now the lit-tle bird's a-rise, Chirp-ing gai-ly in the skies; There their tin-y voic-es raise, In the ear-ly
4. Thou by whom the birds are fed, Give to me my dai-ly bread; And Thy Ho-ly Spir-it give, Without Whom I

si-lent night.
flow'r he-low.
songs they raise.
can-not live. A-men.

5.
Make me, Lord, obedient, mild,
As becomes a little child,
All day long, in every way,
Teach me what to do and say.

6.
Help me never to forget,
That in Thy great book is set,
All that children think and say,
For the awful Judgment Day.

7.
Let me never say a word
That will make Thee angry, Lord,
Help me so to live in love,
As Thine angels do above.

8.
Make me, Lord, in work and play,
Thine more truly every day,
And when Thou at last shalt come,
Take me to Thy heavenly home.

SWEET HOUR OF PRAYER. L. M. Double.

1.
Sweet hour of prayer! sweet hour of prayer!
That calls me from a world of care,
And bids me at my Father's throne,
Make all my wants and wishes known:
In seasons of distress and grief,
My soul has often found relief,
And oft escaped the tempter's snare,
By thy return, sweet hour of prayer.

2.
Sweet hour of prayer! sweet hour of prayer!
Thy wings shall my petition bear,
To Him whose truth and faithfulness,
Engage the writing soul to bless;
And since He bids me seek His face,
Believe His word, and seek His grace,
I'll cast on Him my every care,
And wait for thee, sweet hour of prayer.

3.
Sweet hour of prayer! sweet hour of prayer!
May I thy consolation share;
Till, from Mount Pisgah's lofty height,
I view my home, and take my flight:
This robe of flesh I'll drop, and rise
To seize the everlasting prize;
And shout, while passing through the air,
Farewell, farewell, sweet hour of prayer.

THERE IS LIFE FOR A LOOK.

Rev. E. G. TAYLOR.
From "Bright Jewels," by per.

1. There is Life for a Look at the cru-ci-fied one, There is life at this moment for thee, Then look, sinner, look un-to Him and be saved, Unto Him who was united to the tree. Look! Look! Look and

REFRAIN.

Live! There is life for a look at the cru-ci-fied one, There is life at this mo-ment for thee.

2 Oh why was He there as the bearer of sin,
   If on Jesus thy guilt was not laid?
  Oh why, from his side, flowed the sin cleansing blood,
   If his dying thy debt has not paid?
      Look! Look! Look, &c.

3 It is not thy tears of repentance, and prayers
   But the *Blood* that atones for thy soul.
  On him, then, who shed it, thou mayest at once,
   Thy weight of iniquities roll.
      Look! Look! Look, &c.

4 Then doubt not thy welcome, since God has declared
   "There remaineth no more to be done;"
  That once in the end of the world, he appeared,
   And completed the work he begun.
      Look! Look! Look, &c.

5 Then take with rejoicing from Jesus at once,
   The life everlasting he gives,
  And know, with assurance, thou never canst die,
   Since Jesus thy righteousness lives.
      Look! Look! Look, &c.

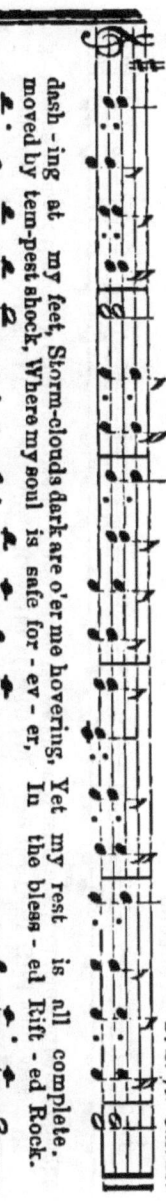

SOUND THE BATTLE CRY!

Words and Music by WM. F. SHERWIN.
From "Bright Jewels," by per.

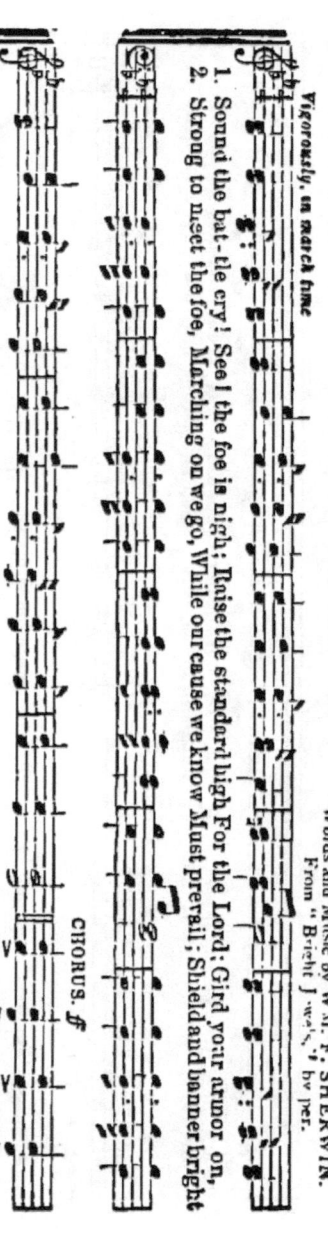

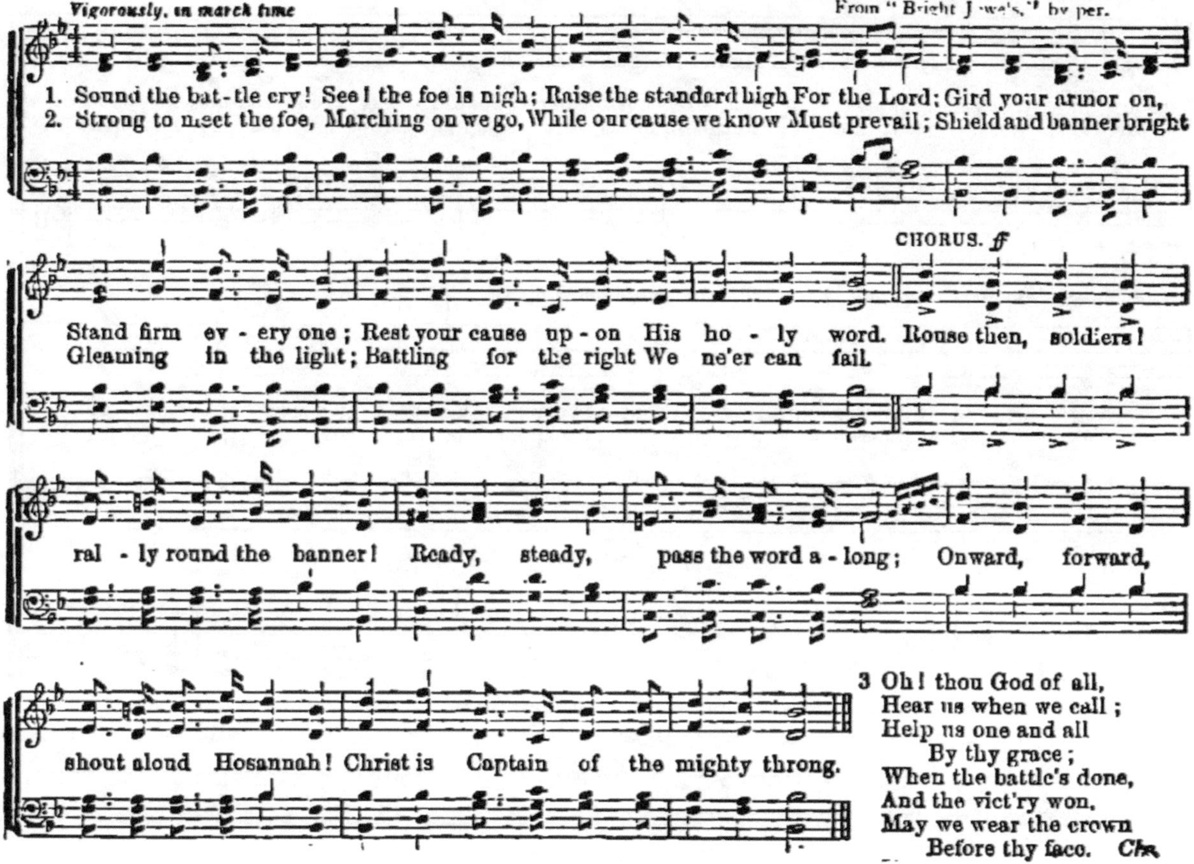

3 Oh! thou God of all,
Hear us when we call;
Help us one and all
By thy grace;
When the battle's done,
And the vict'ry won,
May we wear the crown
Before thy face. Cho.

KEEP PRAYING AS YOU GO.

W. H. DOANE.
From "Pure Gold," by per.

Words written for this work. "Pray without ceasing."—1st Thess. 5:17.

1. Come, burdened souls, with all your guilt, And all your weight of woe, There's mer-cy at a
2. Be - hold the pre-cious Lamb who died For man, his love to show; And while you seek the
3. Young sold-iers, gird your ar - mor on, And bold-ly meet the foe; Let faith di-rect, and
4. Ye pil-grims on the heaven-ly way, Thro' tri-als here be-low, O, nev-er doubt a

throne of grace; Keep pray-ing as you go.
blood-stained cross, Keep pray-ing as you go.
hope in - spire; Keep pray-ing as you go.
Sav - iour's love; Keep pray-ing as you go.

CHORUS.

Keep pray - ing, ev - er pray - ing, Thro'
all our jour-ney be-low; To Je - sus, to Je - sus, Keep pray-ing as you go.

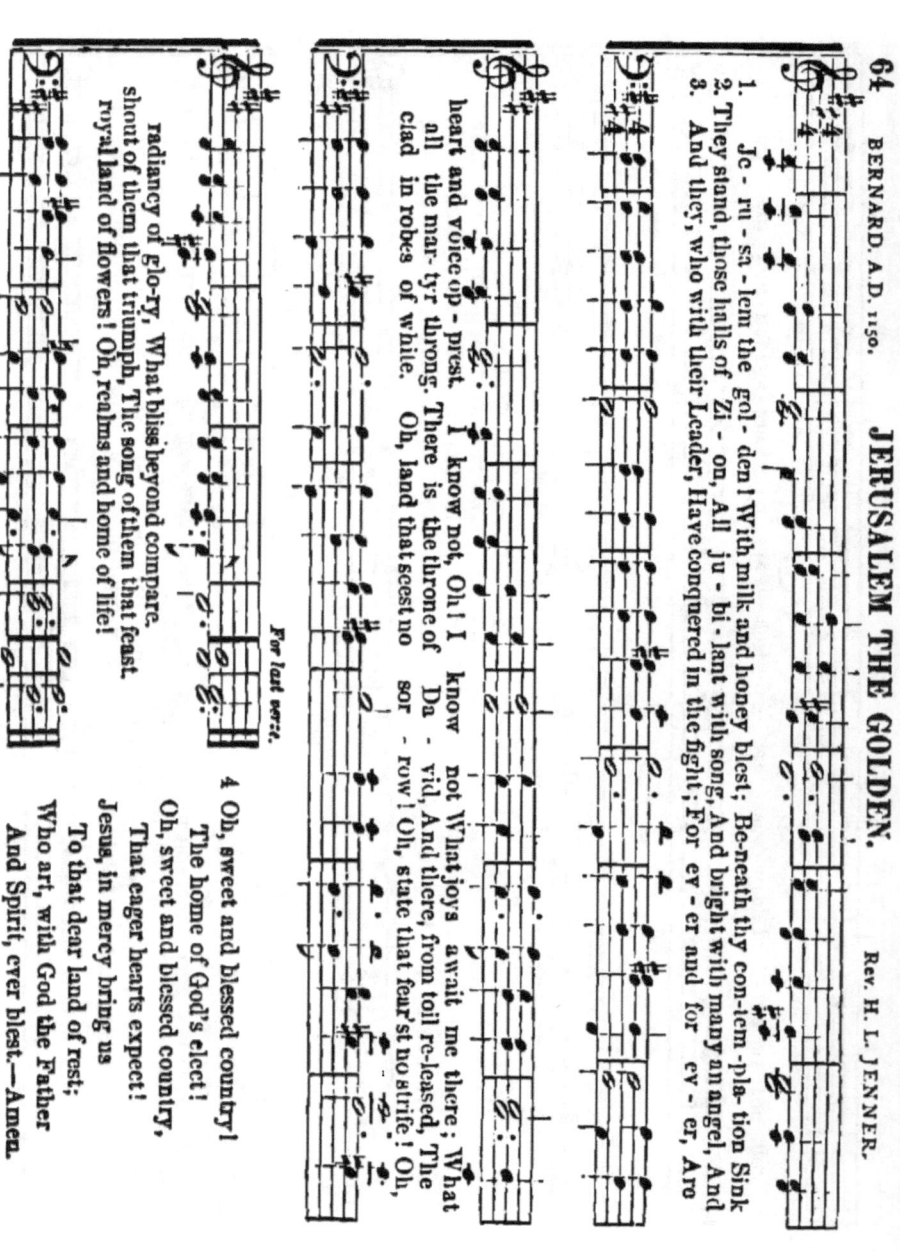

ST. GEORGE.

Dr. G. J. ELVEY.

1. Come, ye thankful people, come, Raise the song of Harvest-home! All is safely gathered in,
2. What is earth but God's own field, Fruit unto His praise to yield? Wheat and tares therein are sown,
3. For we know that Thou wilt come, And wilt take Thy people home; From Thy field will purge away

Ere the winter-storms begin; God our Maker, doth provide, For our wants to be supplied; Come to God's own
Unto joy or sorrow grown; Ripening with a wondrous pow'r, Till the final Harvest-hour. Grant, O Lord of
All that doth offend, that day; And Thine Angels charge at last In the fire the tares to cast, But the fruitful

temple, come; Raise the song of Harvest-home!
life, that we Holy grain and pure may be. A-men.
ears to store In Thy garner evermore.

4.

Come then, Lord of mercy, come,
Bid us sing Thy Harvest-Home!
Let Thy saints be gathered in,
Free from sorrow, free from sin;
All upon the golden floor
Praising Thee for evermore;
Come, with thousand angels, come;
Bid us sing Thy Harvest-Home! Amen

66. LOOKING AT THE CROSS.

Words by Rev. SYDNEY DYER.
Rev. R. LOWRY.
From "Pure Gold," by per.

"Having made peace through the blood of his cross."—Col. 1: 20.

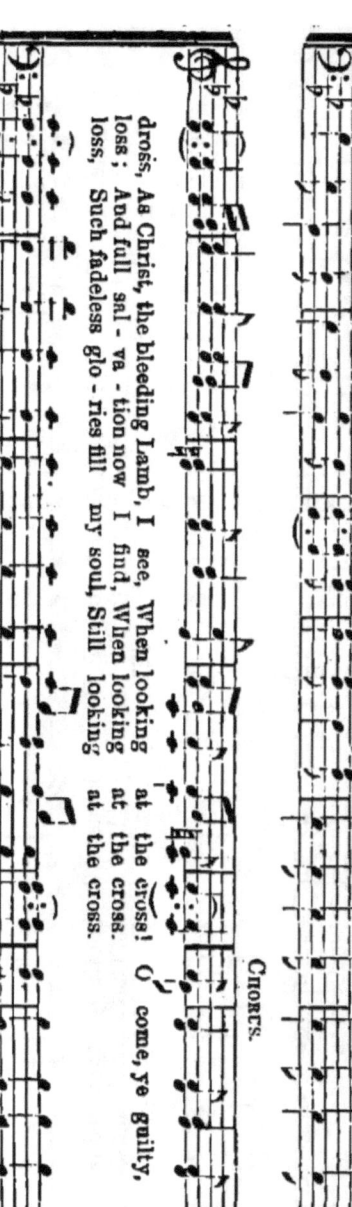
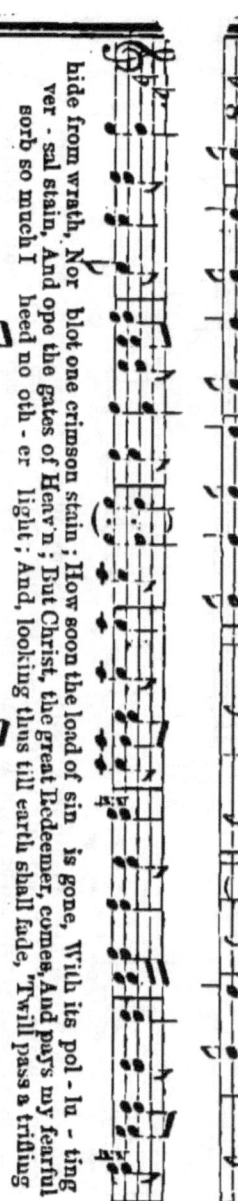

1. When mourning o'er my sense of guilt, My spir-it thrills with pain, Because I can-not hide from wrath, Nor blot one crimson stain; How soon the load of sin is gone, With its pol-lu-ting dross, As Christ, the bleeding Lamb, I see, When looking at the cross!

2. Ah! vain and hope-less each de-vice That wis-dom yet has given, To cleanse the u-ni-ver-sal stain, And ope the gates of Heav'n; But Christ, the great Redeemer, comes, And pays my fearful loss; And full sal-va-tion now I find, When looking at the cross.

3. Here let me fix my stead-fast gaze, And feast my raptured sight, Un-til my eyes ab-sorb so much I heed no oth-er light; And, looking thus till earth shall fade, 'Twill pass a trifling loss, Such fadeless glo-ries fill my soul, Still looking at the cross.

CHORUS.

O come, ye guilty,

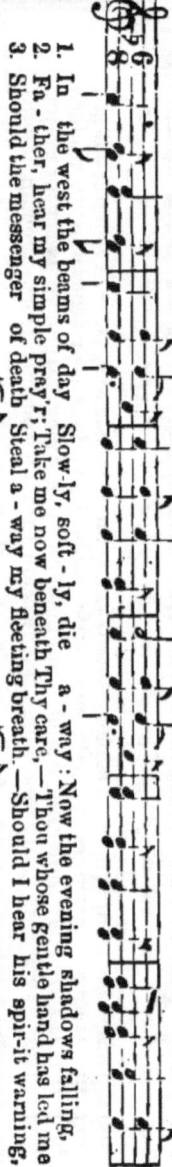

MOUNTAIN OF THE LORD.

FANNY CROSBY.

Rev. R. LOWRY.
From "Pure Gold," by per.

"But in the last days it shall come to pass, that the mountain of the house of the Lord shall be established In the top of the mountains, and it shall be exalted above the hills."—Micah. 4:1.

1. Yes! a brighter morn is breaking, Bet-ter days are coming on; All the world will be a-wak-ing
2. In the day of com-ing glo-ry, Men will show fra-ter-nal hand; Each will tell to each the sto-ry,
3. On the top of Zi-on's mountain, God prepares His house again; At its threshold springs a fountain,
4. From the earth's remotest stations, Men will come to hear the word; And, in all the world, the na-tions

CHORUS.

In the new and gold-en dawn. And ma - ny na - tions shall come, and say, Come
Till it spreads to ev - er-y land.
Flowing for the souls of men.
Shall be na-tions of the Lord.

And ma-ny na - tions shall come and say,

let us go up to the moun-tain of the Lord, Let us go up to the

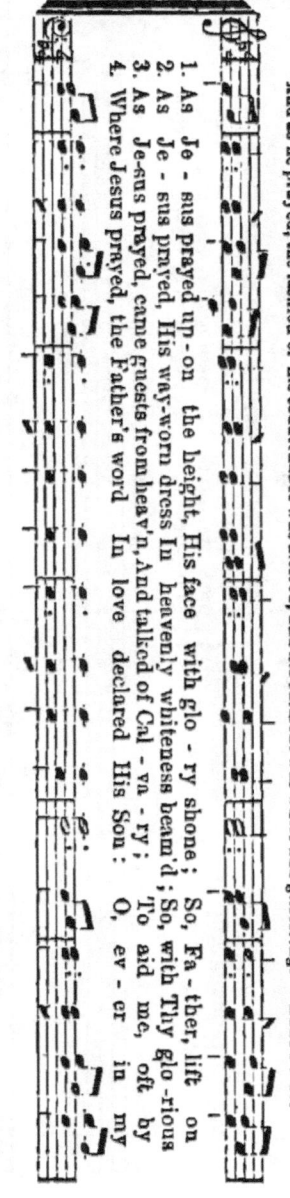

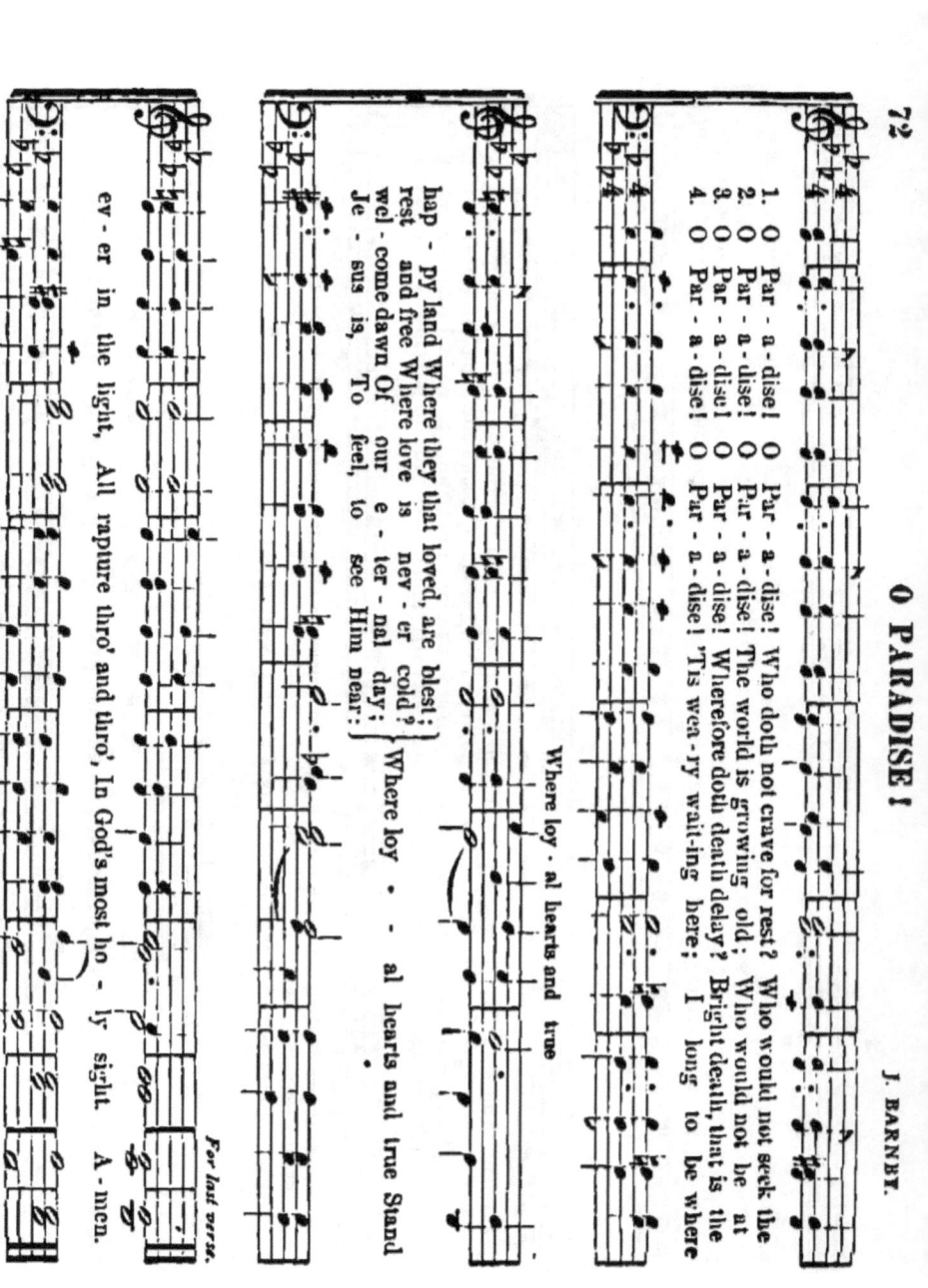

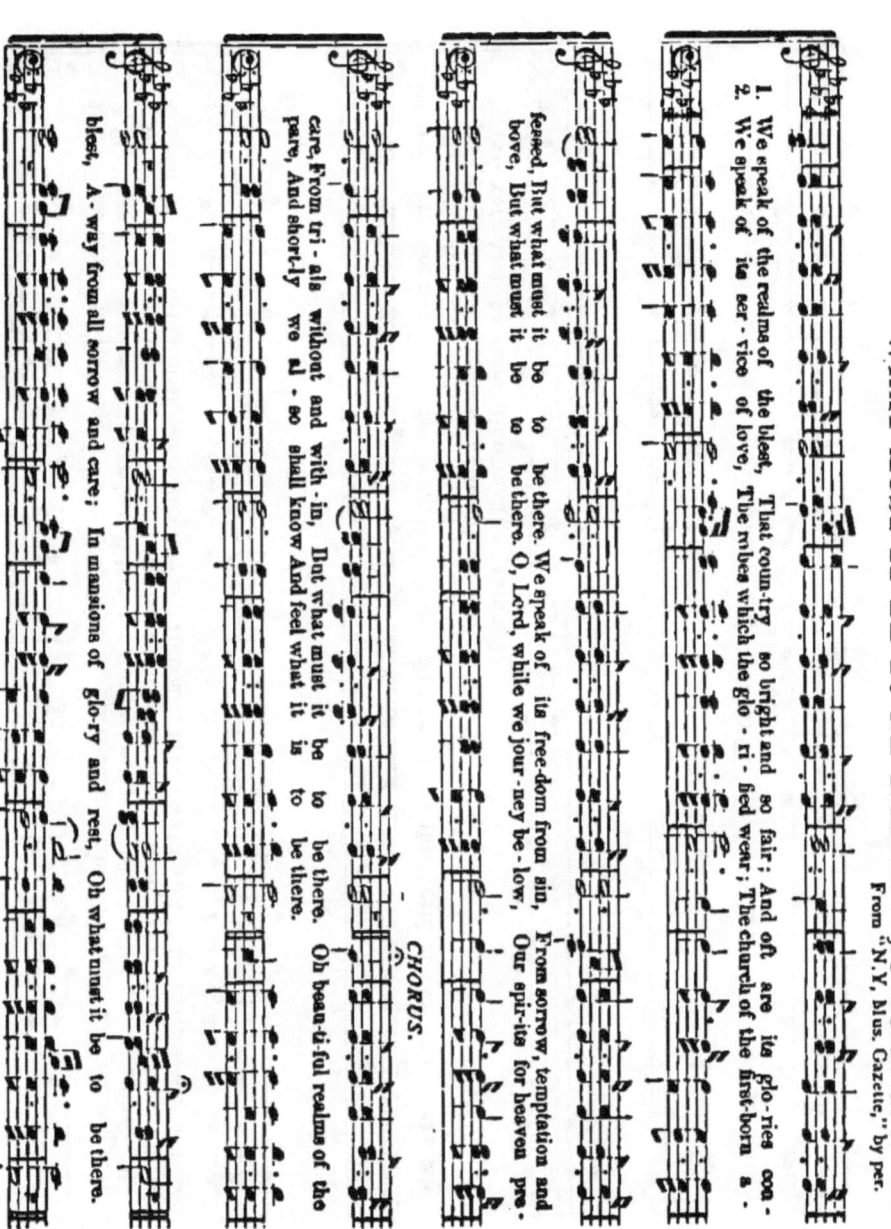

JESUS LOVES A LITTLE CHILD.

W. F. SHERWIN.

Words by W. BENNETT.

From "N. Y. Mus. Gazette," by per.

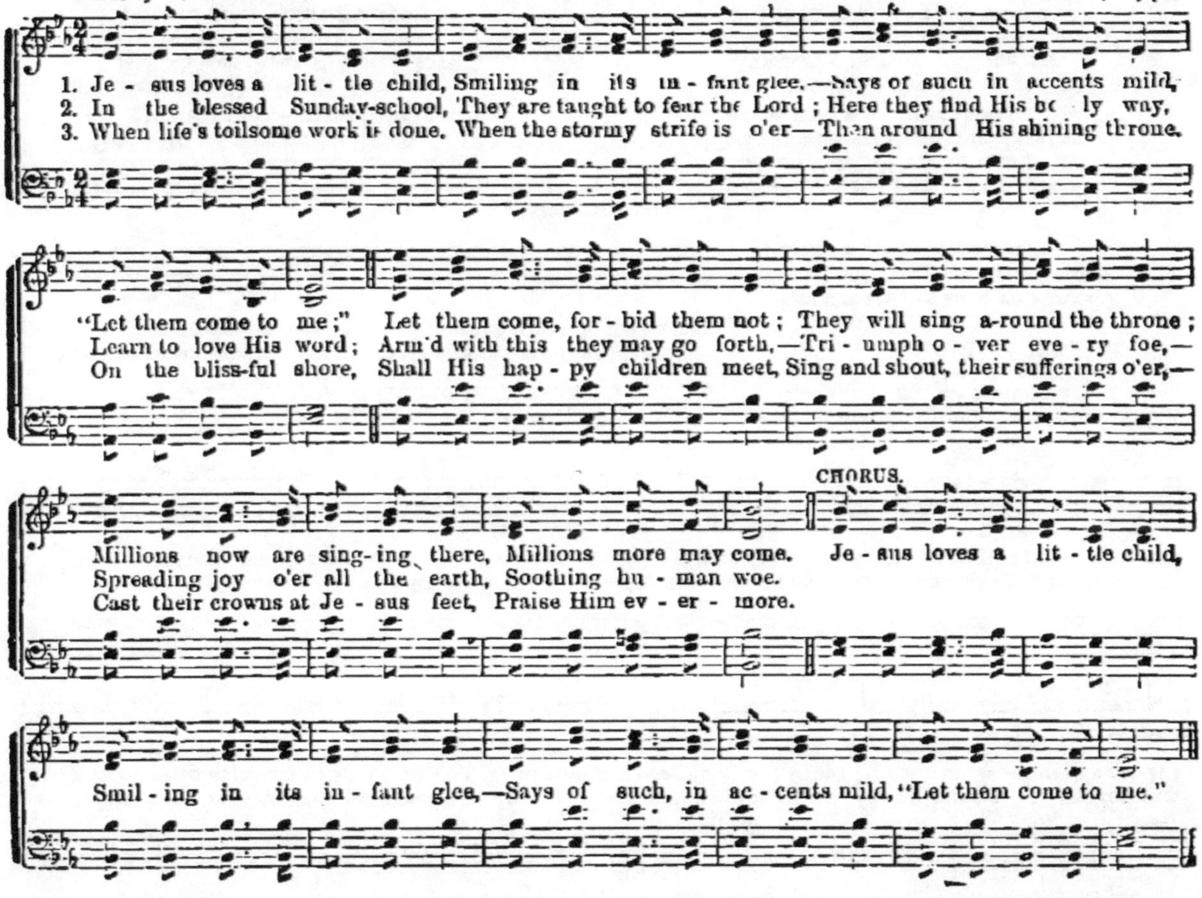

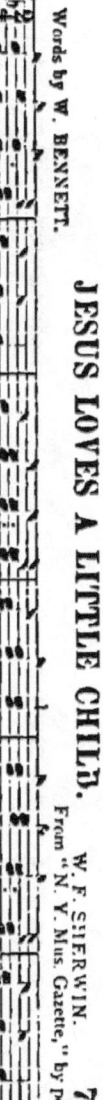

LATTER DAY. 8s & 7s.

From "Plymouth Coll." by per.

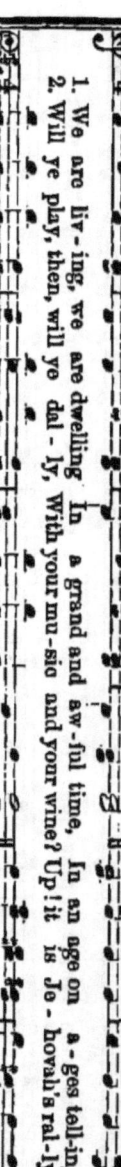

1. We are liv-ing, we are dwelling In a grand and aw-ful time, In an age on a-ges tell-ing,
2. Will ye play, then, will ye dal-ly, With your mu-sic and your wine? Up! it is Je-hovah's ral-ly!

To be liv-ing is sub-lime. Hark! the waking up of na-tions, Gog and Ma-gog to the fray;
God's own arm hath need of thine. Hark! the on-set! will ye fold your Faith-clad arms in la-zy lock?

Hark! what soundeth? is creation Groaning for its lat-ter day.
Up, O up, thou drowsy soldier; Worlds are charging to the shock.

1 Onward, Christian, though the region
 Where thou art be drear and lone;
God hath set a guardian legion
 Very near thee,—press thou on!
2 Listen, Christian, their Hosanna
 Rolleth o'er thee,—"God is love,"
Write upon thy red-cross banner,
 "Upward ever,—heaven's above."

SECOND HYMN.

3 By the thorn-road and none other,
 Is the mount of vision won;
Tread it without shrinking, brother,
 Jesus trod it,—press thou on!
4 By thy trustful, calm endeavor,
 Guiding, cheering, like the sun,
Earth-bound hearts thou shalt deliver,
 For their sake, O press thou on!

3 Worlds are charging—heaven beholding
 Thou hast but an hour to fight;
Now the blazoned cross unfolding,
 On—right onward, for the right.
On! let all the soul within you
 For the truth's sake go abroad!
Strike! let every nerve and sinew
 Tell on ages—tell for God!

ONE MORE DAY'S WORK FOR JESUS.

Rev. R. LOWRY.
From "Bright Jewels," by per.

1. One more day's work for Je-sus, One less of life for me! But heav'n is near-er, And Christ is
2. One more day's work for Je-sus: How glorious is my King! 'Tis joy, not du-ty, To speak his

dear-er, Than yes-ter-day, to me; His love and light Fill all my soul to-night. One more day's work for
beau-ty; My soul mounts on the wing At the mere tho't How Christ my life has bought.

CHORUS.

Je-sus, One more day's work for Jesus, One more day's work for Je-sus, One less of life for me.

3. One more day's work for Jesus;
   How sweet the work has been,
   To tell the story,
   To show the glory,
   Where Christ's flock enter in!
   How it did shine
   In this poor heart of mine!
      One more, &c.

4. One more day's work for Jesus—
   O, yes, a weary day;
   But heaven shines clearer
   And rest comes nearer,
   At each step of the way;
   And Christ in all—
   Before his face I fall.
      One more, &c.

5. O, blessed work for Jesus!
   O, rest at Jesus' feet!
   There toil seems pleasure,
   My wants are treasure,
   And pain for Him is sweet.
   Lord, if I may,
   I'll serve another day!
      One more, &c.

CROWN HIM WITH MANY CROWNS.

Matthew Bridges. 14,3
Dr. J. G. Elvey.

1. Crown Him with many crowns, The Lamb upon His throne; Hark, how the heavenly anthem drowns All music but its own:
A-wake, my son, and sing Of Him who died for thee, And hail Him as thy matchless King Through all eter-ni-ty.

2. Crown Him the Lord of love:
Behold His hands and side,
Rich wounds yet visible above
In beauty glorified:
No angel in the sky
Can fully bear that sight,
But downward bends his burning eye
At mysteries so bright.

3. Crown Him the Lord of peace:
Whose power a sceptre sways
From pole to pole, that wars may cease,
And all be prayer and praise;
His reign shall know no end,
And round His pierced feet
Fair flowers of Paradise extend
Their fragrance ever sweet.

4. Crown Him the Lord of years,
The Potentate of time,
Creator of the rolling spheres,
Ineffably sublime.
All hail, Redeemer, hail!
For Thou hast died for me;
Thy praise shall never, never fail
Throughout eternity.

SUNDAY-SCHOOL ARMY. 27 Trio.

1. O, do not be discouraged,
For Jesus is your Friend,
O, do not be discouraged,
For Jesus is your Friend.
He will giv;, you grace to conquer,
He will give you grace to conquer,
And keep you to the end.

Cho.—I am glad I'm in this army,
Yes, I'm glad I'm in this army.

2. Fight on, ye little soldiers,
The battle you shall win;
Fight on, ye little soldiers,
The battle you shall win.
For the Saviour is your Captain,
For the Saviour is your Captain,
And He has vanquished sin.—Cho.

3. And when the conflict's over,
Before him you shall stand;
And when the conflict's over,
Before him you shall stand.
You shall sing His praise for ever,
You shall sing His praise for ever,
In Canaan's happy land.

Cho.—I am glad, &c.

THE OLD, OLD STORY.

"Who loved me, and gave Himself for me."—Gal. 2: 20.

W. H. DOANE.
From "Songs of Devotion," by per.

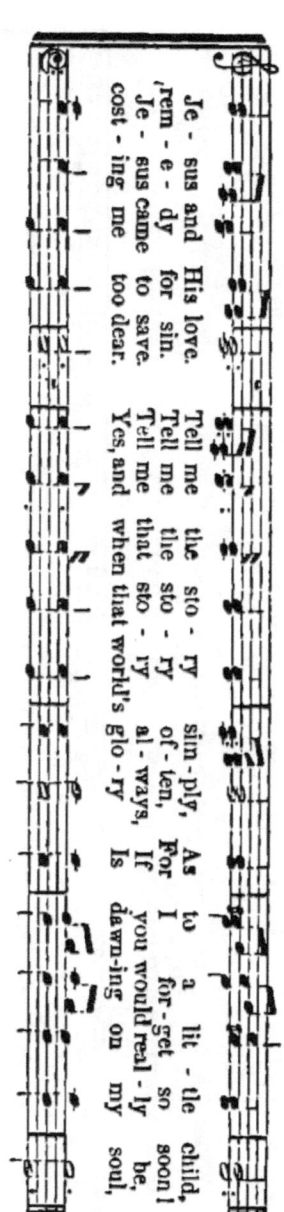
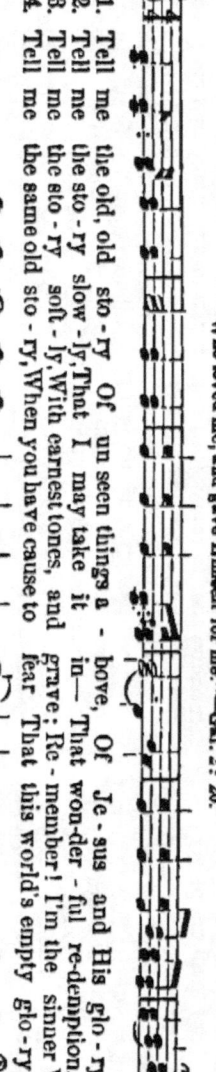

1. Tell me the old, old sto-ry Of un-seen things a-bove, Of Je-sus and His glo-ry Of
2. Tell me the sto-ry slow-ly, That I may take it in— That won-der-ful re-demption, God's
3. Tell me the sto-ry soft-ly, With earnest tones, and grave; Re-member! I'm the sinner Whom
4. Tell me the same old sto-ry, When you have cause to fear That this world's empty glo-ry Is

Je-sus and His love. Tell me the sto-ry sim-ply, As to a lit-tle child,
'rem-e-dy for sin. Tell me the sto-ry of-ten, For I for-get so soon!
Je-sus came to save. Tell me that sto-ry al-ways, If you would real-ly be,
cost-ing me too dear. Yes, and when that world's glo-ry Is dawn-ing on my soul,

CHORUS.

For I am weak and wea-ry, And help-less and de-filed. Tell me the old, old sto-ry,
The "ear-ly dew" of morning Has passed a-way at noon.
In a-ny time of trou-ble, A com-fort-er to me.
Tell me the old, old sto-ry: "Christ Jesus makes thee whole."

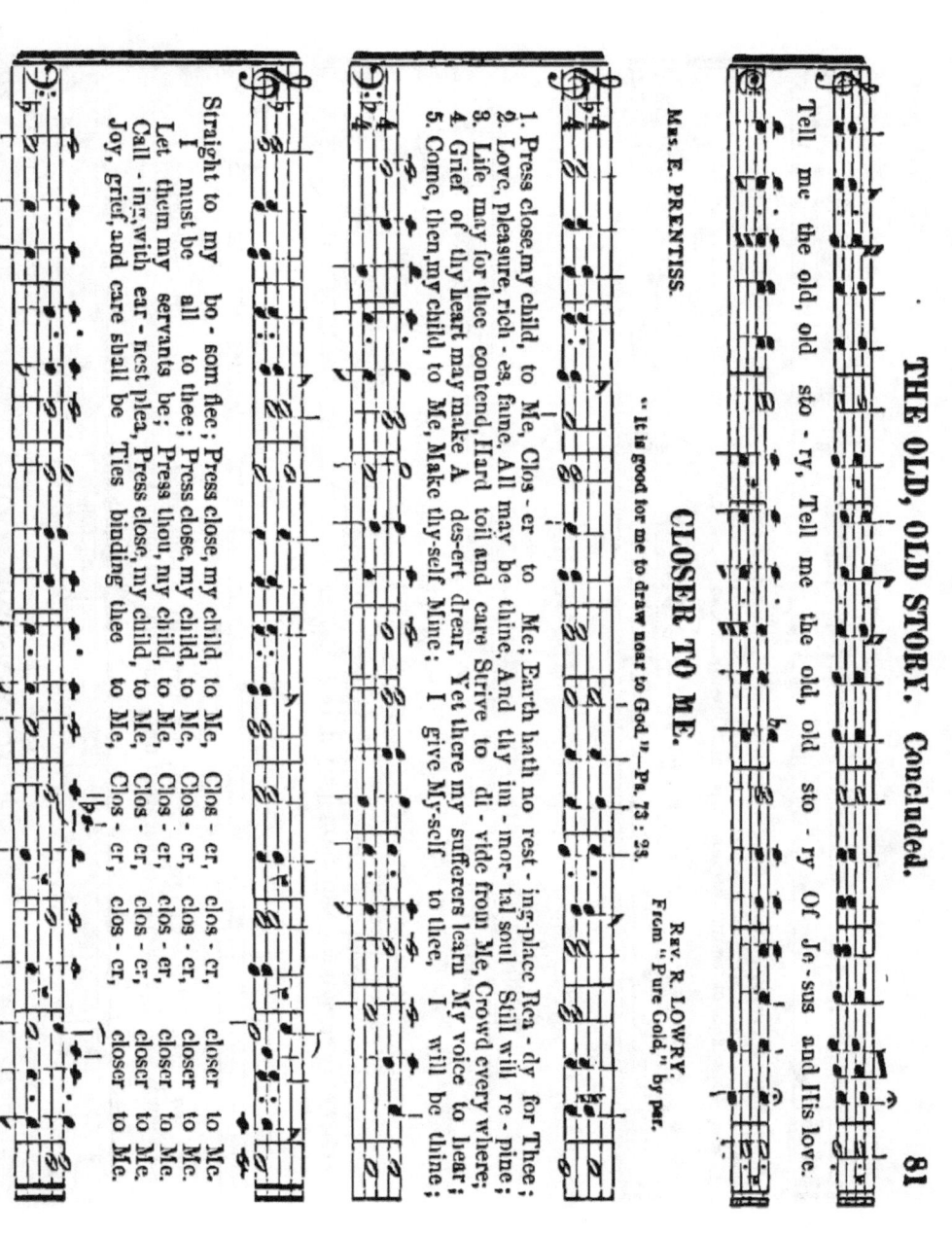

82

WAITING SAVIOUR.

Words by W. BENNETT.

"Behold, I stand at the door."—Rev. 3; 20.

WM. F. SHERWIN.
From "Pure Gold." By per.

1. See Jesus standing at the door; O, hear Him pleading ev-er-more; He waits for
2. He bore the cru-cl cross for thee, He died on rug-ged Cal-va-ry; Say, wea-ry
thee, O heart of sin, Wilt thou not let Him in?
heart oppress'd with sin, Wilt thou not let Him in?

3 He'll bring thee joy from heaven above,
 He'll bring thee pardon, peace and love,
 And wash thy soul from every sin;
 O let the Saviour in!

4 O shall He plead with thee in vain?
 Remember all His grief and pain;
 His death atones for all thy sin,
 O rise, and let Him in.

SUBMISSION.

H. N. WHITNEY.
By per.

1. Come to Jesus, err-ing one; Come to Jesus now; Humbly at His gracious throne, In submission bow.
2. At His feet confess your sin; Seek forgiveness there; For His blood can make you clean,— He will hear your prayer.
3. Seek His face without delay; Give Him now your heart; Tarry not, but, while you may, Choose the better part.

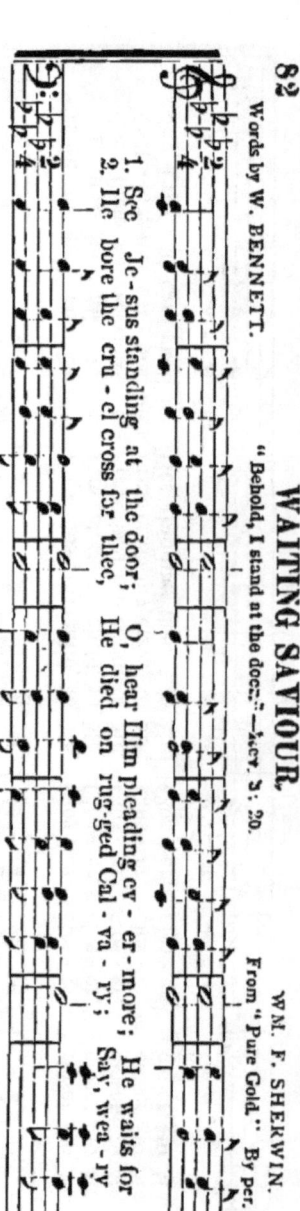

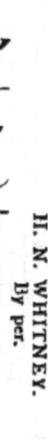

I AM WAITING BY THE RIVER.

Dr. TH. HASTINGS.

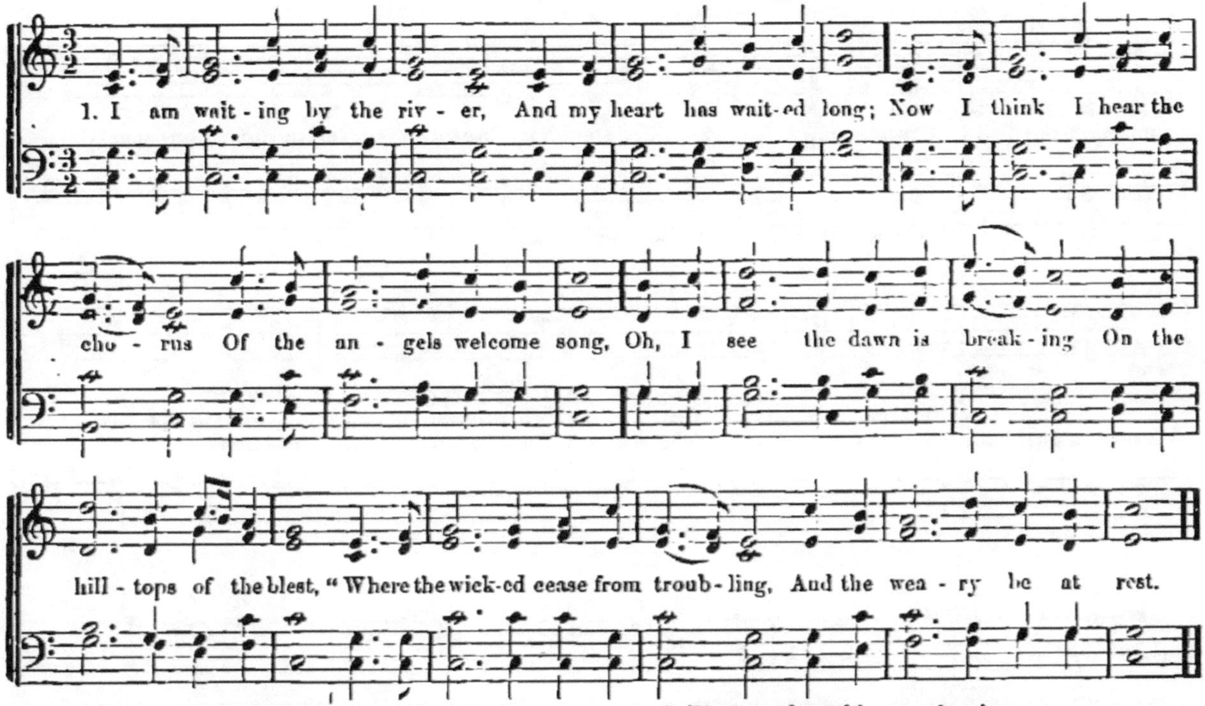

1. I am wait-ing by the riv-er, And my heart has wait-ed long; Now I think I hear the cho-rus Of the an-gels welcome song. Oh, I see the dawn is break-ing On the hill-tops of the blest, "Where the wick-ed cease from troub-ling, And the wea-ry be at rest.

2 Far away beyond the shadows
Of this weary vale of tears,
There the tide of bliss is sweeping
Through the bright and changeless years,
O! I long to be with Jesus,
In the mansions of the blest,
"Where the wicked cease from troubling,
And the weary be at rest."

3 They are launching on the river,
From the calm and quiet shore,
And they soon will bear my spirit
Where the weary sigh no more;
For the tide is swiftly flowing,
And I long to greet the blest,
"Where the wicked cease from troubling,
And the weary be at rest."

THE BEAUTEOUS DAY.

GEO. F. ROOT.
By per. of Root & Cady.

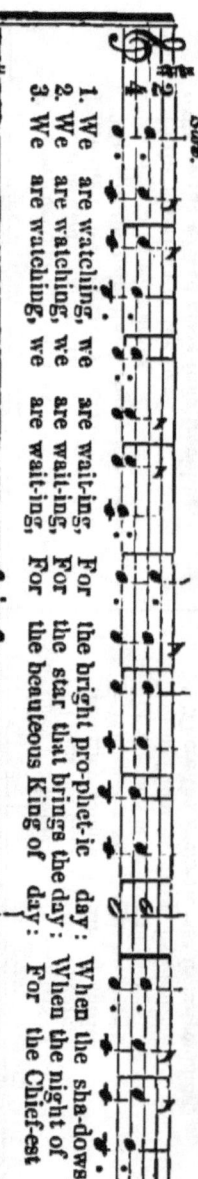

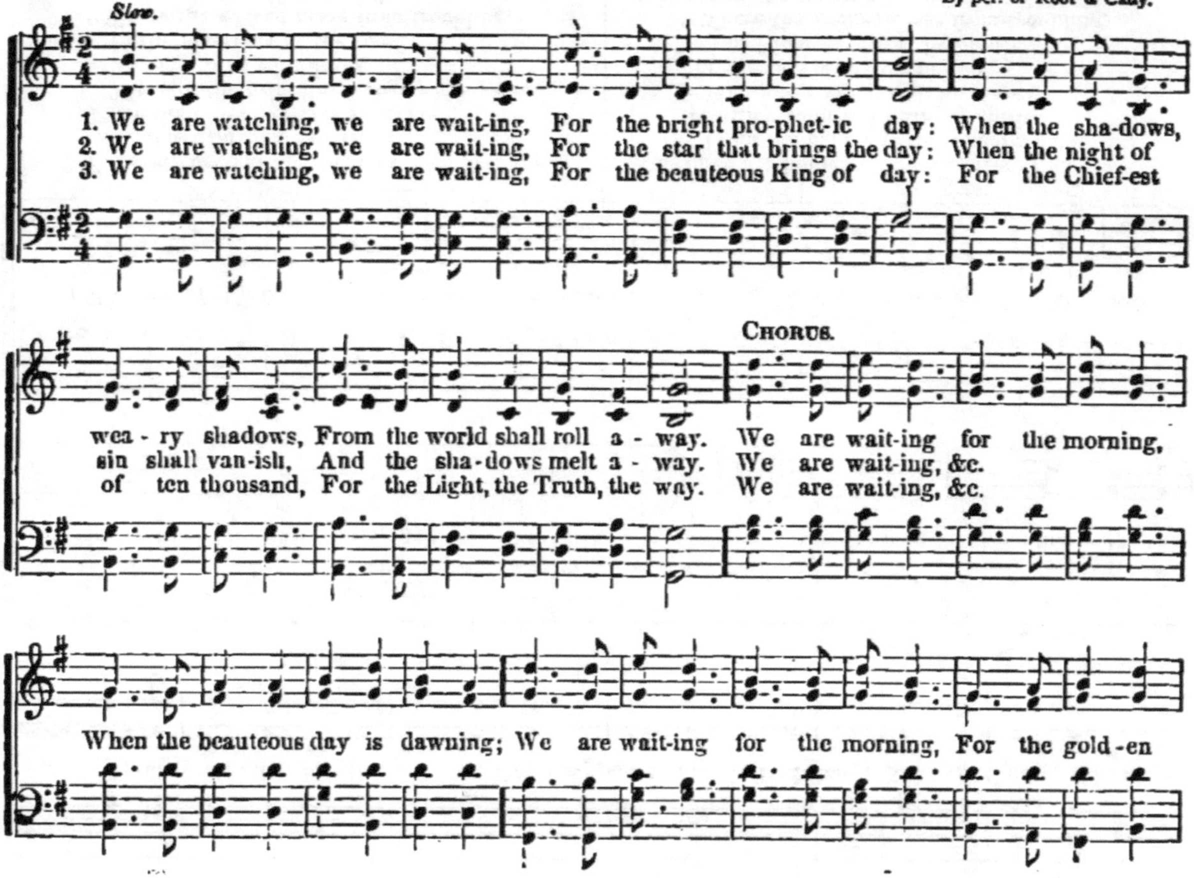

THE BEAUTEOUS DAY, Concluded.

spires of day. Lo! He comes! see the King draw near; Zi - on, shout, the Lord is here.

ESSEX. 7s.

T. CLARK.

1. Songs of praise the an - gels sang, Heav'n with hal - le - lu - jah's rang, When Je - ho - vah's
2. Songs of praise a - woke the morn, When the Prince of Peace was born; Songs of praise a -
3. Heav'n and earth must pass a - way,—Songs of praise shall crown that day; God will make new
4. Men, redeemed with heart and voice, Here in songs of praise re - joice; And a - midst e -

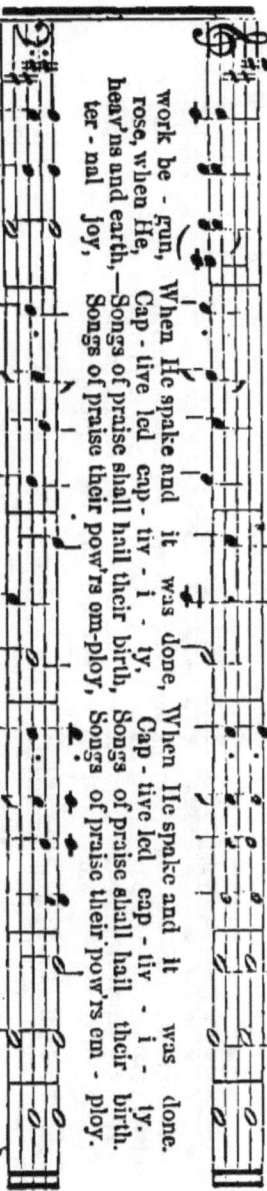

work be - gun, When He spake and it was done, When He spake and it was done.
rose, when He, Cap - tive led cap - tiv - i - ty, Cap - tive led cap - tiv - i - ty.
heav'ns and earth,—Songs of praise shall hail their birth, Songs of praise shall hail their birth.
ter - nal joy, Songs of praise their pow'rs em - ploy, Songs of praise their pow'rs em - ploy.

BEAUTIFUL ZION.

WM. B. BRADBURY, by per.

1. Beauti-ful Zi-on built a-bove, Beautiful ci-ty that I love, Beauti-ful gates of pearly white,
2. Beauti-ful heav'n, where all is light, Beautiful angels, clothed in white, Beautiful strains that never tire,
3. Beautiful crowns on every brow, Beautiful palms the conquerors show, Beautiful robes the ransom'd wear,
4. Beauti-ful throne of Christ our King, Beautiful songs the angels sing, Beautiful rest, all wandering cease,

Beauti-ful tem-ple—God its light; He who was slain on Cal-va-ry, Opens those pearly gates to me.
Beauti-ful harps thro' all the choir; There shall I join the chorus sweet, Worshipping at the Saviour's feet.
Beauti-ful all who en-ter there; Thither I press with eager feet, There shall my rest be long and sweet.
Beauti-ful home of perfect peace; There shall my eyes the Saviour see; Haste to this heav'nly home with me.

SWEET STORY. Concluded.

called lit-tle child-ren as lambs to His fold, I should like to have been with them then.
I might have seen His kind look when He said, "Let the lit-tle ones come un-to me."
if I thus ear-nest-ly seek Him be-low, I shall see Him and hear Him a-bove.
ma-ny dear child-ren are gath-er-ing there, "For of such is the king-dom of heaven."

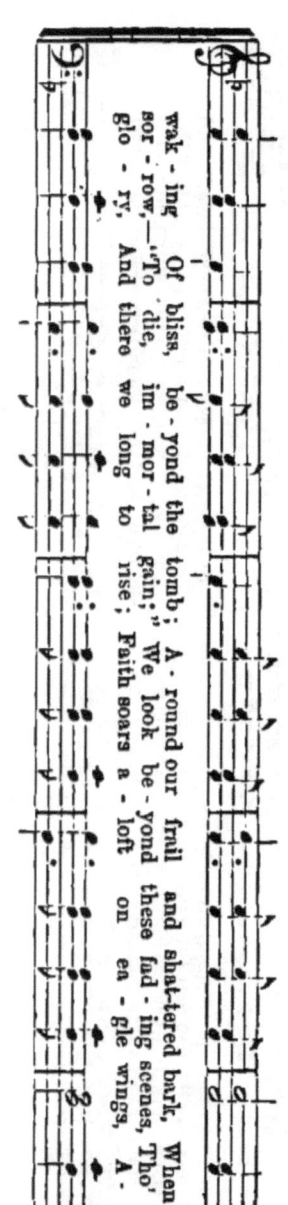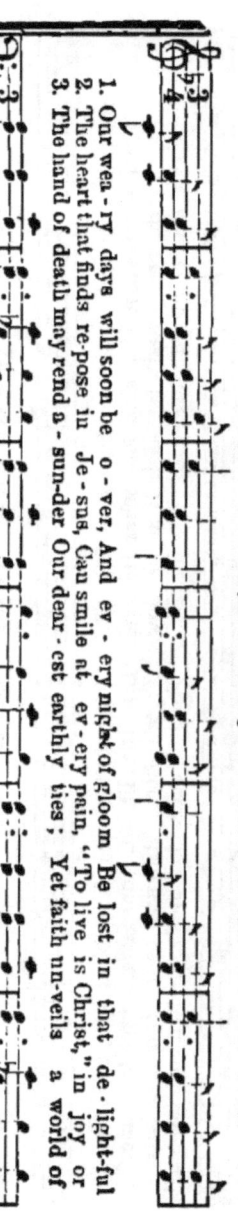

JACOB'S PRAYER.

Words by A. DICKINSON.
WM. B. BRADBURY.
From "Fresh Laurels," by per.

1. All night long till break of day, Ja-cob wept his bit-ter pray'r, Till the An - gel on his way, Christ the An-gel blest him there, I'm a need - y sin - ner too, Torn with an-guish, guilt and fear, I to Je - sus too will go, Go and bathe his feet with tears.
2. Je - sus, at Thy cross I lie All night long till break of day; Per-ish here, if I must die— Un - for - giv'n, go not a - way. Sav-iour, wilt thou take my heart? It is all I have to give, Sin-de-filed in ev - ery part, Such a gift wilt Thou re - ceive?
3. Oh, how kind-ly Je - sus spoke: "Go in peace—all is for-given, Will thou all for me for- sake, Love, and fol - low me to heav'n." Je - sus, I thy goodness bless, And with wondering love a - dore; Let me nev - er love Thee less, Let me love Thee more and more.

WE ARE COMING, BLESSED SAVIOUR.

WM. B. BRADBURY.

Words by Mrs. LYDIA BAXTER.

From "Golden Censer," by per.

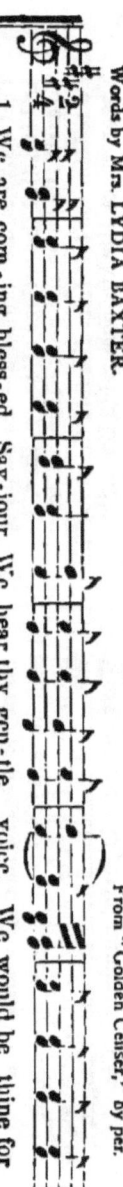

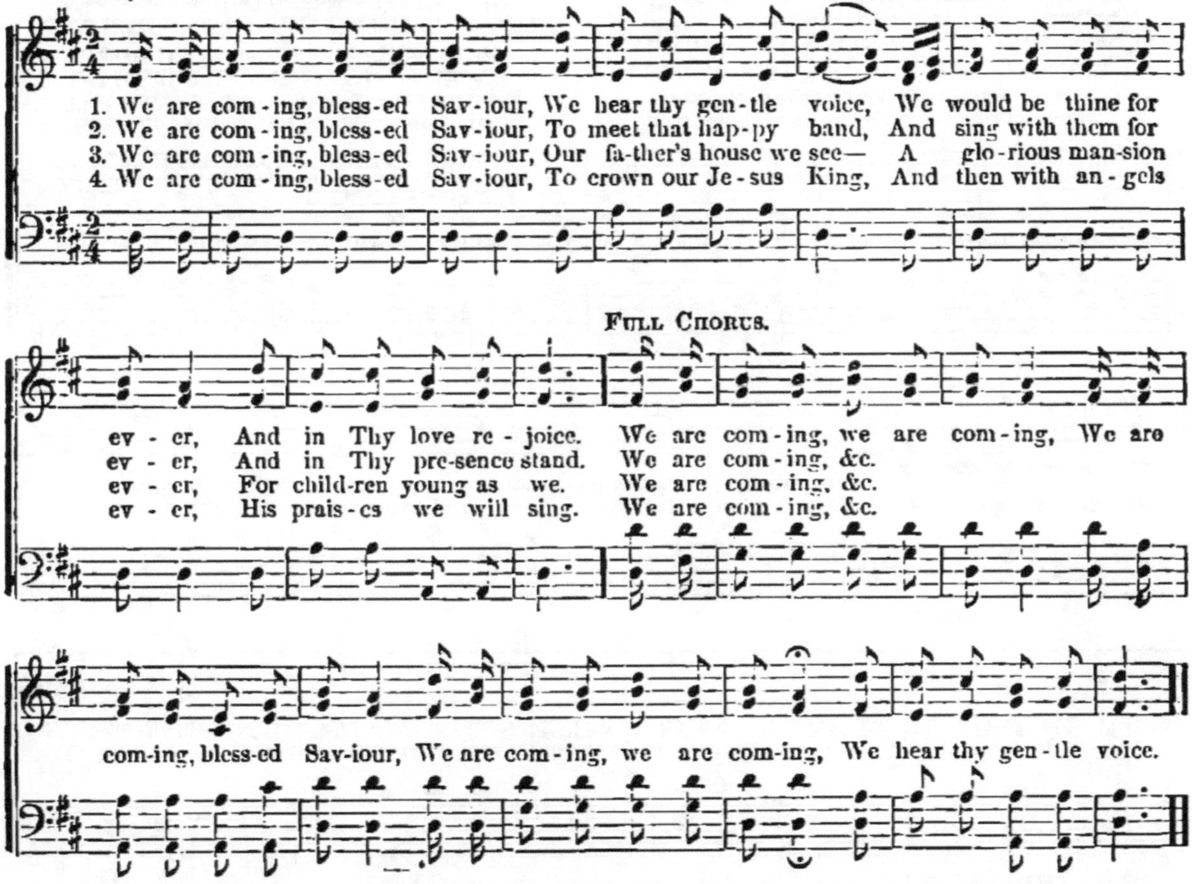

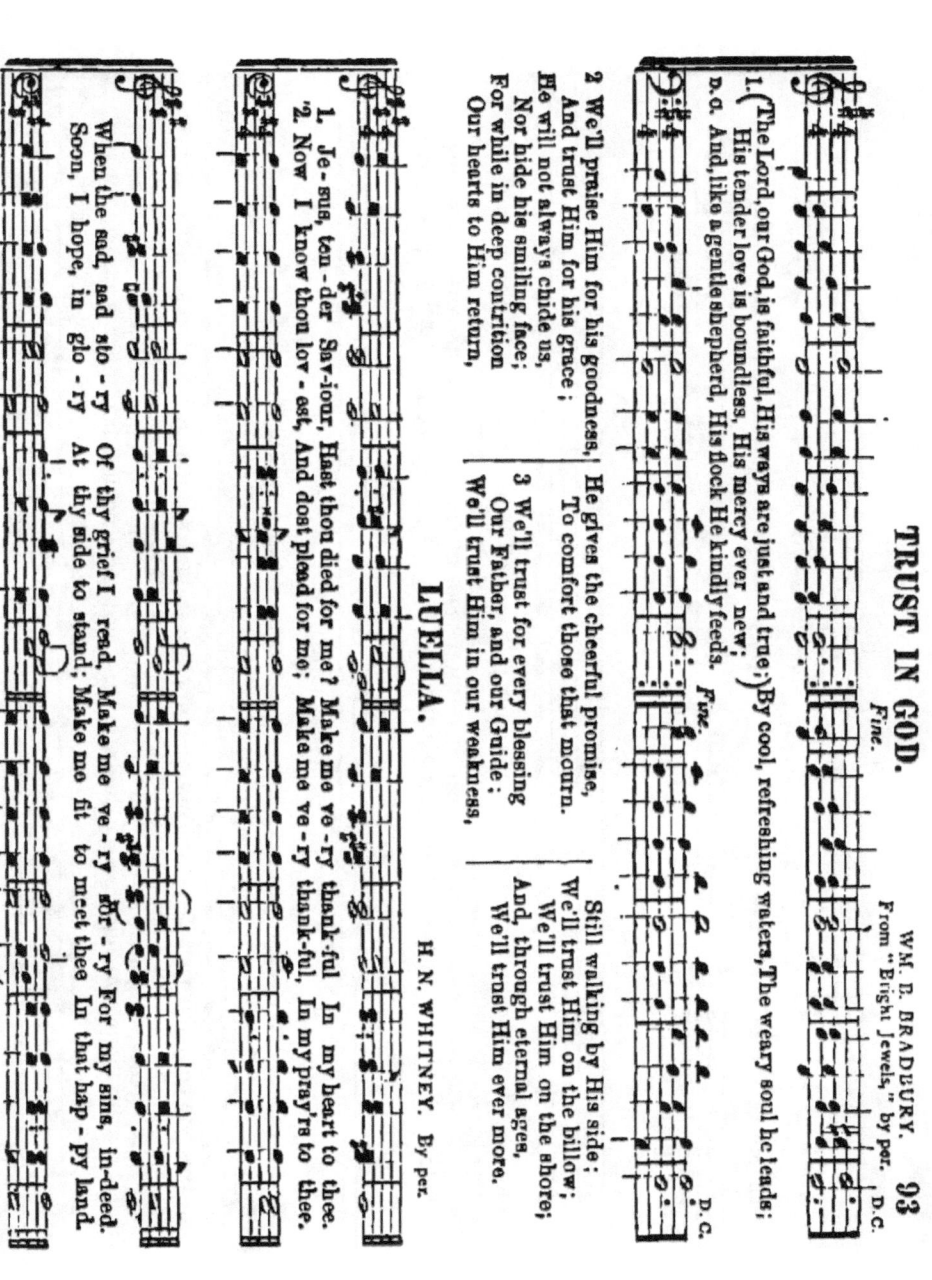

MARCHING ALONG.

Words by R. P. CLARK.

WM. B. BRADBURY.
From "Golden Chain." By permission.

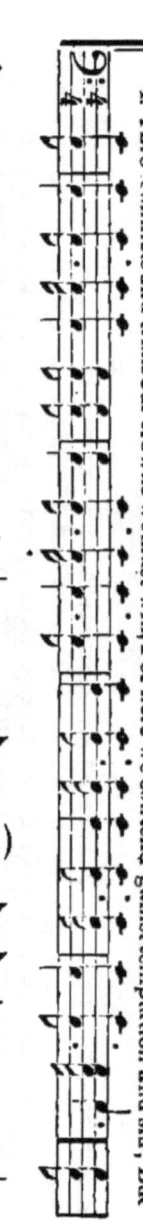

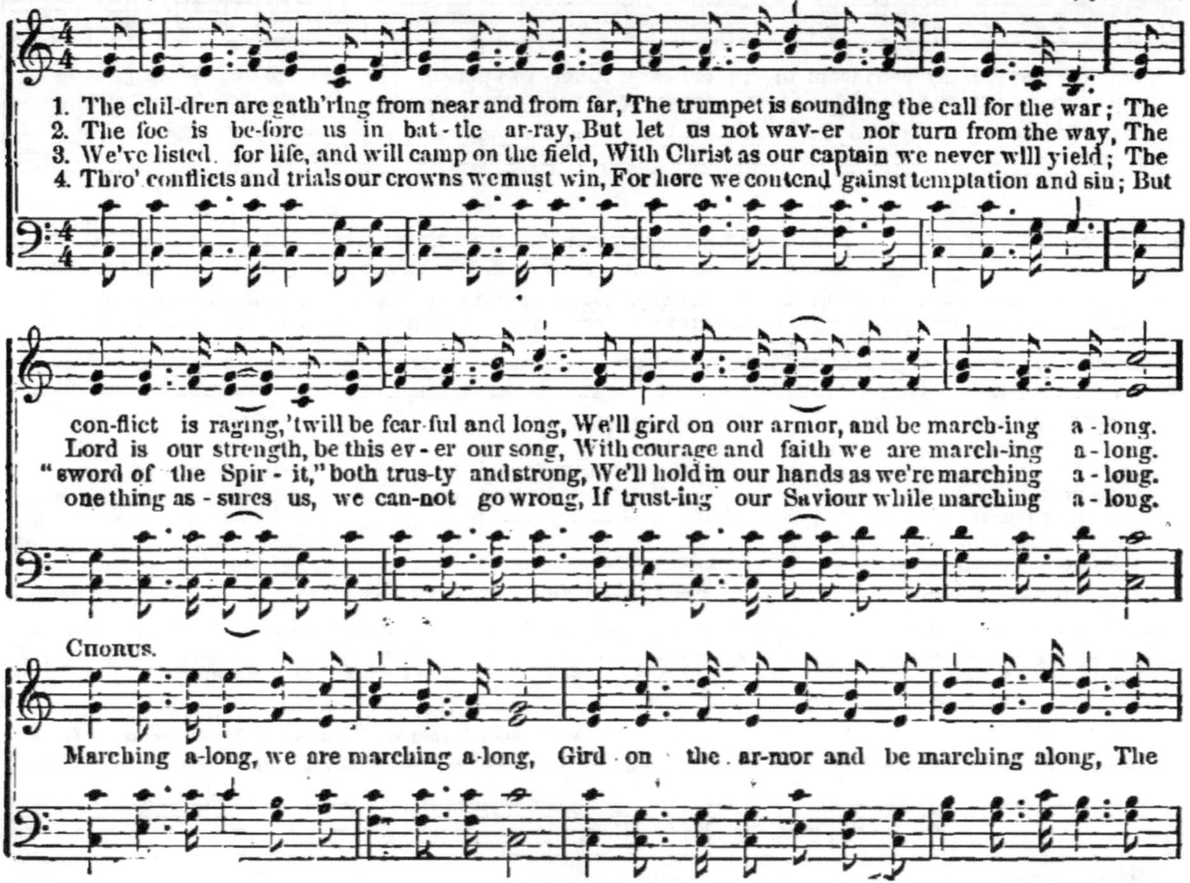

1. The chil-dren are gath'ring from near and from far, The trumpet is sounding the call for the war; The
2. The foe is be-fore us in bat-tle ar-ray, But let us not wav-er nor turn from the way, The
3. We've listed for life, and will camp on the field, With Christ as our captain we never will yield; The
4. Thro' conflicts and trials our crowns we must win, For here we contend 'gainst temptation and sin; But

con-flict is raging, 'twill be fear-ful and long, We'll gird on our armor, and be march-ing a-long.
Lord is our strength, be this ev-er our song, With courage and faith we are march-ing a-long.
"sword of the Spir-it," both trus-ty and strong, We'll hold in our hands as we're marching a-long.
one thing as-sures us, we can-not go wrong, If trust-ing our Saviour while marching a-long.

Chorus.

Marching a-long, we are marching a-long, Gird on the ar-mor and be marching along, The

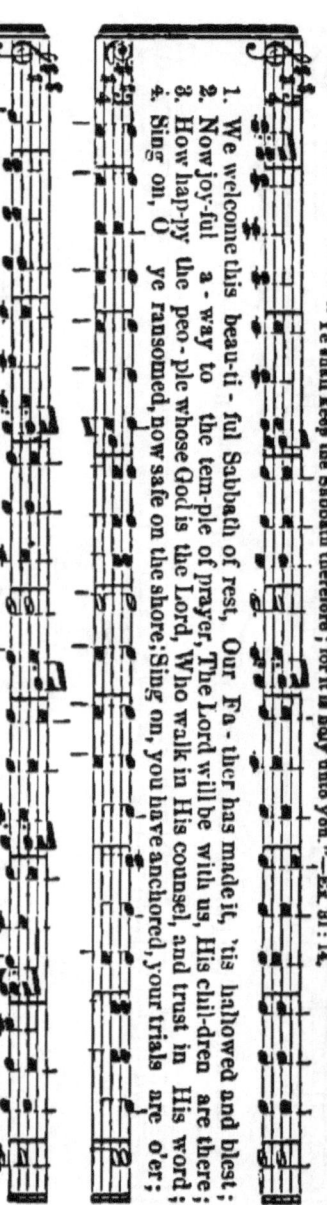

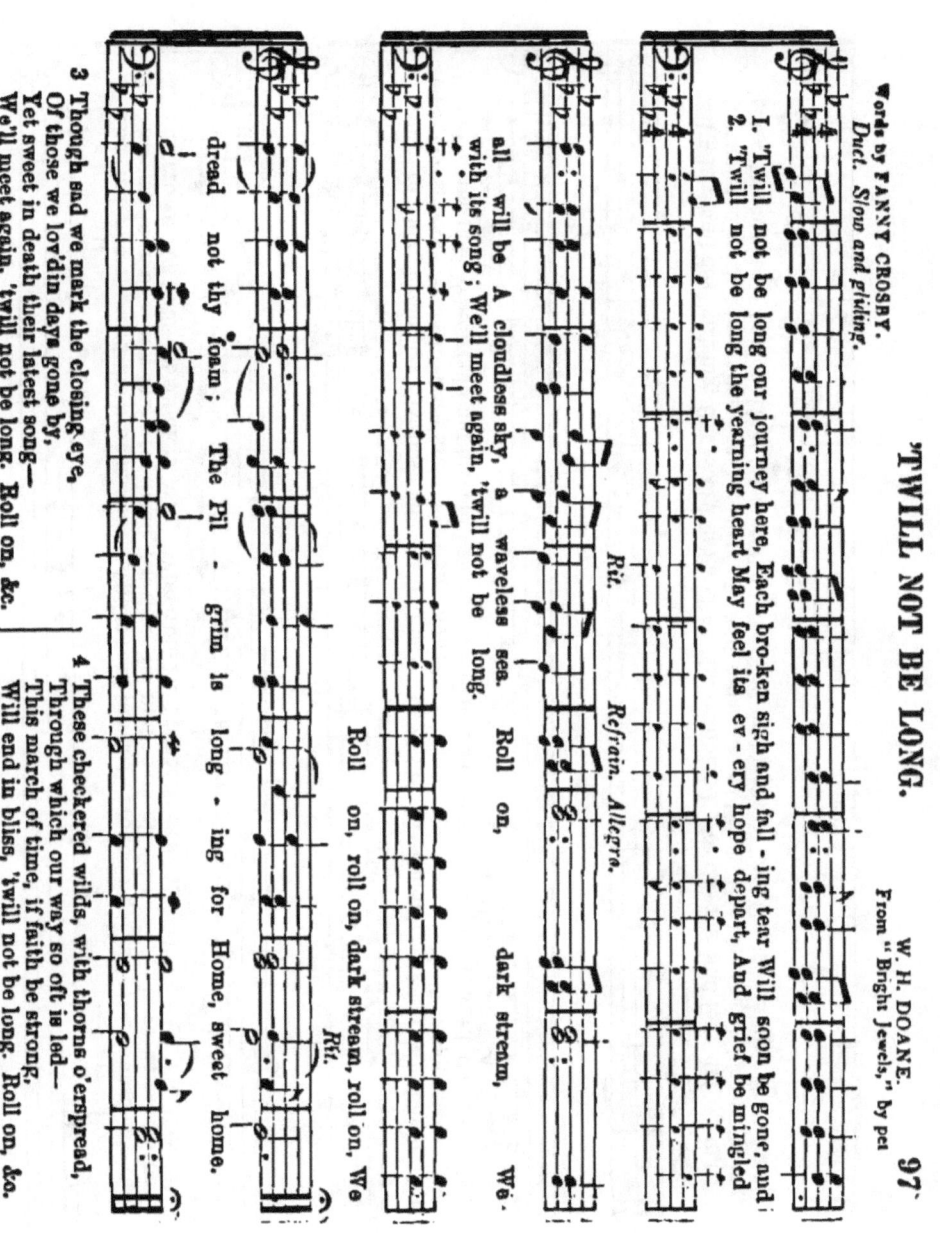

98 Words by R. W. RAYMOND.   BATTLE SONG.   From the German.
Arr. by J. R. H.

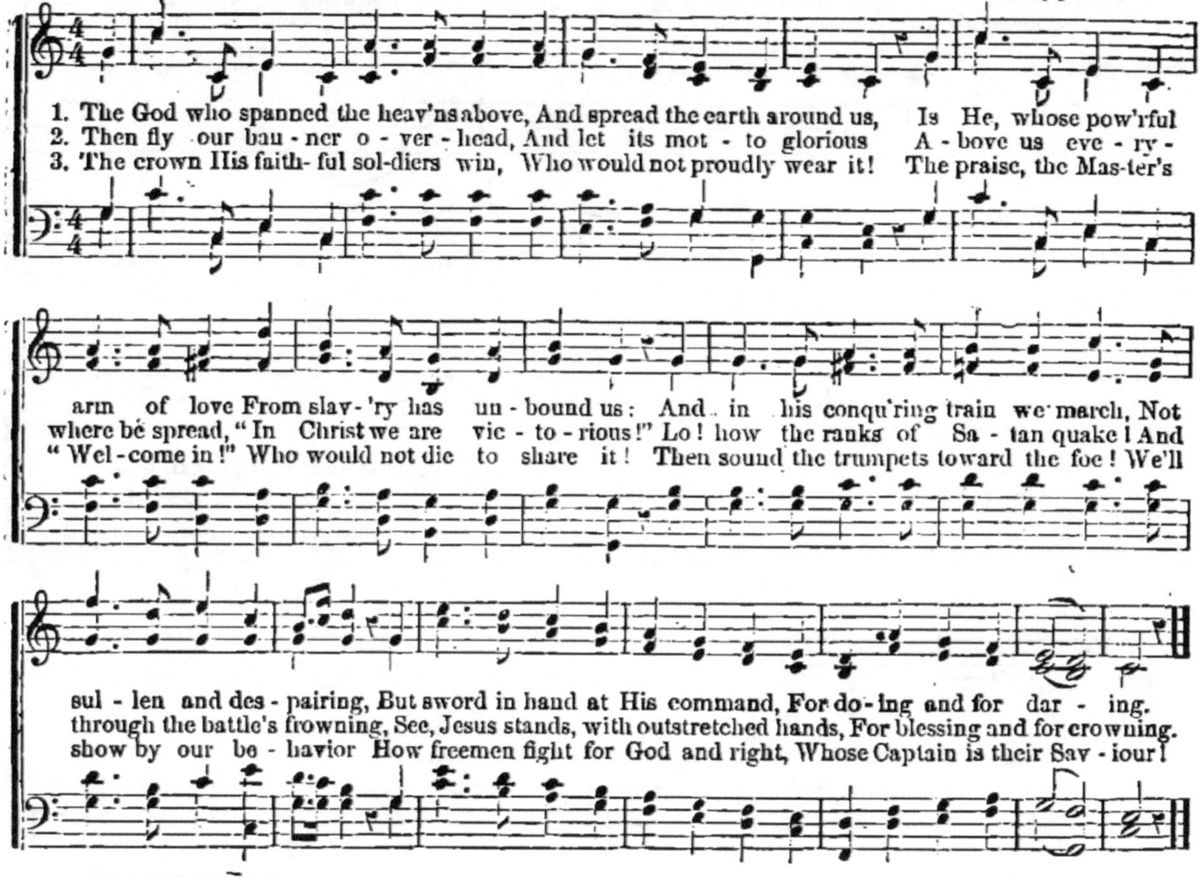

1. The God who spanned the heav'ns above, And spread the earth around us, Is He, whose pow'rful
2. Then fly our ban-ner o-ver-head, And let its mot-to glorious A-bove us eve-ry-
3. The crown His faith-ful sol-diers win, Who would not proudly wear it! The praise, the Mas-ter's

arn of love From slav-'ry has un-bound us; And, in his conqu'ring train we march, Not
where be spread, "In Christ we are vic-to-rious!" Lo! how the ranks of Sa-tan quake! And
"Wel-come in!" Who would not die to share it! Then sound the trumpets toward the foe! We'll

sul-len and des-pairing, But sword in hand at His command, For do-ing and for dar-ing,
through the battle's frowning, See, Jesus stands, with outstretched hands, For blessing and for crowning.
show by our be-havior How freemen fight for God and right, Whose Captain is their Sav-iour!

THE PRAISE OF JESUS' NAME.

FANNY CROSBY.　　　　　　　　　　　　　　CHESTER G. ALLEN.

1. Loud swell in cho-ral numbers The praise of Je-sus' name, His goodness, truth and mer-cy Let young and old proclaim. Ex-alt Him, O ye na-tions, And crown Him while ye sing: The Lord of life e-ter-nal, Cre-a-tor, Saviour, King.

2. We blend our hap-py voi-ces, We lift our hearts a-bove; We thank our kind Pro-tec-tor For all His ten-der love. How bright the year de-part-ed With blessings passed away; Loud swell our choral numbers On this glad, festive day.

CHORUS.

"How blessed are the peo-ple That know the joyful sound," Whose strains shall yet be waft-ed To earth's re-mot-est bound. How blessed, &c.

3 Hosanna in the highest,
  Our grateful songs shall be;
  Hosanna in the highest,
  Our Saviour God, to Thee:
  And when, with all the ransomed,
  Around Thy throne we meet,
  We'll cast our crowns before Thee,
  And worship at Thy feet.—Cro.

THEY ARE GOING DOWN THE VALLEY.

Rev. R. LOWRY.
From "Bright Jewels," by per.

Slow and solemn.

1. Gone to the grave is our loved one, Gone with a youthful bloom; Lowly we bend, schoolmate and friend
2. Oft we have mingled to-geth-er, Sometimes in prayer and song; Now when we meet, this one we greet

Pass-ing a-way to the tomb. They are going down the val-ley, The deep, dark val-ley; We'll
Nev-er a-gain in our throng.

CHORUS.

see their fa-ces nev-er more, Till we pass down the val-ley, The dark, death val-ley, And

meet them on the oth-er shore.

3. Sweetly the form will be sleeping,
Under the cypress shade;
Sad though we be, fondly will we
Cherish the name of the dead. *Cho.*

4. Down in the valley they're going,
Down to the other shore;
But with the blest—fair land of rest—
Weeping will come never more. *Cho.*

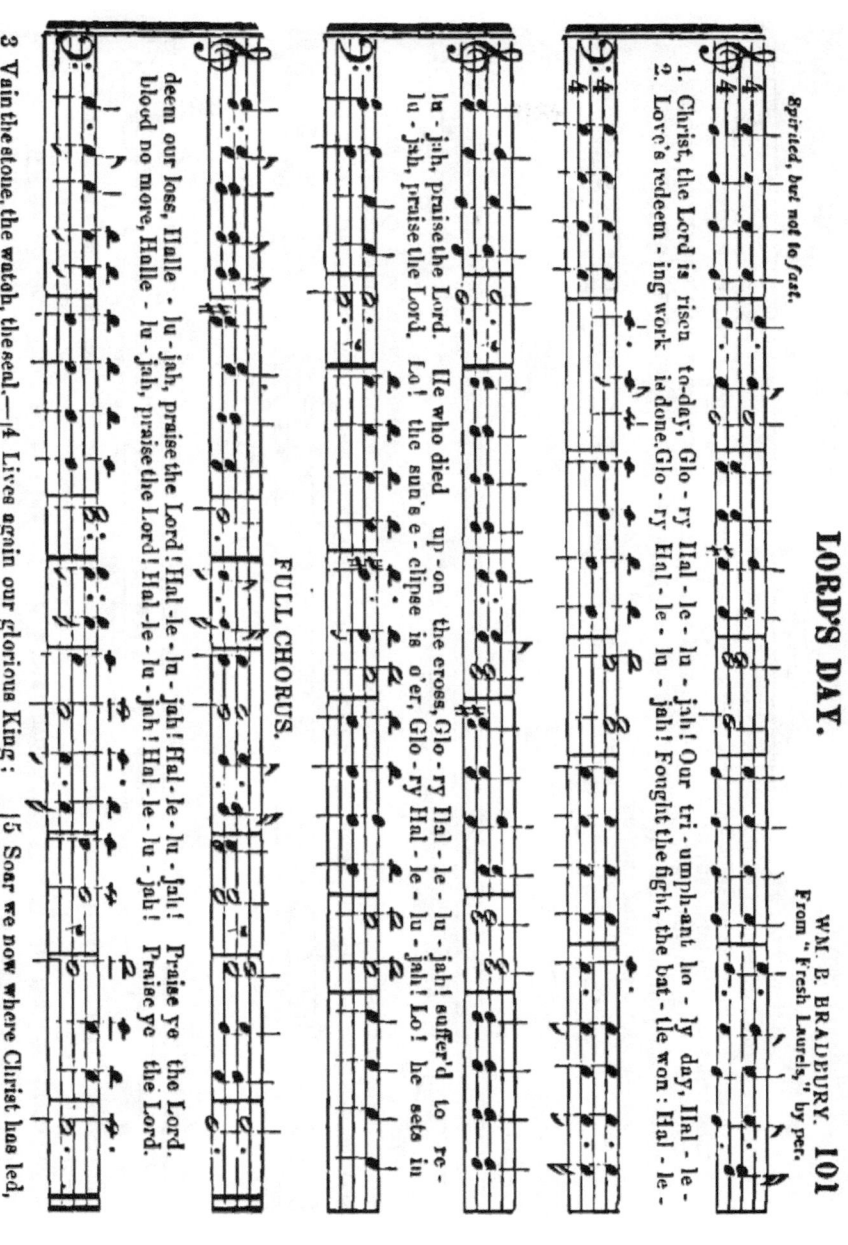

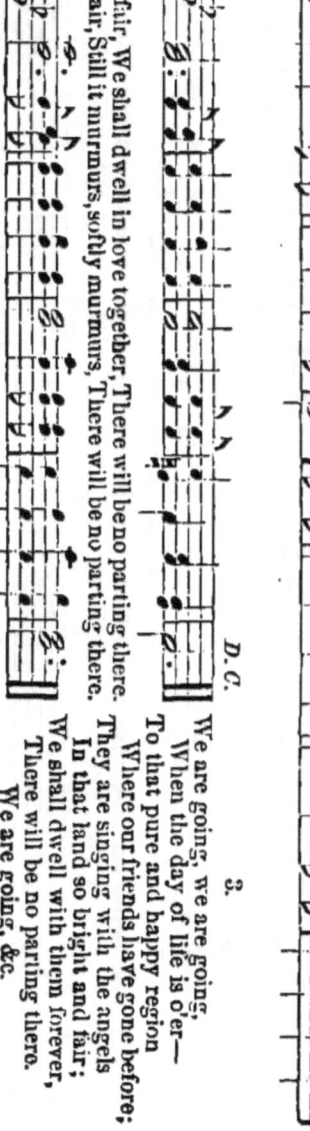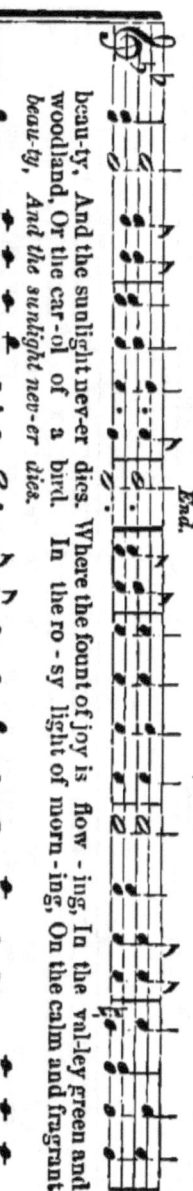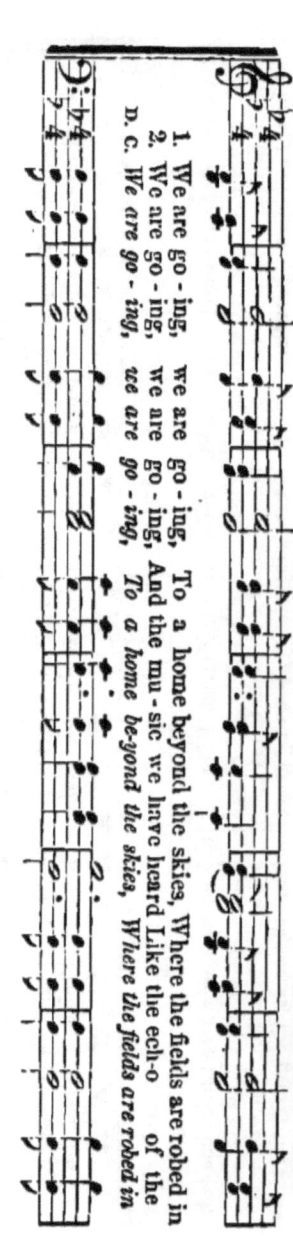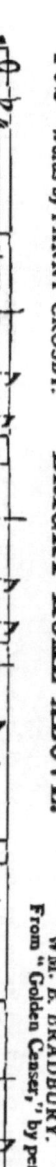

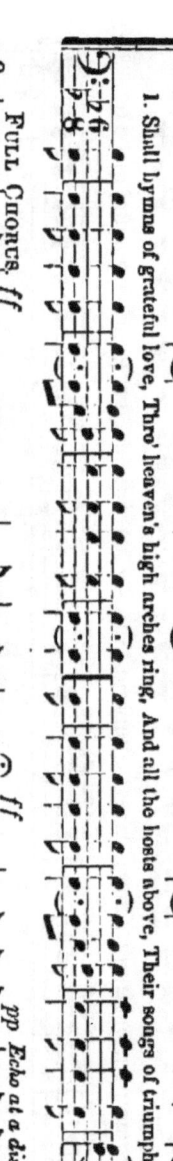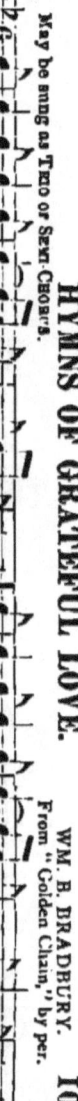

GLORY, GLORY TO THE LAMB.

WM. B. BRADBURY.
From "Golden Censer." By per.

1. Hark, the sweetest notes of angels singing, Glo-ry, glo-ry to the Lamb, All the hosts of heav'n their
2. Ye for whom His precious life was giv'n, Sacred themes to you belong; Come, and join the glorious
3. Endless life in Christ our Lord possessing, Let us praise His precious name; Glo-ry, hon-or, rich-es

trib-ute bringing, Raising high the Saviour's name.
choir of hea-ven, Join the ev-er-last-ing song.
power, and blessing, Be for-ev-er to the Lamb.

REFRAIN.

We will join the beau-ti-ful an-gels,

We will join the beautiful an-gels, Singing a-way, Singing a-way, Glo-ry, glo-ry to the Lamb.

SHALL WE SING IN HEAVEN?

WM. B. BRADBURY.
From "Golden Chain," by per.

1. Shall we sing in heaven for ev - er—Shall we sing? Shall we sing in heaven for ev - er,
2. Shall we sing with ho - ly an - gels In that land? In that land? Shall we sing with ho - ly an-gels
3. Shall we rest from care and sor-row, In that land? In that land? Shall we rest from care and sorrow,

In that hap-py land. Yes! oh, yes! in that land, that hap-py land, They that meet shall sing for ever,
In that hap-py land. Yes! oh, yes! in that land, that hap-py land, Saints and an-gels sing for ev - er,
In that hap-py land. Yes! oh, yes! in that land, that hap-py land, They that meet shall rest for ever,

REFRAIN.

Far be-yond the roll-ing riv - er, Meet to sing and love for ev - er, In that hap - py land.

4. Shall we meet our dear, lost children
In that land? In that land?
Shall we meet our dear, lost children
In that happy land?
Yes! oh, yes! in that land, that happy land,
Children meet and sing for ever
Far beyond the rolling river,
Meet to sing and love for ever,
In that happy land.

5. Shall we know our blessed Saviour
In that land? In that land?
Shall we know our blessed Saviour
In that happy land?
Yes! oh, yes! in that land, that happy land,
We shall know our blessed Saviour,
Far beyond the rolling river,
Love and serve him there for ever,
In that happy land.

106　MAY I COME IN?　WM. F. SHERWIN. By per.

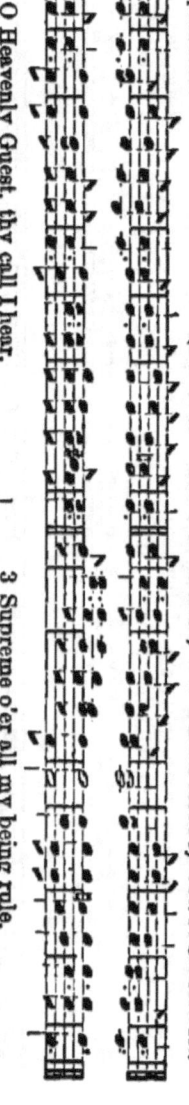

By permission.

1 Behold me standing at the door,
  And hear me pleading ever-more
  With gentle voice above the din,
  "May I come in?" "May I come in?"
2 I fought for thee with death's dark wave,
  I burst the dungeons of the grave;
  I would my rightful guerdon win—
  "May I come in?" "May I come in?"
3 I wore the cruel thorns for thee;
  I listen long and patiently

To bear thy footsteps from within,
  "May I come in?" "May I come in?"
4 There's surely room within thy breast
  For one more loving than the rest;
  More loving far than earthly kin—
  "May I come in?" "May I come in?"
5 I would not have thee beat in vain
  My Father's door, and plead in pain
  When Heaven and all its joys begin—
  "May I come in?" "May I come in?"

O LAMB OF GOD, COME IN!

(Answer to "MAY I COME IN?")　Words and Music by WM. F. SHERWIN.

1 O Heavenly Guest, thy call I hear,
  Thy pleadings move my soul within;
  My heart is open now to Thee;
  O Lamb of God, come in, come in.
2 Here let thy dwelling ever be,
  And for remove my every sin;
  Thrice welcome to my longing soul!
  Thou Best of Friends, come in, come in.

3 Supreme o'er all my being rule,
  That earth no more my love may win;
  Abide with me till life depart;
  O Blessed One, come in, come, in.
4 Help me to love thee more and more;
  Now let the work of grace begin;
  My strength, my hope, my Saviour dear,
  Thou All in All, come in, come in.

Words by JOSEPHINE POLLARD.

I STOOD OUTSIDE THE GATE.

HUBERT P. MAIN.

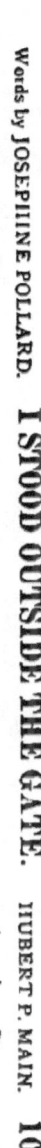

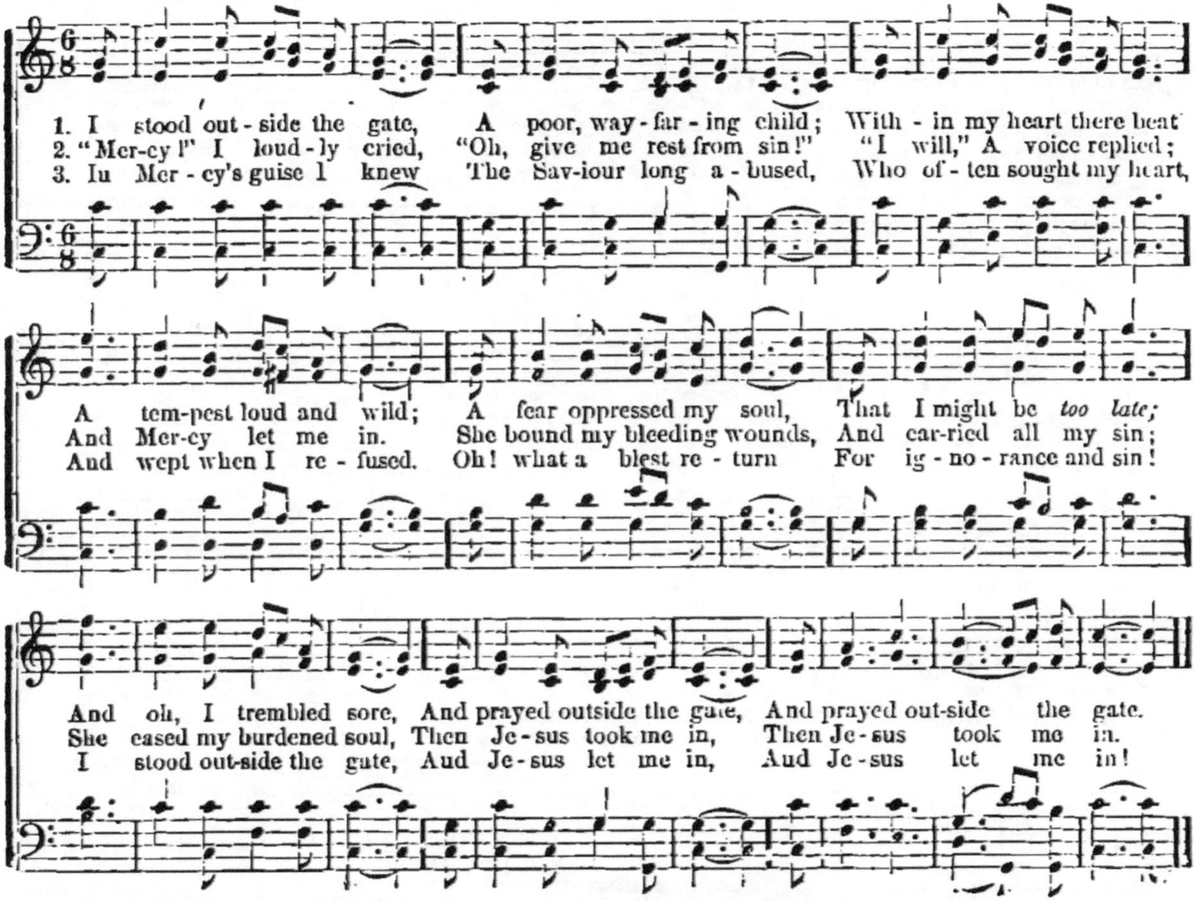

108. HARK! THE VOICE OF JESUS.

MISSION SONG.

Words by Y. A.
P. P. VAN ARSDALE.
From "Bright Jewels," by per.

1. Hark! the voice of Je-sus calling,—Who will go and work to-day? Fields are white, the harvest waiting,
2. If you cannot cross the ocean And the heathen lands explore, You can find the heathen nearer,
3. If you cannot speak like angels, If you cannot preach like Paul, You can tell the love of Jesus,

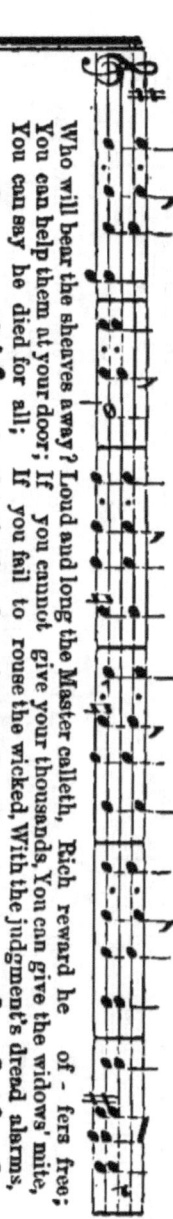

Who will bear the sheaves away? Loud and long the Master calleth, Rich reward he of-fers free;
You can help them at your door; If you cannot give your thousands, You can give the widows' mite,
You can say be died for all; If you fail to rouse the wicked, With the judgment's dread alarms,

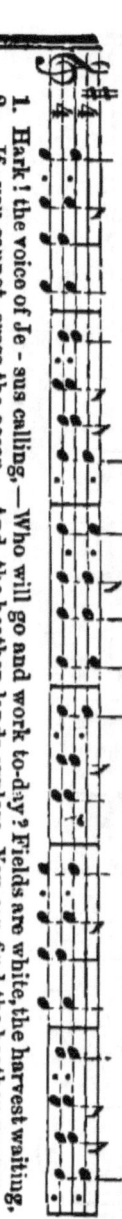

Who will answer, gladly saying, "Here am I, O Lord, send me."
And the least you do for Jesus Will be precious in his sight.
You may lead the lit-tle children To the Saviour's waiting arms.

4. While the souls of men are dying,
   And the Master calls for you,
   Let none hear you idly saying,
   "There is nothing I can do."
   Gladly take the task he gives you,
   Let his work your pleasure be
   Answer quickly when he calleth,
   "Here am I, O Lord, send me."

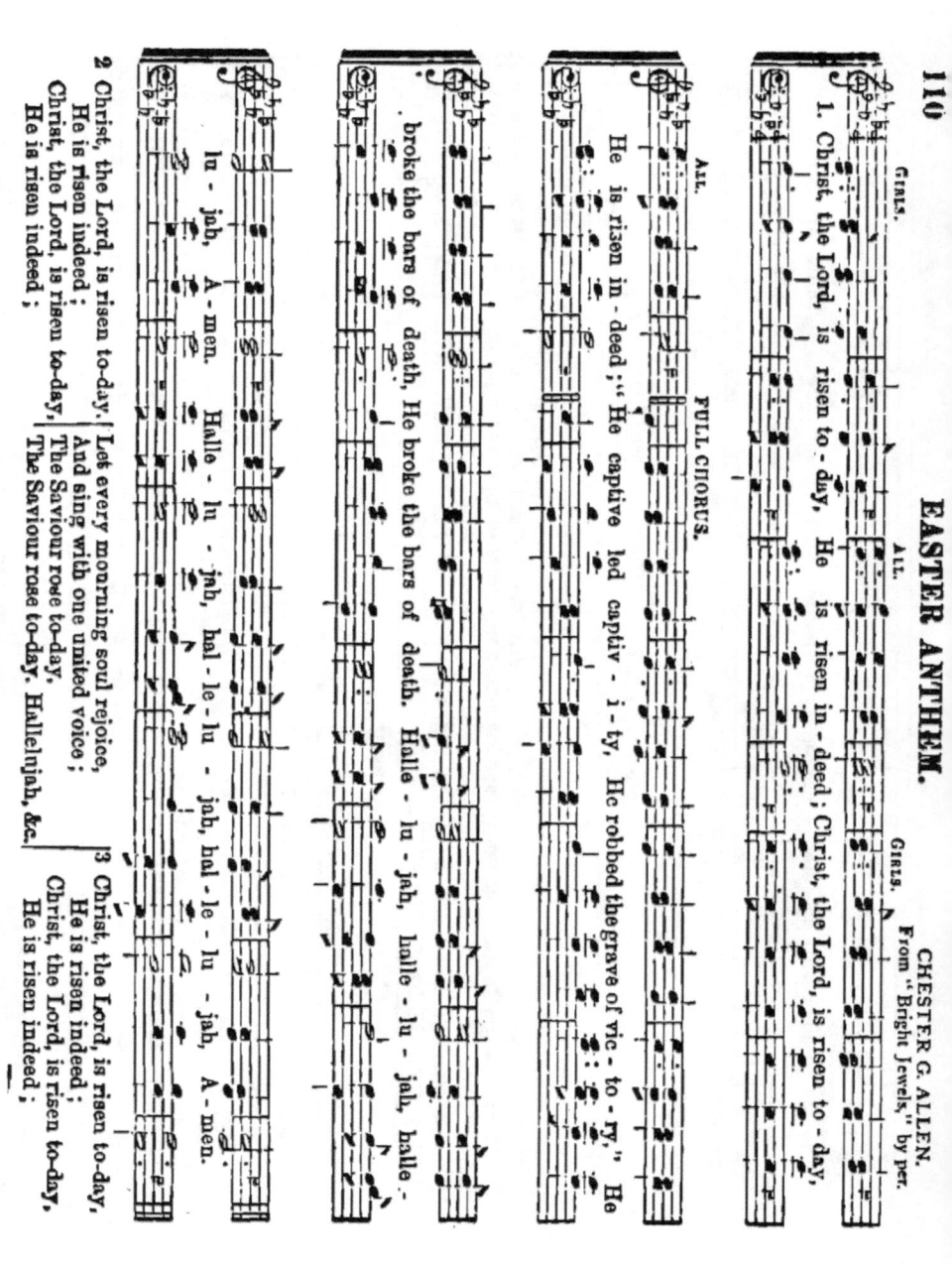

EASTER ANTHEM. Concluded.

The great and glorious work is done,
Free grace to all through Christ, the Son;
Hosanna to His name,
Hosanna to His name. Hallelujah, &c.

4 Christ, the Lord, is risen to-day,
He is risen indeed;

Christ, the Lord, is risen to-day,
He is risen indeed;
Let all that fill the earth and sea,
Break forth in tuneful melody,
And swell the mighty song,
And swell the mighty song. Hallelujah, &c.

THE LAND TO WHICH WE GO.

Words by FANNY CROSBY.

WM. F. SHERWIN.
Written for this Work.

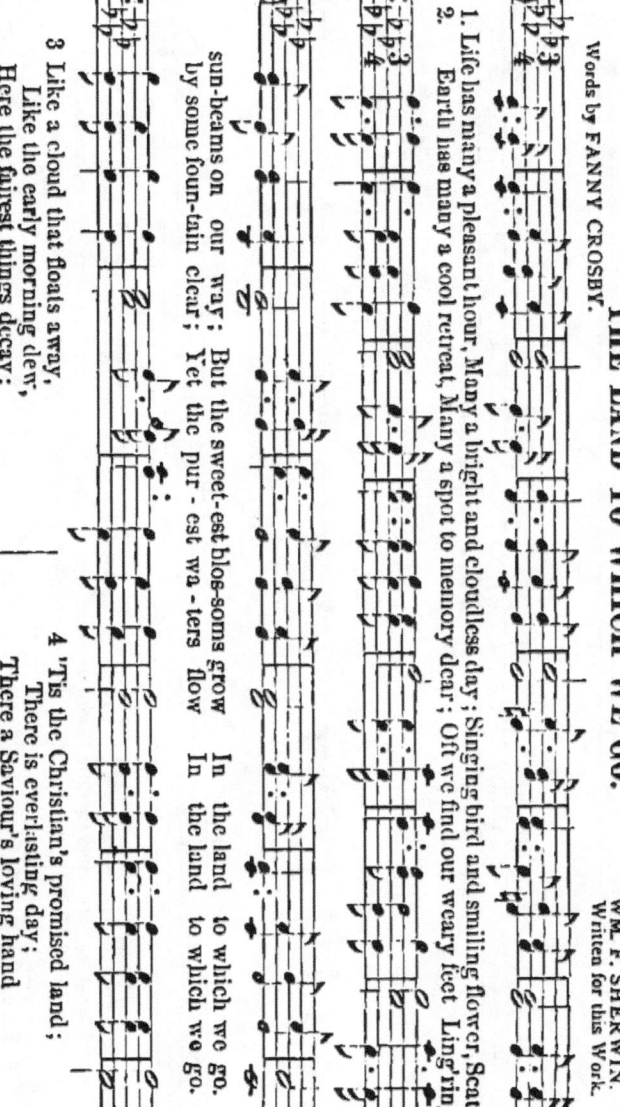

1. Life has many a pleasant hour, Many a bright and cloudless day; Singing bird and smiling flower, Scatter sun-beams on our way; But the sweet-est blos-soms grow In the land to which we go.
2. Earth has many a cool retreat, Many a spot to memory dear; Oft we find our weary feet Lingering by some foun-tain clear; Yet the pur - est wa - ters flow In the land to which we go.

3 Like a cloud that floats away,
Like the early morning dew;
Here the fairest things decay;
There, are pleasures ever new;
Only joy the heart will know
In the land to which we go.

4 "Tis the Christian's promised land;
There is everlasting day;
There a Saviour's loving hand
Wipes the mourner's tears away;
Oh! the rapture we shall know
In the land to which we go.

111

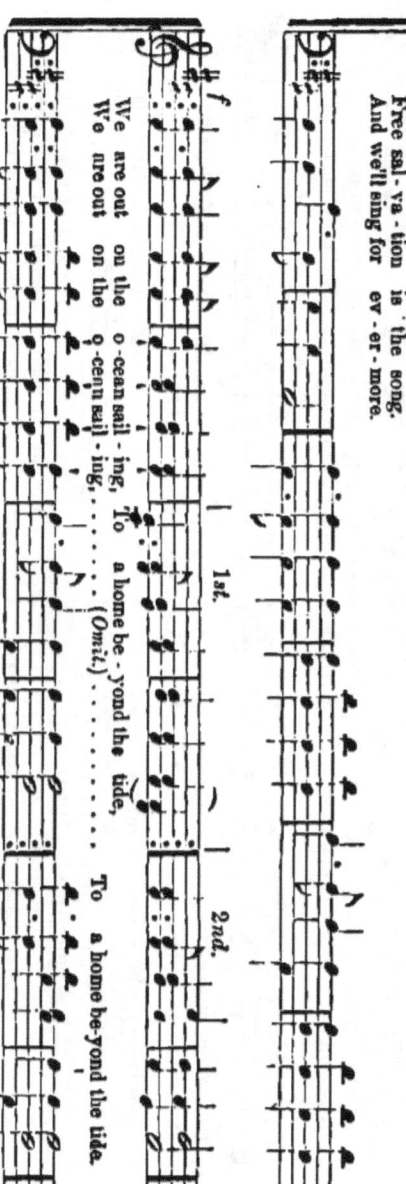

THE BETTER LAND.

"But now they desire a better country, that is an heavenly."—*Paul.*

WM. B. BRADBURY. 113
From the "Golden Chain," by per.

CHORUS.

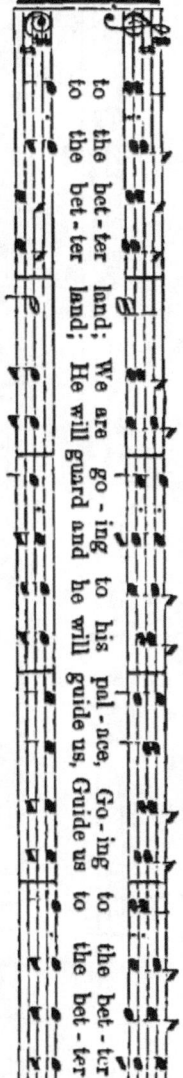

Boys. 1. (Whither, pilgrims, are you go - ing, Going each with staff in hand?)
Girls.   (We are go - ing on a journey, Going at our king's command.)
Boys. 2. (Fear ye not the way so lone - ly, You, a lit - tle, fee-ble band?)
Girls.   (No, for friends unseen are near us, Ho-ly an - gels round us stand.) Christ our lead - er, walks be-

val - leys, We are go - ing to his pal - ace, We are go - ing to his pal - ace, Go - ing
side us, He will guard, and He will guide us, He will guard, and He will guide us, Guide us

to the bet - ter land; We are go - ing to his pal - ace, Go - ing to the bet - ter land.
to the bet - ter land; He will guard and he will guide us, Guide us to the bet - ter land.

Boys. 3 Tell me, pilgrims, what you hope for
    In that far-off, better land?
Girls. Spotless robes and crowns of glory
    From a Saviour's loving hand;
All. We shall drink of life's clear river
    We shall dwell with God forever,
    We shall dwell with God forever
    In that bright, that better land.

Boys. 4 Pilgrims, may we travel with you
    To that bright and better land?
Girls. Come and welcome, come and welcome,
    Welcome to our pilgrim band.
All. Come, O come! and do not leave us,
    Christ is waiting to receive us,
    Christ is waiting to receive us,
    In that bright, that better land.

114 BALMY DEW.

Arr. by Rev. CHAS. BEECHER.

1. I know that my Re-deem-er lives, O glo-ry, hal-le-lu-jah! What comfort this sweet sentence gives, O glo-ry, hal-le-lu-jah! He lives, He lives who once was dead, O glo-ry, hal-le-lu-jah! He lives, my ev-er-liv-ing Head, O glo-ry, hal-le-lu-jah!
2. He lives to bless me with His love, O glo-ry, hal-le-lu-jah! He lives to plead for me a-bove, O glo-ry, hal-le-lu-jah! He lives my hun-gry soul to feed, O glo-ry, hal-le-lu-jah! He lives to help in time of need, O glo-ry, hal-le-lu-jah!
3. He lives to si-lence all my fears, O glo-ry, hal-le-lu-jah! He lives to wipe a-way my tears, O glo-ry, hal-le-lu-jah! He lives to calm my troubled heart, O glo-ry, hal-le-lu-jah! He lives all bless-ings to im-part, O glo-ry, hal-le-lu-jah!

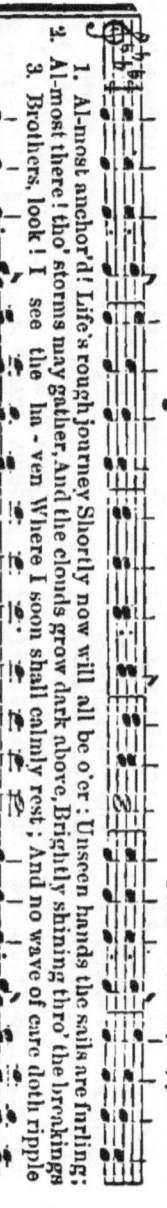

116 FLEMMING.

1. O ho-ly Sav-iour, Friend un - seen, Since on Thine arm Thou bidst me lean,
2. What tho' the world de-ceit - ful prove, And earthly friends and hopes re - move;
3. If e'er I seem to tread a - lone Life's wea-ry waste, with thorns o'er - grown,
4. If faith and hope are oft - en tried, I'll ask not, need not, aught be - side;

Help me throughout life's chang-ing scene, By faith to cling to Thee!
With pa-tient, un - com - plain-ing love, Still would I cling to Thee!
Thy voice of love in gen-tlest tone, Still whispers, "cling to Me!"
So safe, so calm, so sat - is - fied, The soul that clings to Thee!

1 Praise ye the Father! for His loving kindness,
Tenderly cares He for His erring children,
Praise Him, ye angels, praise Him in the heavens,
Praise ye Jehovah!

2 Praise ye the Saviour! great is His compassion,
Graciously cares He for His chosen people;

SECOND HYMN.

Young men and maidens, ye old men and children,
Praise ye the Saviour!

3 Praise ye the Spirit! comforter of Israel,
Sent of the Father, and the Son to bless us;
Praise ye the Father, Son, and Holy Spirit,
Praise ye the Triune God!

GOD OF MERCY, THRONED ON HIGH.

From "Cantica Sacra." 117

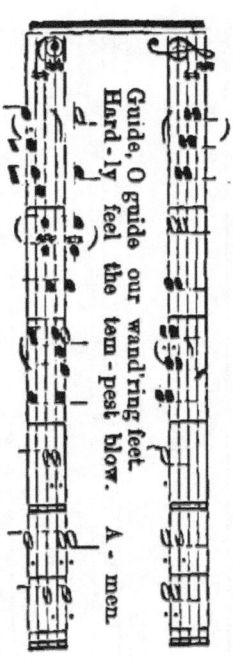

1. God of mer-cy, throned on high, Lis-ten from Thy loft-y seat; Hear, oh hear our fee-ble cry;
2. Young and erring travel-ers we All our dan-gers do not know; Scarcely fear the storm-y sea,

Guide, O guide our wand'ring feet.
Hard-ly feel the tem-pest blow. A-men.

3 Jesus, Lover of the young,
  Cleanse us with Thy Blood divine
  Ere the tide of sin grow strong;
  Save us, keep us, make us Thine.

4 Saviour, give us faith, and pour
  Hope and Love on every soul,—
  Hope, till time shall be no more ;
  Love, while endless ages roll. Amen.

THINE, LORD, FOREVER!

Words by W. BENNETT. HUBERT P. MAIN, by per.

1. Thine, Lord, for-ev-er! Purchas'd by blood di-vine, Rescued and saved by Thee, Lord, I am Thine!
2. Thine, Lord, for-ev-er! Thro' storm and tempest wild, Trusting con-fid-ing-ly, I am Thy child.

3 Thine, Lord, forever!
  Cheered by Thy precious word,
  Thro' darkness, doubts, and fears,
  Thine, thine, O Lord!

4 Thine, Lord, forever!
  Tho' death shall lay me low,
  Even in that dreadful hour
  Thine, Lord, I know!

5 Thine, Lord, forever!
  When safe before Thy throne
  I stand, forevermore
  Thine, thine alone!

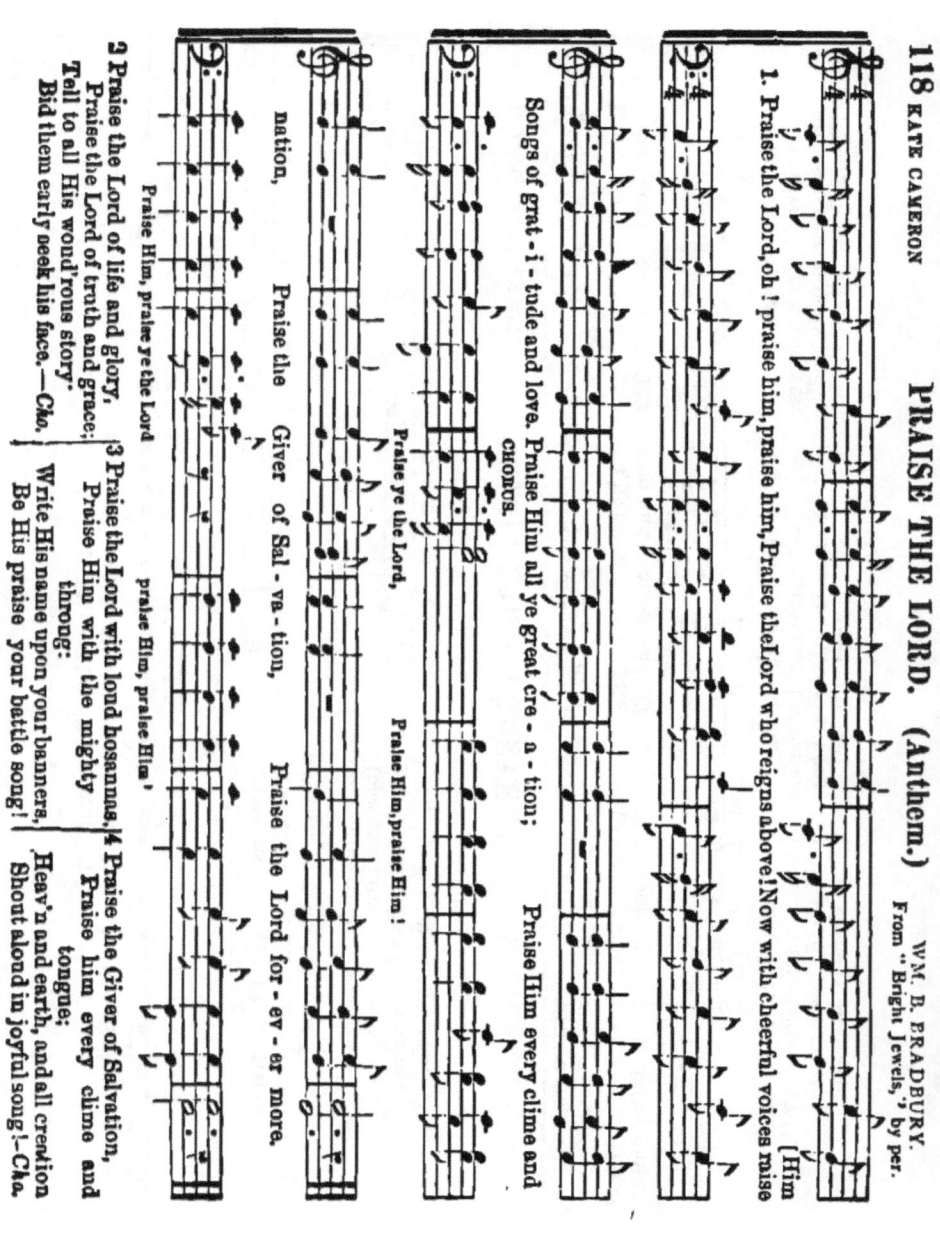

WITH GLADSOME FEET WE PRESS.

CORBET SINGLETON. 1867.
G. A. McFARREN.

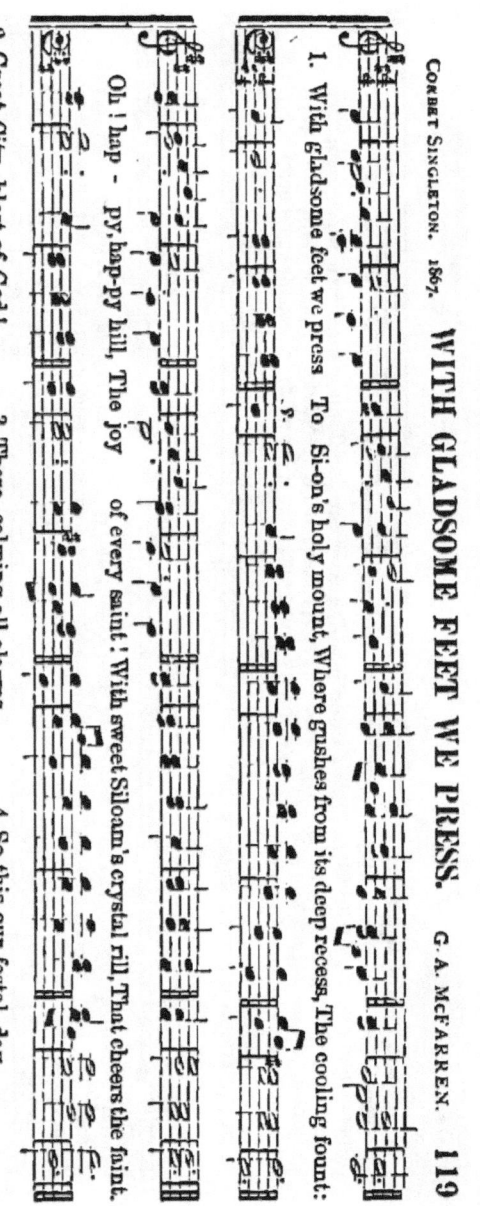

1. With gladsome feet we press To Sion's holy mount, Where gushes from its deep recess, The cooling fount: Oh! hap-py, hap-py hill, The joy of every saint! With sweet Siloam's crystal rill, That cheers the faint.

2. Great City, blest of God!
Jerusalem the free!
With ceaseless step the path be trod
That leads to Thee!
The martyr's bleeding feet,
The saints with woundless breast,
Alike have sought Thy golden seat,
To win their rest.

3. There, calming all alarms,
Thy Cross of Love is traced,
Outstretching salutary arms,
To bless the waste;
The sinner there can plead
In ever listening Ears;
On hope and Thee, can sweetly feed,
And dry his tears.

4. So this our festal day
Celestial joy shall raise,
While lips and hearts, conjoined, essay
To hymn Thy praise!
The very stones shall ring,
Resound each holy wall, [Spring,
With Thee, Thyself the Rock, the
Our Heaven, our All!

HOLLY. 7s.

GEO. HEWS.

1. Softly now the light of day Fades upon my sight away; Free from care, from labor free, Lord I would commune with Thee.
2. Soon for me the light of day Shall forever pass away; Then from sin, and sorrow free, Take me, Lord, to dwell with Thee.

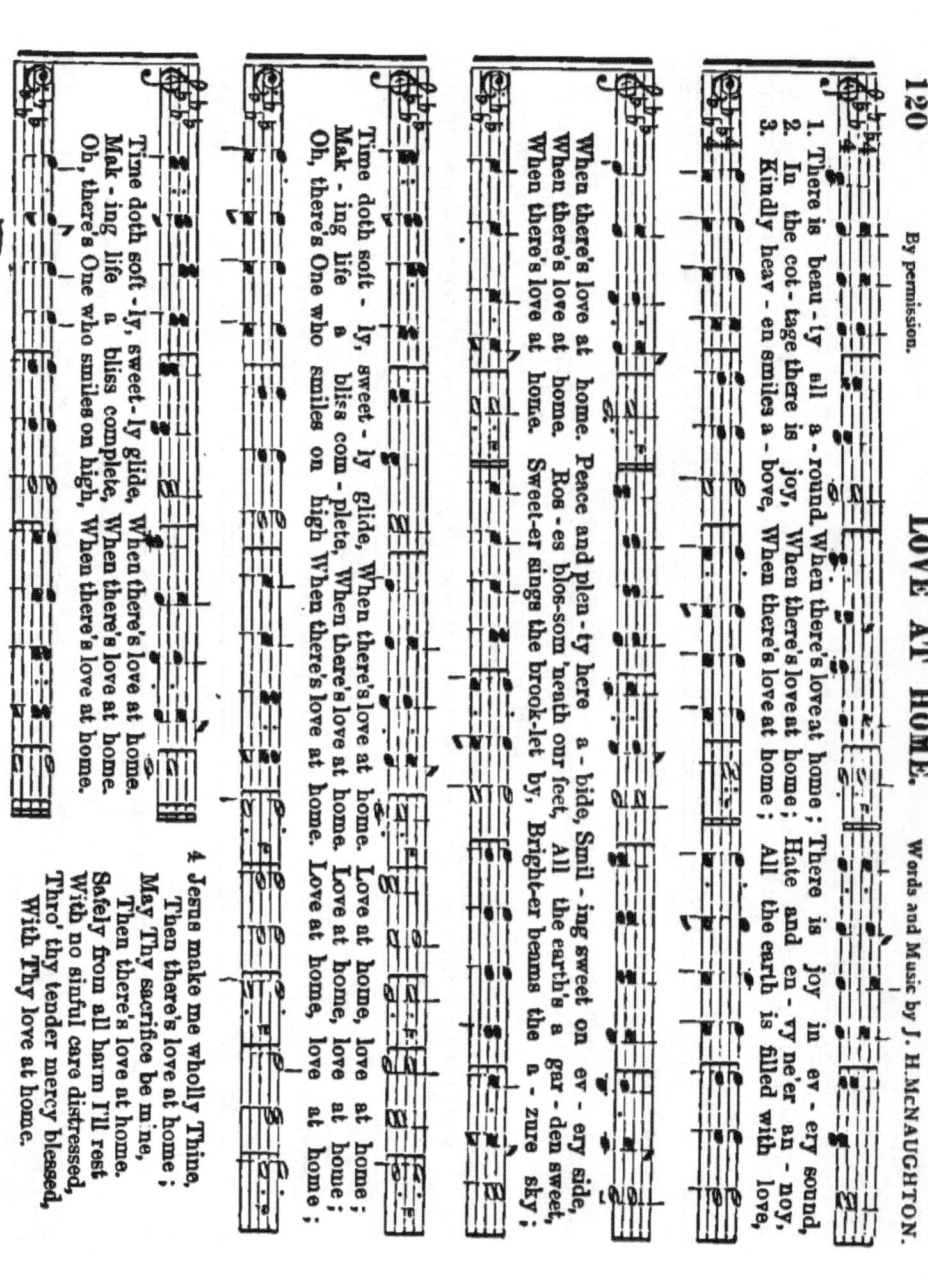

GUIDANCE. 8s & 6s.

Arr. from Flotow.

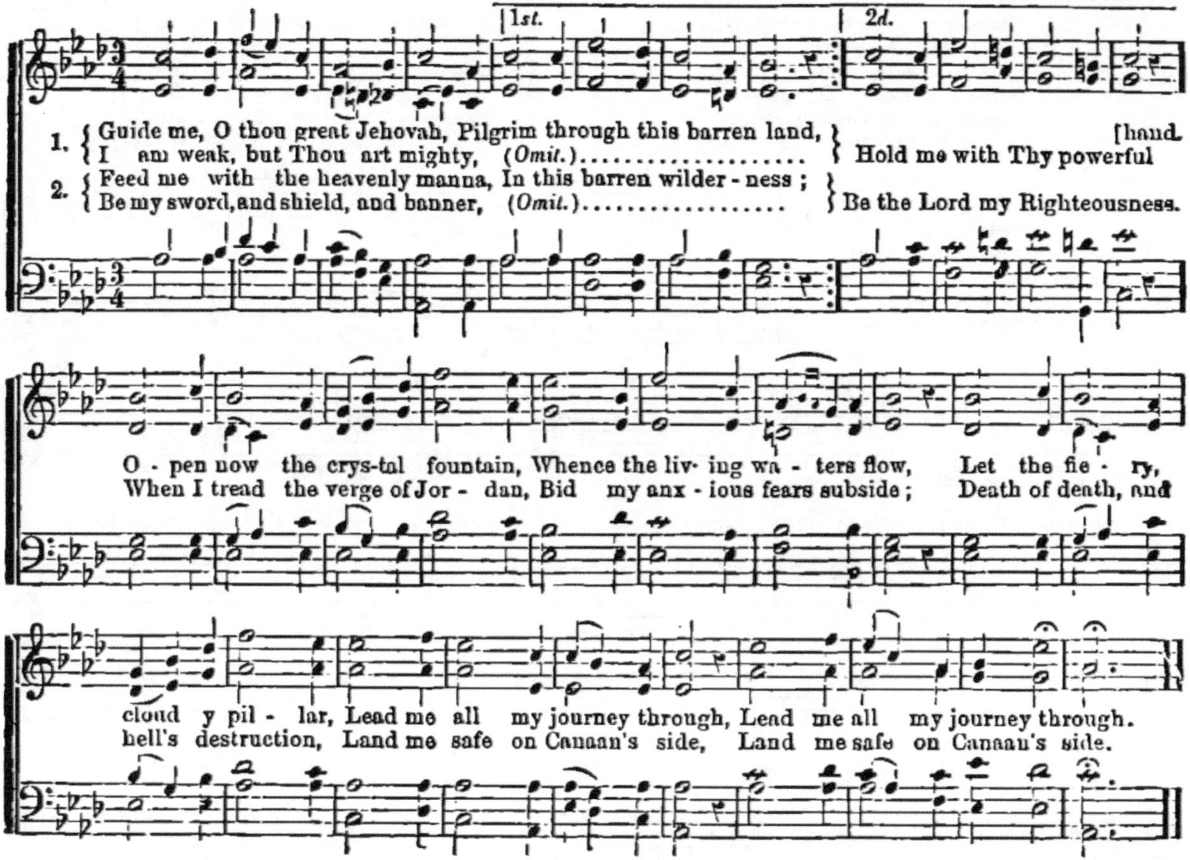
1st.
2d.
1. { Guide me, O thou great Jehovah, Pilgrim through this barren land,
I am weak, but Thou art mighty, (Omit.)...................... } Hold me with Thy powerful [hand.
2. { Feed me with the heavenly manna, In this barren wilder - ness ;
Be my sword, and shield, and banner, (Omit.).................. } Be the Lord my Righteousness.
O - pen now the crys-tal fountain, Whence the liv- ing wa - ters flow, Let the fie - ry,
When I tread the verge of Jor - dan, Bid my anx - ious fears subside ; Death of death, and
cloud y pil - lar, Lead me all my journey through, Lead me all my journey through.
hell's destruction, Land me safe on Canaan's side, Land me safe on Canaan's side.

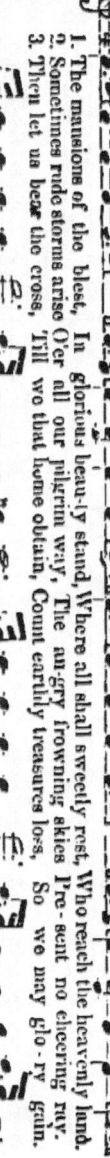

124. MY HOME IS THERE.

Words by Mrs. M. A. Kidder.

Wm. B. Bradbury.
From "Fresh Laurels," by per.

1. A-bove the waves of earth-ly strife, Above the ills and cares of life, Where all is peace - ful, bright, and fair; My home is there, My home is there. My beau-ti-ful home,...... My beau-ti-ful home,.... In the land where the glo-ri-fied ev - er shall beau-ti-ful home,....

2. Where liv-ing foun - tains sweet-ly flow, Where buds and flowers im-mortal grow, Where trees their fruits ce - les - tial bear; My home is there, My home is there. My beau-ti-ful

CHORUS.

My beau-ti-ful home, My beau-ti-ful home, In the land where the glo-ri-fied ev - er shall

MY HOME IS THERE. Concluded.

roam, Where angels bright...... wear crowns of light..... My home is there, my home is there.

roam, Where angels, angels bright, wear crowns, wear crowns of light, My home is there, my home is there.

3 Away from sorrow, doubt and pain,
Away from worldly loss and gain,
From all temptation, tears and care;
My home is there, my home is there. *Cho.*

4 Beyond the bright and pearly gates,
Where Jesus, loving Saviour, waits,
Where all is peaceful, bright, and fair;
My home is there, my home is there. *Cho.*

JESUS, WE THY LAMBS WOULD BE.

C. A. MARVIN.

1. Jesus we thy lambs would be, Humbly we would follow thee, Waiting for the joy-ful day, When all care will pass away,
2. Now the field with grain is white, Now the day in dawning bright.—Brighter far the sky will be, When our Master we shall see,
3. May we wait, and watch, and pray, For the coming of that day, When the wheat shall sifted be, And the chaff be driv'n from thee.

When the reaping time shall come, And angels about the harvest home, When the reaping time shall come, And angels about the harvest home.

NEVER ALONE.

Words by R. W. RAYMOND.
F. SILCHER.

1. Far out on the des-o-late bil-low, The sail-or sails the sea; A-
2. Far down in the earth's dark bo-som, The min-er mines the ore; Death
3. Lord, grant as we sail. life's o-cean, Or delve in its mines of woe; Or

lone with the night and the tempest, Where countless dan-gers be.
lurks in the dark be-hind him, And hides in the rock be-fore.
fight in its ter-ri-ble con-flict, This com-fort all to know,

CHORUS.

Yet, nev-er a-lone is the
That nev-er a-lone, &c.

Christian, Who lives by faith and prayer; For God is a friend un-fail-ing, And God is ev'ry-where.

AMERICA. (National Hymn.) 103 Trio.

1.
My country, 'tis of thee,
Sweet land of liberty,
Of thee I sing;
Land where my fathers died,
Land of the pilgrim's pride,
From ev'ry mountain side
Let freedom ring.

2.
My native country! thee,
Land of the noble free,
Thy name I love;
I love thy rocks and rills,
Thy woods and templed hills,
My heart with rapture thrills,
Like that above.

3.
Let music swell the breeze,
And ring from all the trees
Sweet freedom's song:
Let mortal tongues awake,
Let all that breathe partake,
Let rocks their silence break,
The sound prolong.

REV. S. F. SMITH. 1831.

4.
Our father's God, to thee,
Author of liberty,
To thee we sing:
Long may our land be bright
With freedom's holy light;
Protect us by thy might,
Great God, our King.

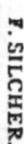

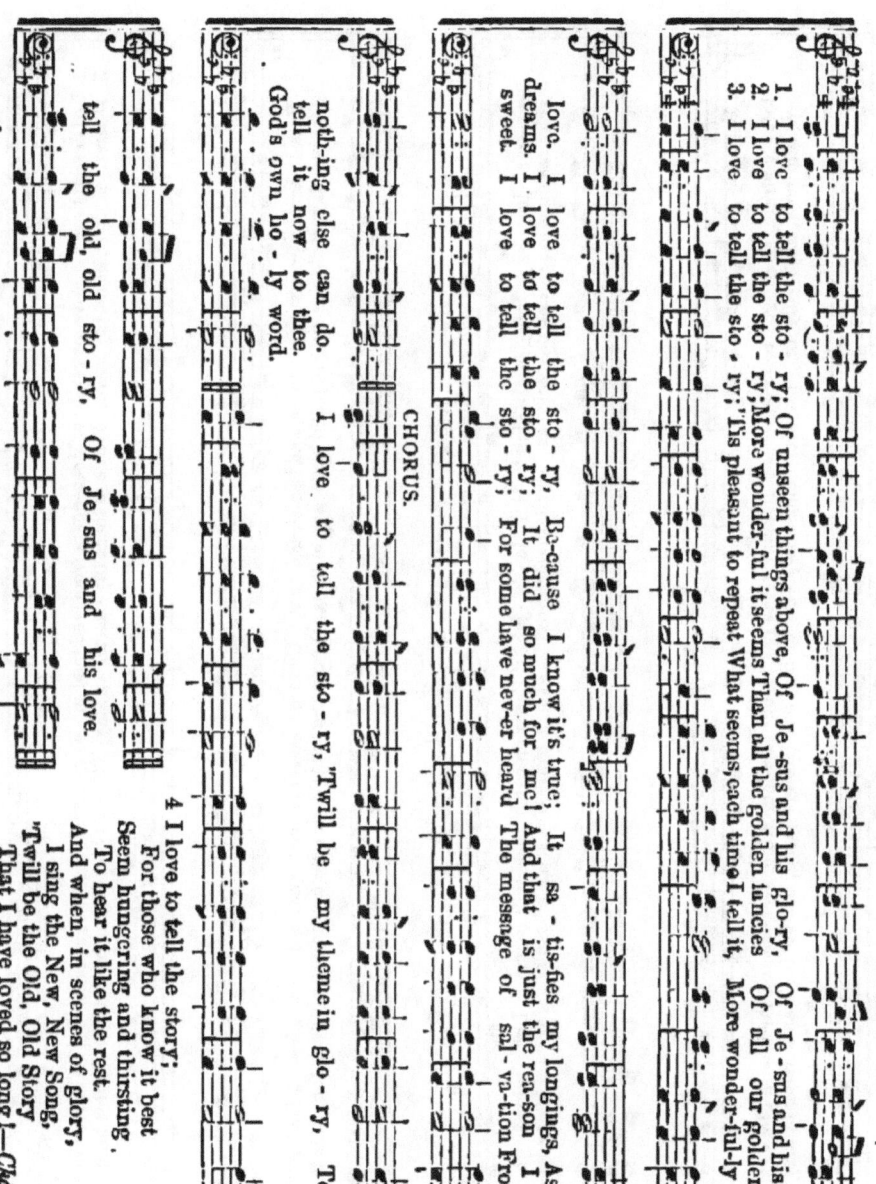

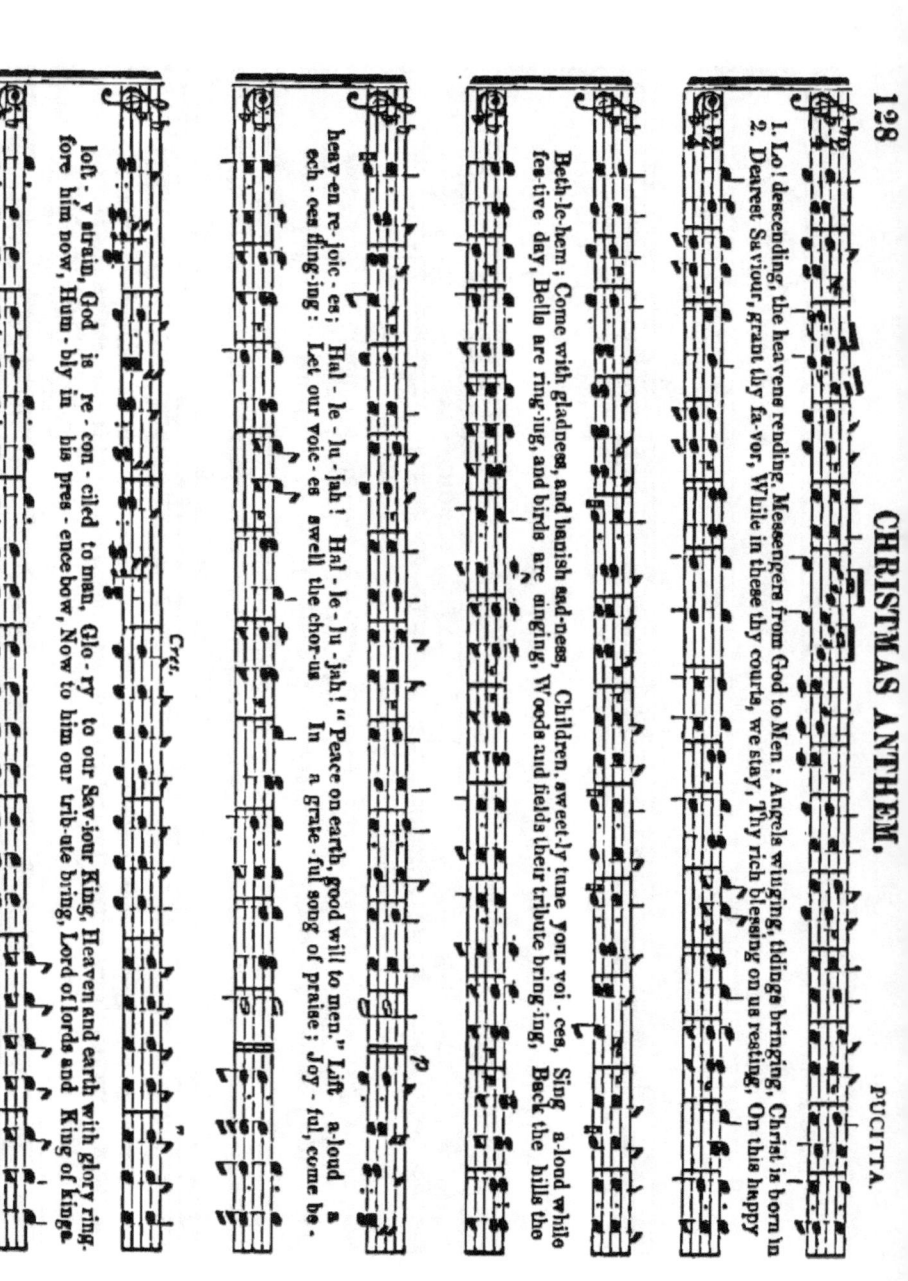

CHRISTMAS ANTHEM. Concluded.

Praise him, Praise him, The Lord Jehovah praise, Praise him, Praise him, The Lord Jehovah praise, Hosanna! Hosanna. Praise him, Praise him, Ye grateful children, praise, Praise him, Praise him, Ye grateful children, praise, Hosanna! Hosanna.

STILL PRESSING ON.

Words by FANNY C.
Music by WM. B. BRADBURY. By per.

1. Not dreary the world we in-hab-it, Or lone-ly the path that we tread; Our Father his blessings around us In richest pro-fus-ion has spread. Still we're pressing on To reach a brighter shore, Where pleasure like a ri-ver flows, And the good shall part no more.
2. The mercies of God are unbounded; Like sunbeams they tenderly fall; And while from his hand we receive them We'll praise him and thank him for all.

ff REFRAIN.

3 Our sky may be clouded a moment,
But soon 'twill be lovely and bright;
The joy will return with the morning,
Our sorrow will last but a night.—*Ref.*

4 Not dreary the world we inhabit,
Yet here, as we journey along,
We'll think of the brighter and better,
And tell of its glory in song.—*Ref.*

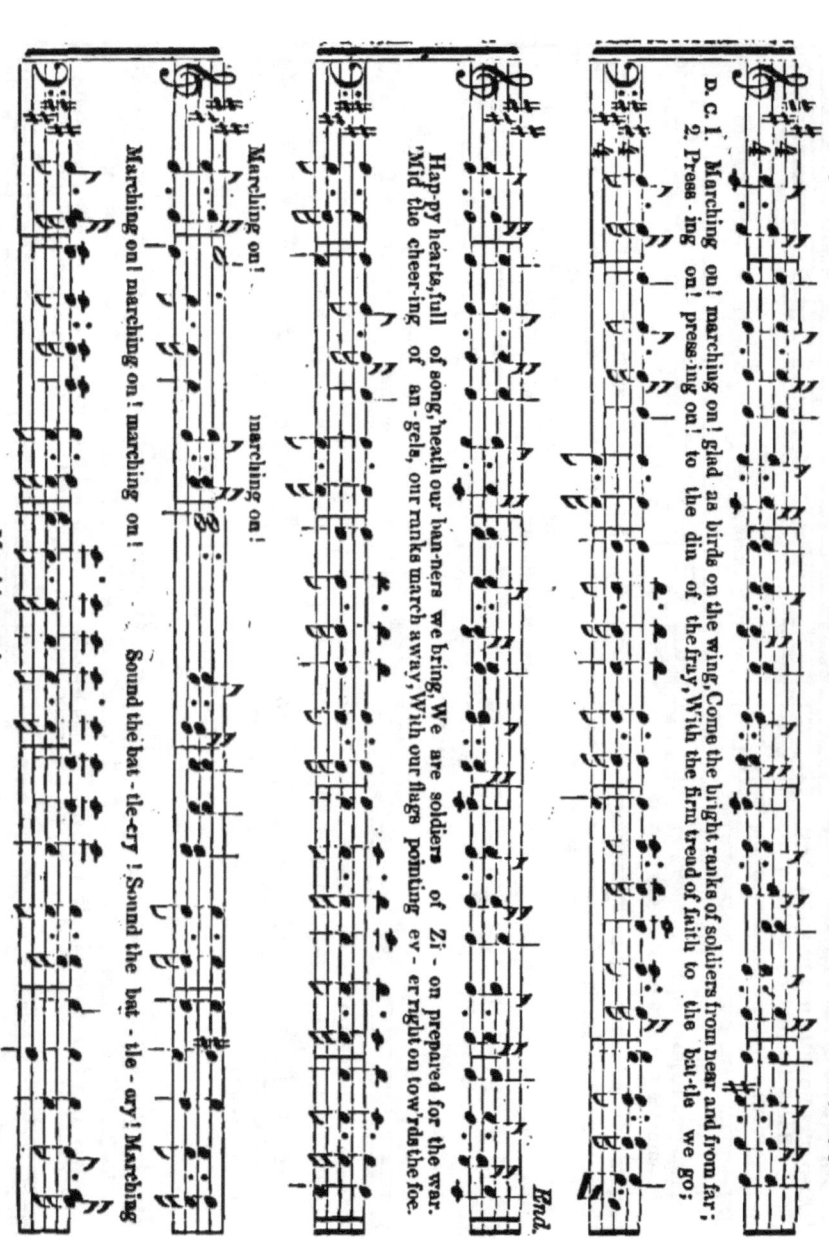

MARCHING ON! Concluded.

on! marching on! marching on! marching on! Shout the victo-ry, the vic-to-ry, the vic-to-ry!

D. C.

3.
Fighting on! fighting on! in the midst of the strife,
At the call of our Captain, we draw ev'ry sword;
We are battling for God, we are struggling for life,
Let us strike ev'ry rebel that fights 'gainst the Lord.
Cho.—Marching on, &c.

4.
Singing on! singing on! from the battle we come,
Ev'ry flag bears a wreath, ev'ry soldier renown;
Heav'nly angels are waiting to welcome us home,
And the Saviour will give us a robe and a crown.
Cho.—Marching on, &c.

COME, COME TO JESUS!

Words by Rev. GEO. R. PECK.   HUBERT P. MAIN. By per.
Tenderly.

1. Come, come to Jesus! He waits to welcome thee, O wand'rer, ea-ger-ly; Come, come to Jesus!
2. Come, come to Jesus! He waits to ransom thee, O slave! e-ter-nal-ly; Come, come to Jesus!
3. Come, come to Jesus! He waits to lighten thee, O burdened! trustingly; Come, come to Jesus!

4 Come, come to Jesus!
   He waits to give to thee,
O blind! a vision free;
   Come, come to Jesus!

5 Come, come to Jesus!
   He waits to shelter thee,
O weary! blessedly;
   Come, come to Jesus!

6 Come, come to Jesus!
   He waits to carry thee,
O lamb! so lovingly;
   Come, come to Jesus!

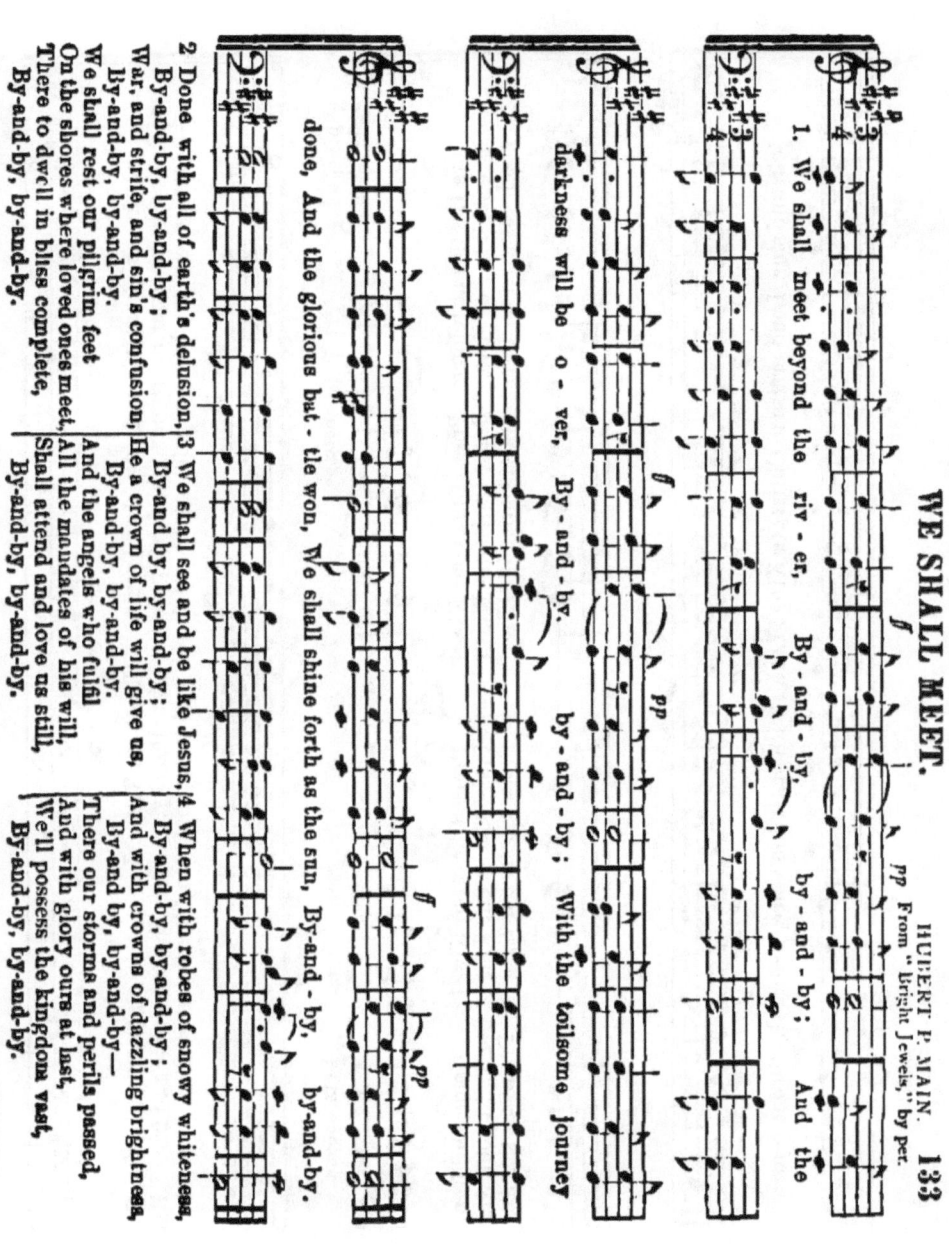

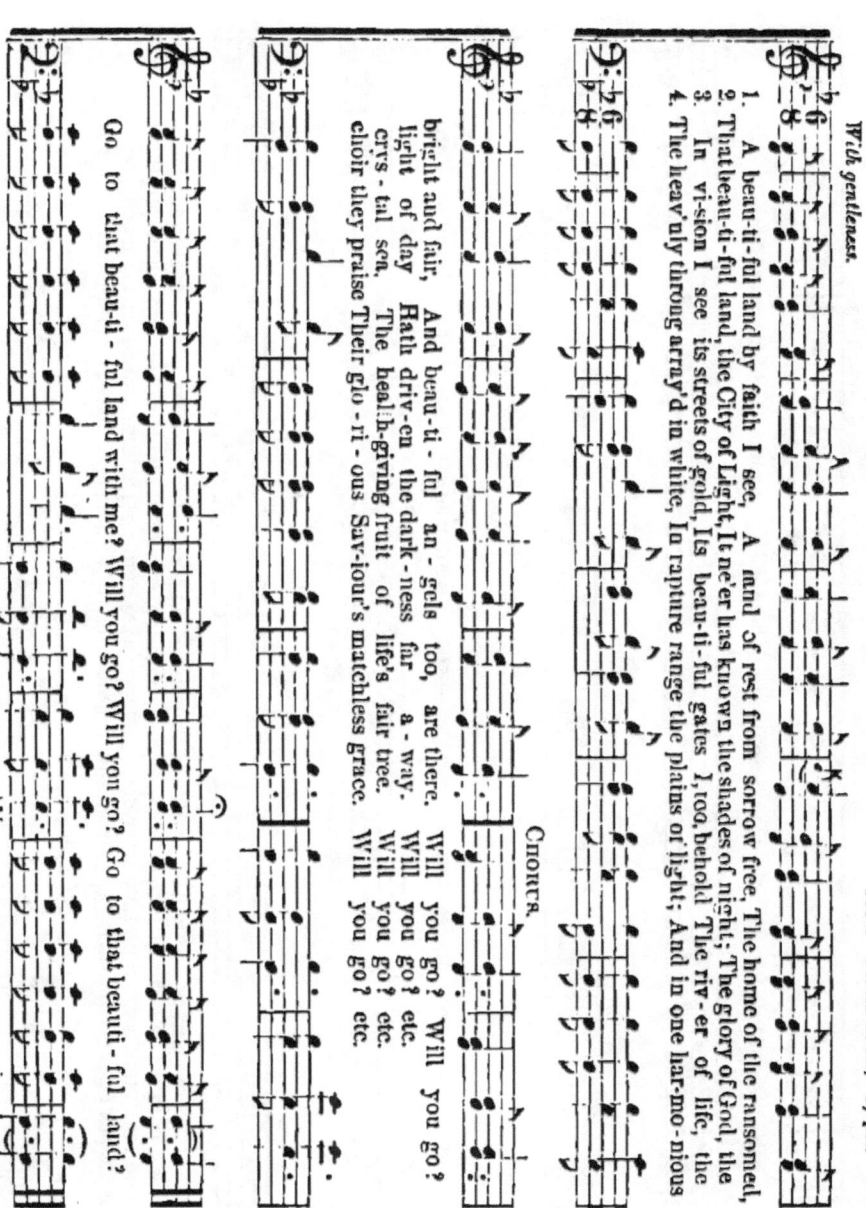

ZION'S HILL.

WM. B. BRADBURY.
From "Golden Chain." By permission.

1. What are these soul-reviving strains Which echo thus from Salem's plains? What anthems loud and louder
2. Lo! 'tis an in-fant chorus sings, Hosanna to the King of kings, The Saviour comes! and babes pro-
3. Messiah's name shall joy impart, Alike to Jew and Gentile heart; He bled for me, He bled for
4. Proclaim hosannas loud and clear; See David's Son and Lord appear! All praise on earth to Him be

CHORUS.—*Very spirited.*

still, So sweet-ly sound from Zi - on's hill? Ho-san - na, ho-san-na, ho-san-na to the
claim Sal - va-tion sent in Je-sus' name.
you, And we will sing ho-san - na too.
given, And glo - ry shout thro' highest heaven.

Lamb of God! Ho-sanna, ho-san-na, ho-sanna, in the high-est, in the high - est, in the high - est.

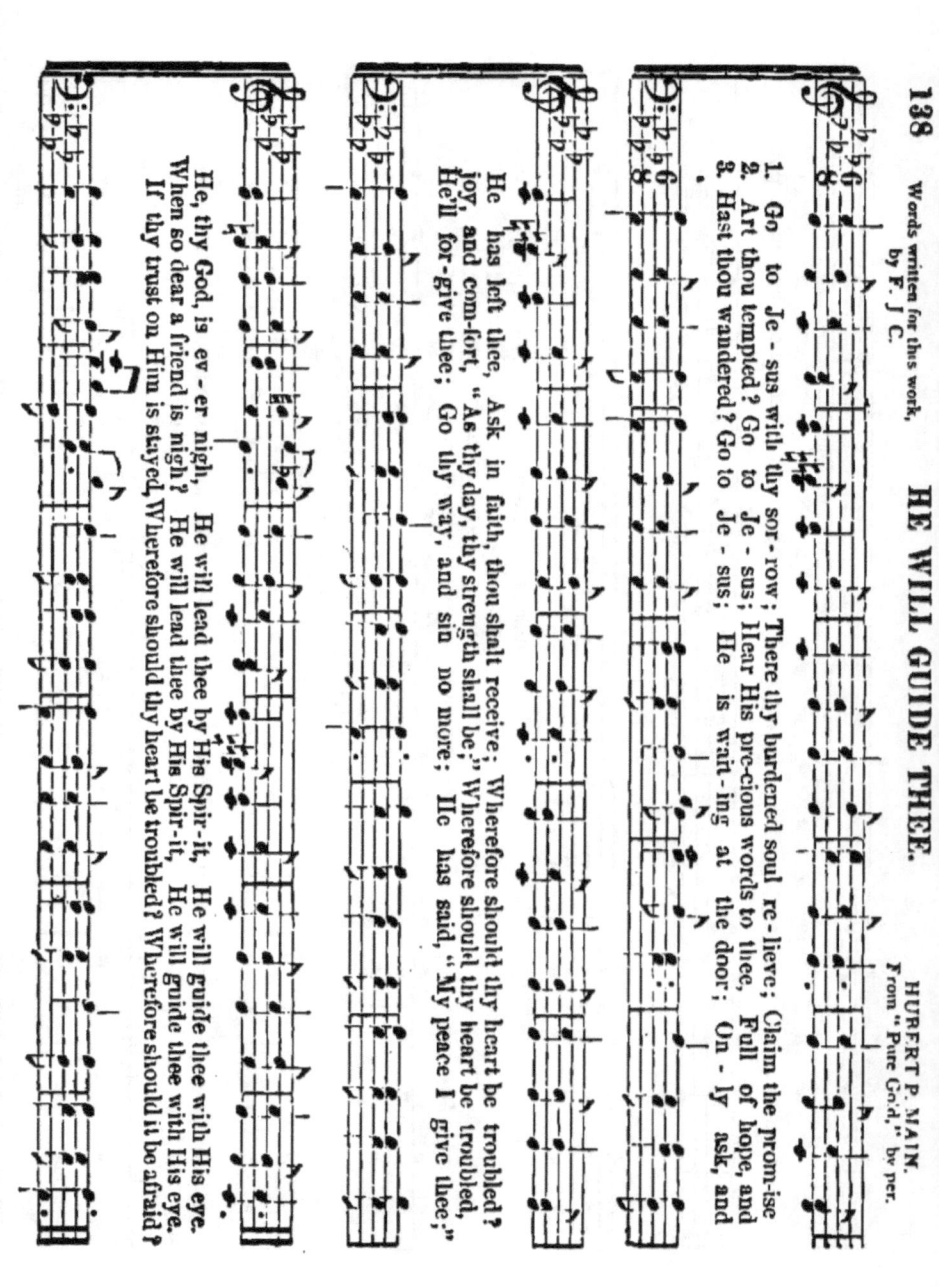

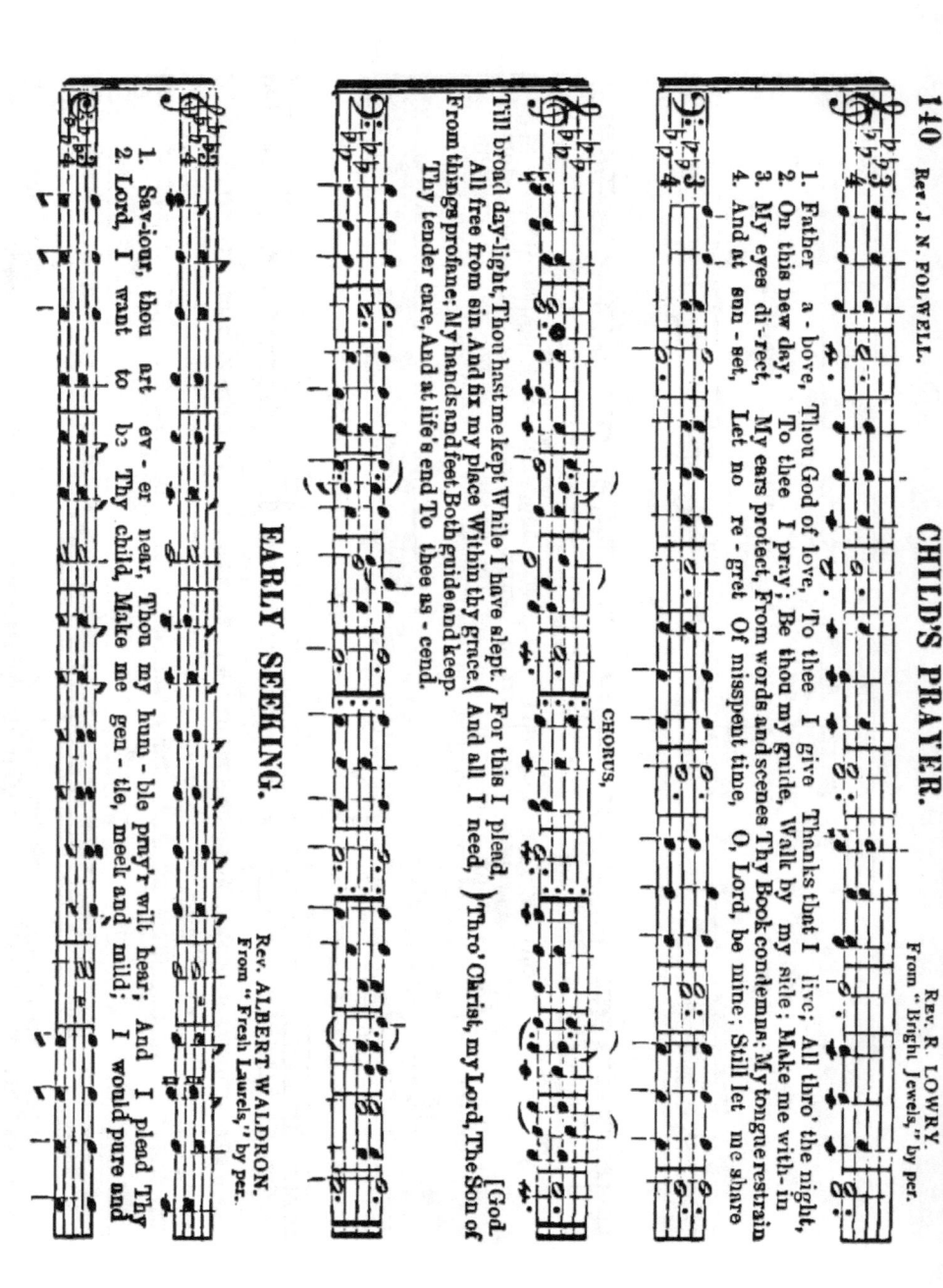

HOLY, HOLY! LORD GOD ALMIGHTY!

Rev. J. B. DYKES.

1. Ho-ly, Ho-ly, Ho-ly! Lord God Al-migh-ty! Ear-ly in the morning our song shall rise to Thee;
2. Ho-ly, Ho-ly, Ho-ly! all the saints adore Thee, Casting down their golden crowns around the glassy sea;

Ho-ly, Ho-ly, Ho-ly! Mer-ci-ful and Might-y! God in Three Persons, blessed Trin-i-ty!
Che-ru-bim and Ser-aphim falling down before Thee, Which wert, and art, and ev-er-more shalt be. A-men.

3 Holy, Holy, Holy! though the darkness hide Thee,
Though the eye of sinful man Thy glory may not see,
Only Thou art Holy, there is none beside Thee
Perfect in power, in love, and purity.

4 Holy, Holy, Holy! Lord God Almighty!
All Thy works shall praise Thy Name in earth, and sky, and sea;
Holy, Holy, Holy! Merciful and Mighty!
God in Three Persons, blessed Trinity! Amen

EARLY SEEKING. Concluded.

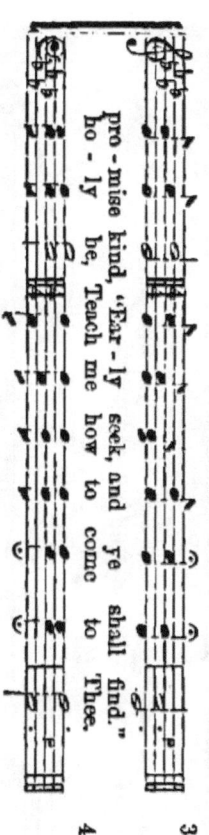

pro-mise kind, "Ear-ly seek, and ye shall find."
ho-ly be, Teach me how to come to Thee.

3 When I go to work or play,
  Be Thou with me day by day;
  When I seek my quiet bed,
  Let Thy wings be o'er me spread.

4 Saviour, hold me lest I fall,
  Deign to bear me whilst I call;
  O, regard my humble cry!
  Save me, Jesus, or I die.

142. THE CHORUS OF PRAISE.

Words by R. W. RAYMOND.
From "Clariona," by per.

1. O what can you tell, little pebble, little pebble, O what can you tell, little pebble, by the sea! The
Ref.—It is the love of God in heaven, The God who made both you and me, And
se-cret of your si-lent life, Now whisper it to me!
every day I think His praise In si-lence by the sea.

D.C. Ref.

2. O what can you tell, little flower, little flower,
O what can you tell, little flower on the lea!
The secret of your sweet perfume,
Now whisper it to me.
Ref.—It is the love of God in heaven,
The God who made both you and me,
And every day I breathe His praise
In fragrance on the lea.

3. O what can you tell, little bird, little bird,
O what can you tell, little bird upon the tree!
The secret of your joyous song,
Now whisper it to me!
Ref.—It is the love of God in heaven,
The God who made both you and me,
And every day I sing His praise
Upon the summer tree.

4. O what can you tell, little child, little child,
O what can you tell, little child upon my knee!
The secret of your happy smile,
Now whisper it to me!
Ref.—It is the love of God in heaven,
The God who made both you and me,
And every day I seek His face
Upon my bended knee!

Full. Cho.—Thus to the love of God in heaven,
The God who made both you and me,
The praise of all things here is given,
And evermore shall be!

WHAT SHALL I DO TO BE SAVED?

WM. B. BRADBURY. 143

From "Golden Shower," by per.

1. O! what shall I do to be saved From the sorrows that burden my soul? Like the waves in the storm When the winds are at war, Chilling floods of dis-tress o'er me roll. What shall I do? what shall I do? O! what shall I do to be saved?
2. O! what shall I do to be saved When the pleasures of youth are all fled? And the friends I have loved, From the earth are re-moved, And I weep o'er the graves of the dead. What shall I do? what shall I do? O! what shall I do to be saved?
3. O! what shall I do to be saved When sickness my strength shall subdue? Or the world in a day, Like a cloud roll a-way, And e-ter-ni-ty o-pens to view? What shall I do? what shall I do? O! what shall I do to be saved?

4.

O! Lord, look in mercy on me,
Come, O come and speak peace to my soul:
Unto whom shall I flee,
Dearest Lord, but to Thee,
Thou canst make my poor broken heart whole.
That will I do! that will I do!
To Jesus I'll go and be saved.

144   Words by Miss THALHEIMER.   MY SHEPHERD.   CRAMER.

1. Thou art my shepherd, Car-ing in ev-ery need, Thy lit-tle lamb to feed, Trusting Thee still;
2. Or if my way lie Where death o'erhanging nigh, My soul would ter-ni-fy With sudden chill,—

In the green pastures low, Where living wa-ters flow, Safe by Thy side I go, Fear-ing no ill.
Yet I am not a-fraid; While softly on my head Thy ten-der hand is laid, I fear no ill!

SECOND HYMN.

1 Lord, do not leave me!
  I'm but a little child,
  Weak, poor, and sin defiled,
    Afraid, alone;
But Thou art strong and wise,
No ill can Thee surprise;
Beneath Thy loving eyes
    Danger is none.

2 If Thou wilt guide me,
  Gladly I'll go with Thee;—
  No harm can come to me,
    Holding Thy hand;
And soon my weary feet,
Safe in the golden street,
Where all who love Thee meet,
    Redeem'd shall stand.

THE SAVIOUR'S PRAISE.

C. A. MARVIN, by per.

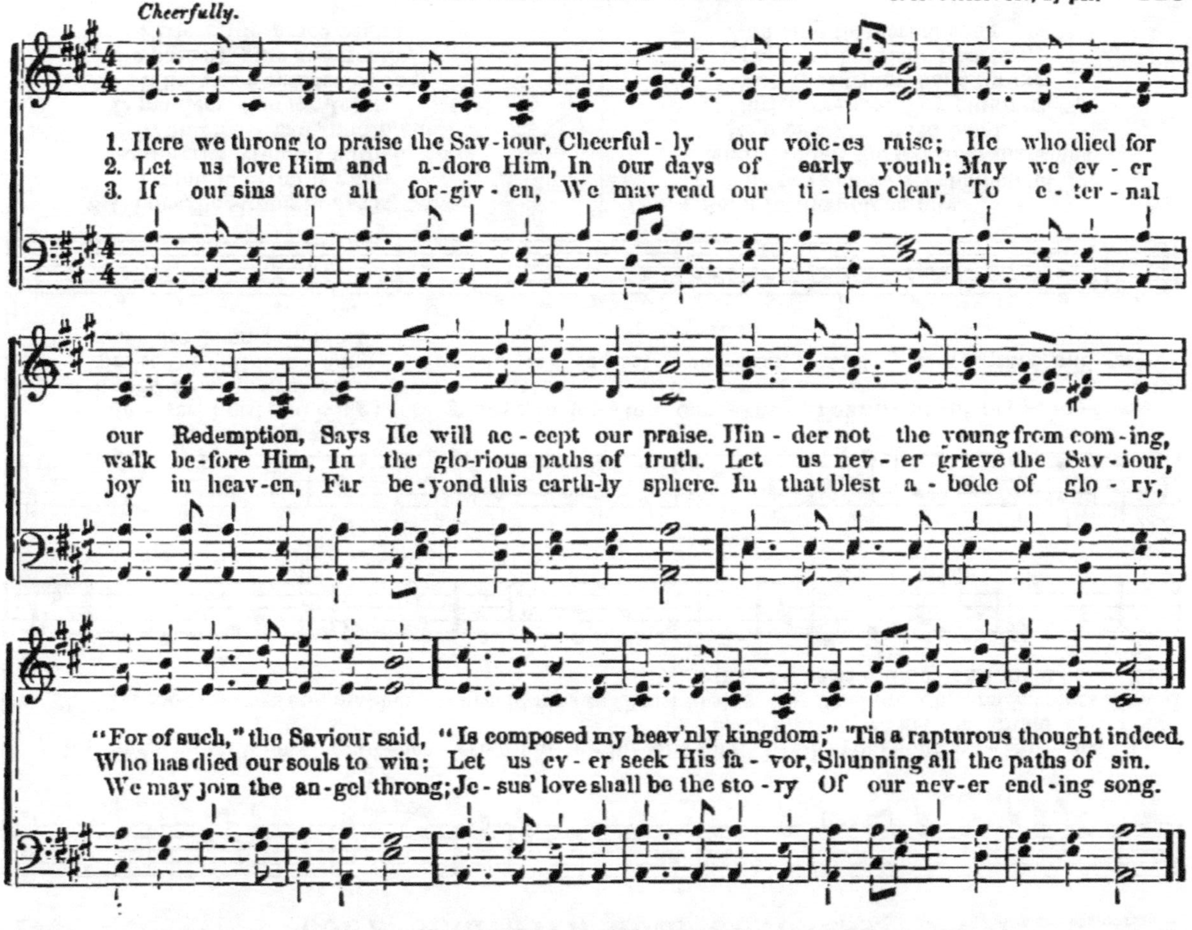

Cheerfully.

1. Here we throng to praise the Saviour, Cheerful-ly our voic-es raise; He who died for
2. Let us love Him and a-dore Him, In our days of early youth; May we ev - er
3. If our sins are all for-giv - en, We may rend our ti - tles clear, To e - ter - nal

our Redemption, Says He will ac - cept our praise. Hin - der not the young from com - ing,
walk be-fore Him, In the glo-rious paths of truth. Let us nev - er grieve the Sav - iour,
joy in heav-en, Far be-yond this earth-ly sphere. In that blest a - bode of glo - ry,

"For of such," the Saviour said, "Is composed my heav'nly kingdom," "Tis a rapturous thought indeed,
Who has died our souls to win; Let us ev - er seek His fa - vor, Shunning all the paths of sin.
We may join the an - gel throng, Je - sus' love shall be the sto - ry Of our nev-er end-ing song.

THE WELCOME HOME.

WM. B. BRADBURY.
From "Golden Shower," by per.

147

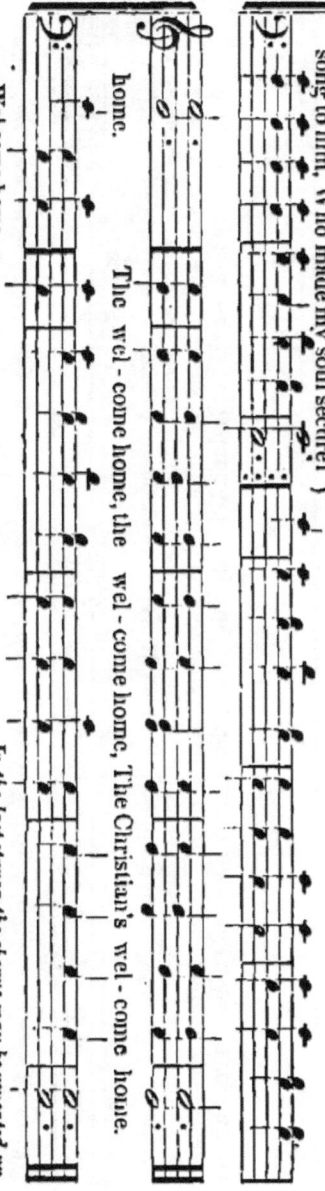

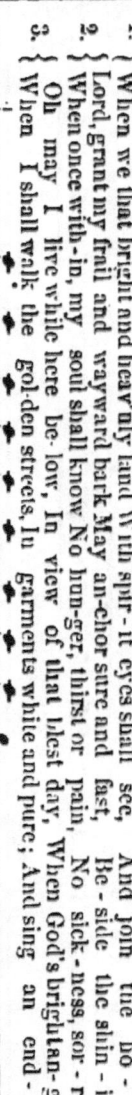

1. How sweet will be the welcome home, When this short life is o'er, When pain and sor - row,
   When we that bright and heav'nly land With spir - it eyes shall see, And join the bo - ly
2. Lord, grant my frail and wayward bark May an - chor sure and fast, Be - side the shin - ing
   When once with - in, my soul shall know No hun - ger, thirst or pain, No sick - ness, sor - row,
3. Oh may I live while here be - low, In view of that blest day, When God's bright an - gels
   When I shall walk the gol - den streets, In garments white and pure; And sing an end - less

Full Chorus.

care and grief Shall dwell with us no more.
angel band, In praise, dear Lord, of thee.   } The welcome home, the welcome home, The Christian's welcome
gates of pearl, Where I may rest at last!
care or death Shall vis - it me a - gain!   } The welcome home, &c.
shall comedown, To bear my soul away!
song to him, Who made my soul secure!   } The welcome home, &c.

home.   The wel - come home, the   wel - come home, The Christian's wel - come home.

Wel-come home.   In the last stanza the chorus may be repeated pp.

COME THOU FOUNT.

Arranged by WM. B. BRADBURY.

CHORUS.

1. Come, thou Fount of ev-ery blessing, Tune my heart to sing thy grace; }
Streams of mer - cy, nev - er ceasing, Call for songs of loudest praise. } I love Jesus, Hal-le - lu-jah,

2. Teach me some me-lodious son-net, Sung by flaming tongues a - bove; }
Praise the mount, I'm fixed up-on it, Mount of thy re-deem-ing love. }

I love Je - sus, yes, I do, I do love Je - sus, he's my Saviour, Je-sus smiles, and loves me too.

3 Jesus sought me, when a stranger,
    Wandering from the fold of God;
  He, to rescue me from danger,
    Interposed his precious blood.—Cho.

4 Prone to wander—Lord, I feel it,
    Prone to leave the God I love;
  Here's my heart—O, take and seal it,
    Seal it for thy courts above.—Cho.

SECOND HYMN.

1 "Mercy, O Thou Son of David!"
    Thus the blind Bartimeus prayed,
  "Others by thy word are saved;
    Now to me afford thine aid."

2 Many for his crying chid him,
    But he called the louder still;
  Till the gracious Saviour bid him
    Come, and ask me what you will.

3 Money was not what he wanted,
    Though by begging used to live;
  But he asked, and Jesus granted,
    Alms which none but He could give.

4 "Lord, remove this grievous blindness,
    Let my eyes behold the day!"
  Straight he saw, and, won by kindness,
    Followed Jesus in the way.

5 Oh! methinks I hear him praising,
    Publishing to all around:
  "Friends, is not my case amazing?
    What a Saviour I have found!

6 "O that all the blind but knew Him,
    And would be advised by me!
  Surely they would hasten to Him,
    He would cause them all to see."

149

COMING TO JESUS. Concluded. 151

CHORUS.

Grant Thy loving care. O God our Father, Christ, our King, Now to thee our hearts we bring, Keep them ever,

Blessed Saviour, Till in heav'n Thy love we sing.

2 Strength is Thine; we often stray
From the pure and holy way;
Wilt Thou guide us, Walk beside us,
Nearer every day!—*Cho.*

3 Thou may we, when life is o'er,
Stand with Thee on yonder shore;
Freed from sinning, Heaven winning,
Praising evermore!—*Cho.*

MILWAUKEE.
JOHN ZUNDEL. By per.

Rather slow and gentle.

1. Sav - iour, who thy flock art feed - ing With the shepherd's kind - est care, All the fee - ble,
2. Now, these lit - tle ones re - ceiv - ing, Fold them in thy gracious arm; There, we know, thy

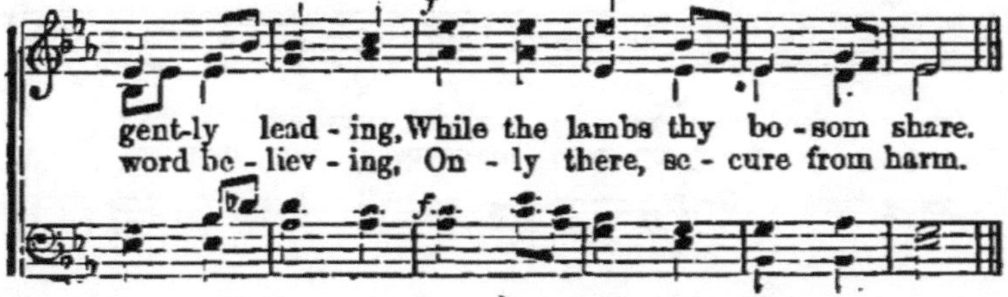

gent - ly lead - ing, While the lambs thy bo - som share,
word be - liev - ing, On - ly there, se - cure from harm.

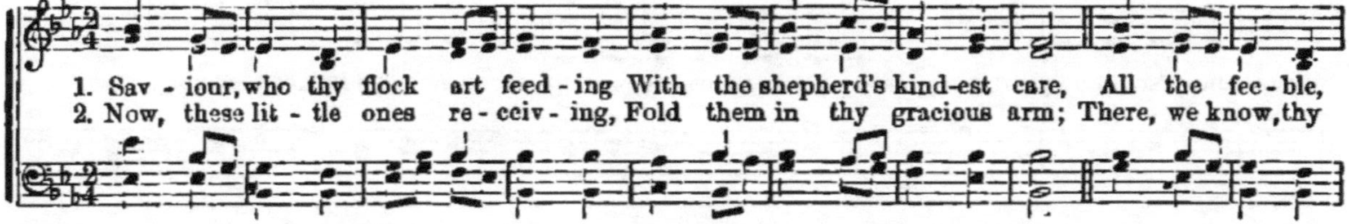

3 Never, from thy pasture roving,
Let them be the lion's prey;
Let thy tenderness, so loving,
Keep them thro' life's dangerous way.

4 Then within thy fold eternal,
Let them find a resting-place,
Feed in pastures ever vernal,
Drink the rivers of thy grace.

152. SAVIOUR, LIKE A SHEPHERD.

WM. B. BRADBURY.
From "Golden Chain," by per.

1. { Saviour, like a shepherd lead us, Much we need thy tend'rest care;
   { In thy pleasant pastures feed us, For our use thy folds pre-pare; } Blessed Je-sus, Blessed
   Jesus, Thou hast bought us, thine we are. Blessed Je-sus, Blessed Je-sus, Thou hast bought us, thine we are.

2. We are thine, do thou befriend us,
   Be the Guardian of our way;
   Keep thy flock, from sin defend us,
   Seek us when we go astray.
   Blessed Jesus,
   Hear, O hear us, when we pray.

3. Thou hast promised to receive us,
   Poor and sinful though we be;
   Thou hast mercy to relieve us,
   Grace to cleanse, and power to free.
   Blessed Jesus,
   We will early turn to thee.

4. Early let us seek thy favor,
   Early let us do thy will;
   Blessed Lord and only Saviour,
   With thy love our bosoms fill.
   Blessed Jesus,
   Thou hast loved us, love us still.

OUR SHEPHERD.

SYLVESTER MAIN.
By per.

Earnestly.

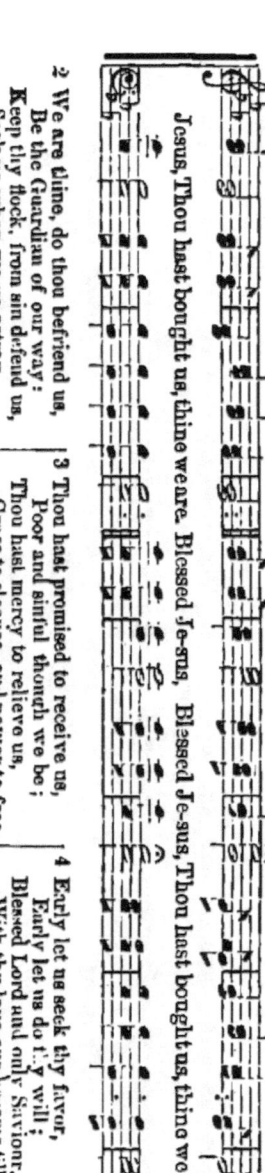

1. Je-sus is our Shepherd, Wiping ev-e-ry tear; Folded in his bosom, What have we to fear?

OUR SHEPHERD. Concluded.

On-ly let us fol-low Whither he doth lead, To the thirs-ty de-sert, Or the dew-y mead.

2. Jesus is our Shepherd;
Well we know his voice,
How its gentlest whisper
Makes our heart rejoice!
Even when he chideth,
Tender is his tone,
None but he shall guide us,
We are his alone.

3. Jesus is our Shepherd,
For the sheep he bled;
Every lamb is sprinkled
With the blood he shed.
Then on each he setteth
His own secret sign:
"They that have my Spirit,
These," saith he, "are mine."

4. Jesus is our Shepherd,
Guided by his arm,
Though the wolves may rave,
None can do us harm.
When we tread death's valley,
Dark with fearful gloom,
We will fear no evil,
Victors o'er the tomb.

PEACEFULLY REST.

WM. B. BRADBURY.
From "Golden Chain," by per.

1. An-other fleeting day is gone; Slow o'er the west the shadows rise; Swift the soft-stealing hours have flown,
2. An-oth-er fleeting day is gone; In solemn silence rest, my soul! Bow down be-fore His awful throne,

And night's dark mantle vails the skies. Peacefully rest, Peacefully rest, Rest till the morning, Peacefully rest.
Who bids the morn and evening roll.

3. Soon shall a darker night descend,
And vail from me yon azure skies;
And soon shall death's oppressive hand
Lie heavy on these languid eyes.

4. Yet when beneath the dreadful shade,
I lay my weary frame to rest,
That night shall not make me afraid;
That bed the dying Saviour pressed.

5. Again emerging from the night,
I, like my risen Lord shall rise;
Again drink in the morning light,
Pure at its fount above the skies.

154 SWEET HOME.

SIR HENRY R. BISHOP.

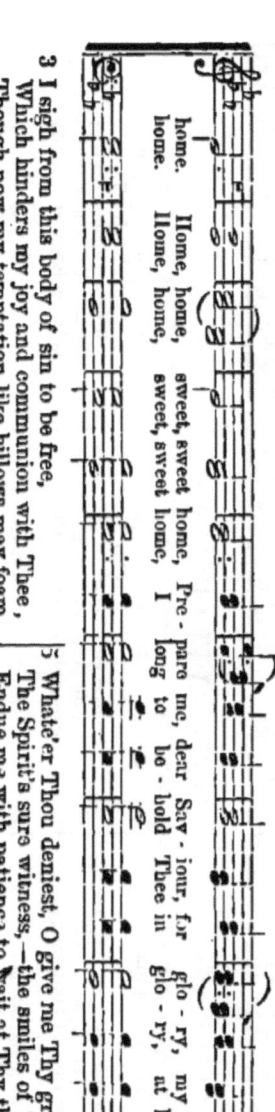

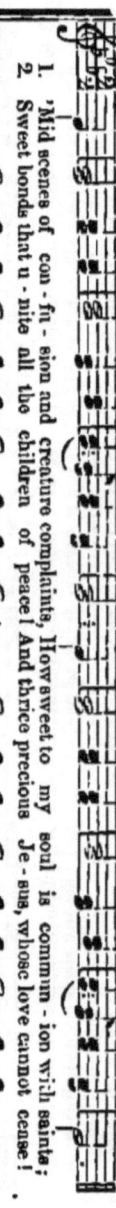

1. 'Mid scenes of con-fu-sion and creature complaints, How sweet to my soul is commun-ion with saints;
2. Sweet bonds that u-nite all the children of peace! And thrice precious Je-sus, whose love cannot cease!

To find at the ban-quet of mer-cy there's room, And feel in the pres-ence of Je-sus at
Tho' oft from Thy pres-ence in sad-ness I roam, I long to be-hold Thee in glo-ry at

Home, home, sweet, sweet home, Pre-pare me, dear Sav-iour, for glo-ry, my home.
home. Home, home, sweet, sweet home, I long to be-hold Thee in glo-ry, at home.

3 I sigh from this body of sin to be free,
 Which hinders my joy and communion with Thee,
 Though now my temptation like billows may foam,
 All, all will be peace, when I'm with Thee at home.

4 While here in the valley of conflict I stay,
 O give me submission, and strength as my day;
 In all my affliction to Thee would I come,
 Rejoicing in hope of my glorious home.

5 Whate'er Thou deniest, O give me Thy grace,
 The Spirit's sure witness,—the smiles of Thy face;
 Endue me with patience to wait at Thy throne,
 And find, even now, a sweet foretaste of home.

6 I long, dearest Lord, in Thy beauties to shine;
 No more an exile in sorrow to pine;
 And in Thy dear image arise from the tomb,
 With glorified millions to praise Thee at home.

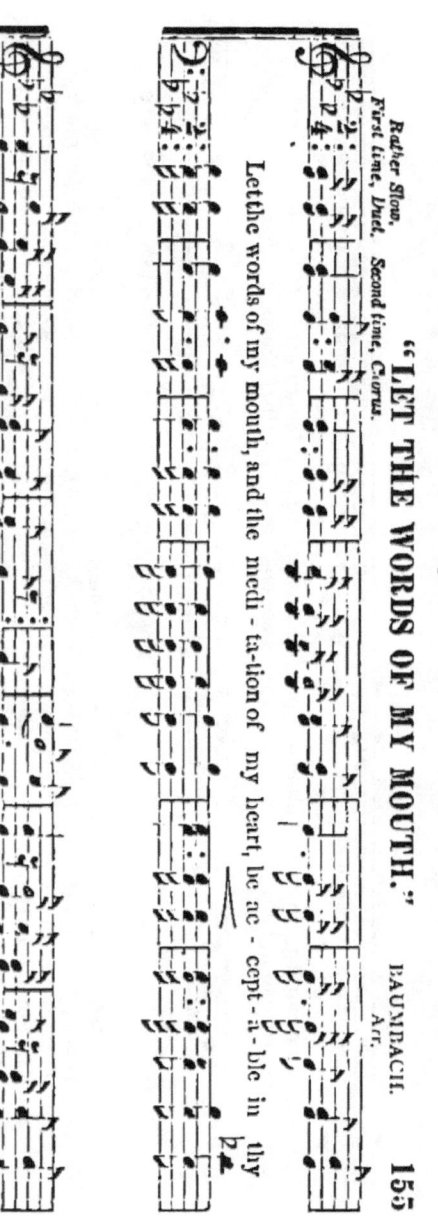

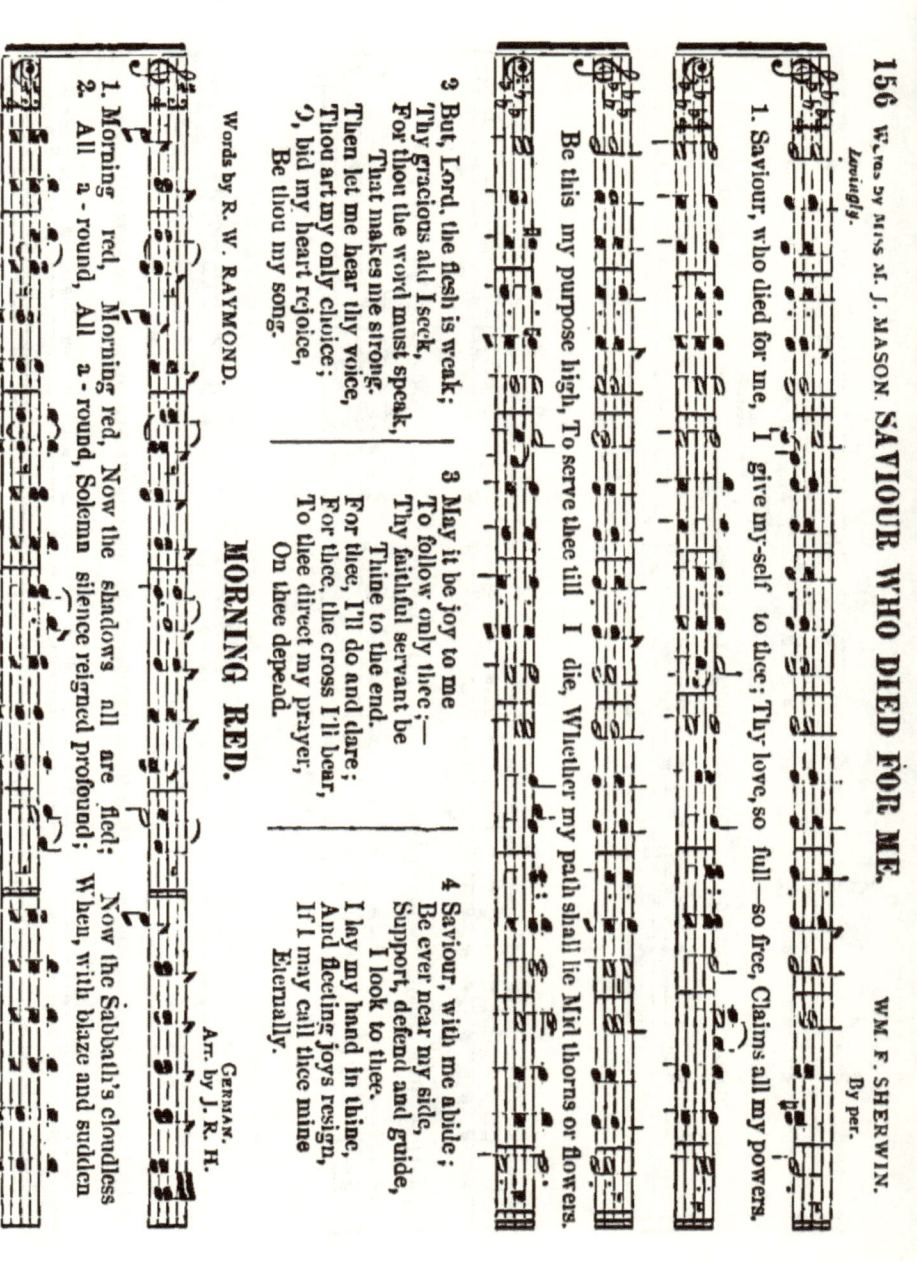

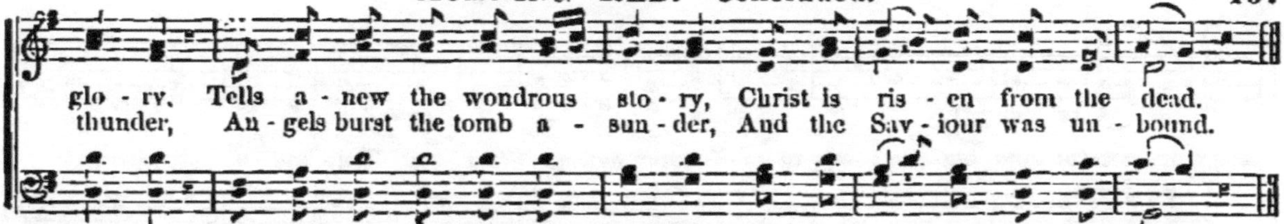

MORNING RED. Concluded.

glo-ry, Tells a-new the wondrous sto-ry, Christ is ris-en from the dead.
thunder, An-gels burst the tomb a-sun-der, And the Sav-iour was un-bound.

3 Forth he came! Forth he came!
  Robed in white, celestial flame!
  Mary, at his empty prison,
  Knew not her Redeemer, risen,
  Till he called her by her name.

4 Morning red! Morning red!
  Christ is risen from the dead!
  Still he walketh in the garden,
  Speaking words of love and pardon,
  Though the crown is on his head.

5 Morning red! Morning red!
  Thou dost light his crowned head
  Brightest jewel of his glory,
  Ever shines that wondrous story,
  Christ is risen from the dead.

I'M A PILGRIM.

GERMAN.

1. I'm a pil-grim, and I'm a stranger: I can tar-ry, I can tar-ry but a night.
D.C. I'm a pil-grim, and I'm a stranger: I can tar-ry, I can tar-ry but a night.

Do not de-tain me, for I am go-ing To where the streamlets are ev-er flow-ing.

2 There the sunbeams are ever shining,
  And I'm longing, and I'm longing for the night;
  Within a country, unknown and dreary,
  I have been wand'ring, forlorn and weary:—Cho.

3 Of that country to which I'm going,
  My Redeemer, my Redeemer is the light?
  There is no sorrow, nor any sighing,
  Nor any sin there, nor any dying:—Cho.

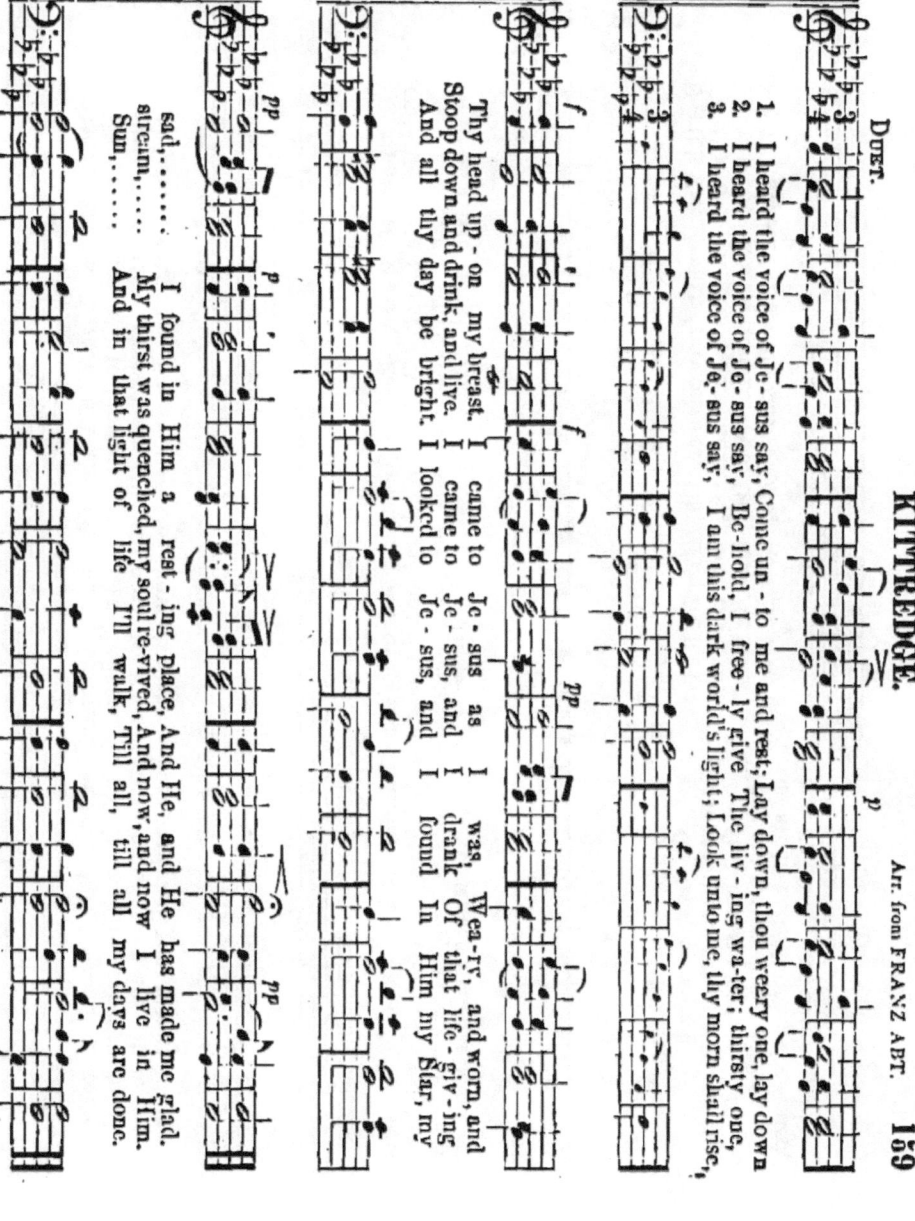

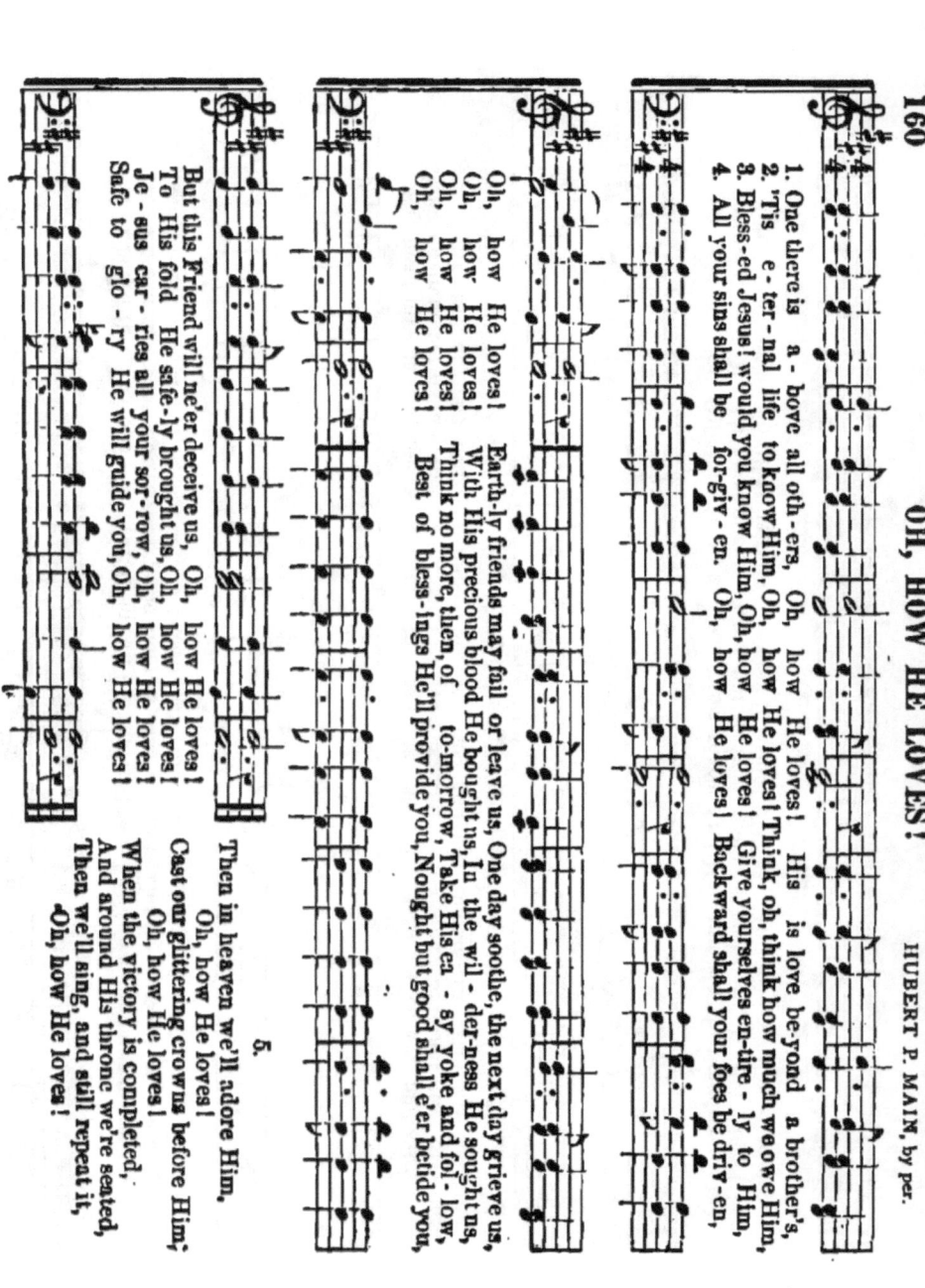

Words by Mrs. WARING.

THALBERG.

S. THALBERG.

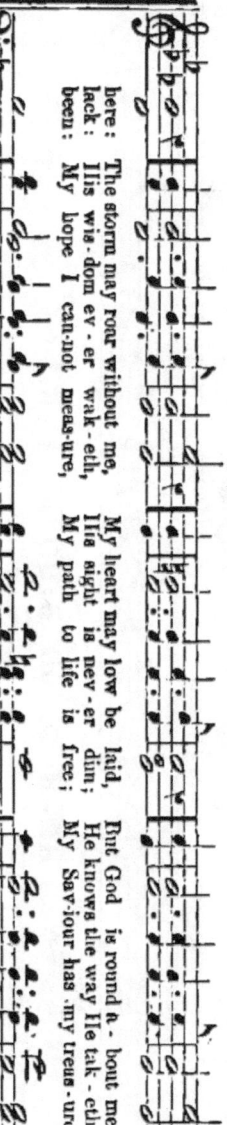

1. In heav'nly love a-bid-ing, No change my heart shall fear, And safe is such confiding, For nothing changes here: The storm may roar without me, My heart may low be laid, But God is round a-bout me, And can I be dis-mayed!
2. Wherev-er He may guide me, No want shall turn me back, My Shepherd is beside me, And nothing can I lack: His wis-dom ev-er wak-eth, His sight is nev-er dim; He knows the way He tak-eth, And I will walk with Him.
3. Green pastures are before me, Which yet I have not seen; Bright skies will soon be o'er me, Where darkest clouds have been; My hope I can-not meas-ure, My path to life is free; My Sav-iour has my treas-ure, And He will walk with me.

SECOND HYMN.

1.

To Thee, our God and Saviour,
Our hearts exulting spring,
Rejoicing in Thy favor,
Thou everlasting King:
We'll celebrate Thy glory,
With all the saints above;
And tell the wondrous story
Of Thy redeeming love.

2.

By Thee through life supported,
We pass the dang'rous road,
By heavenly hosts escorted,
Up to their bright abode;
There cast our crowns before Thee,
Our toils and conflicts o'er,
And day and night adore Thee,
Forever, evermore.

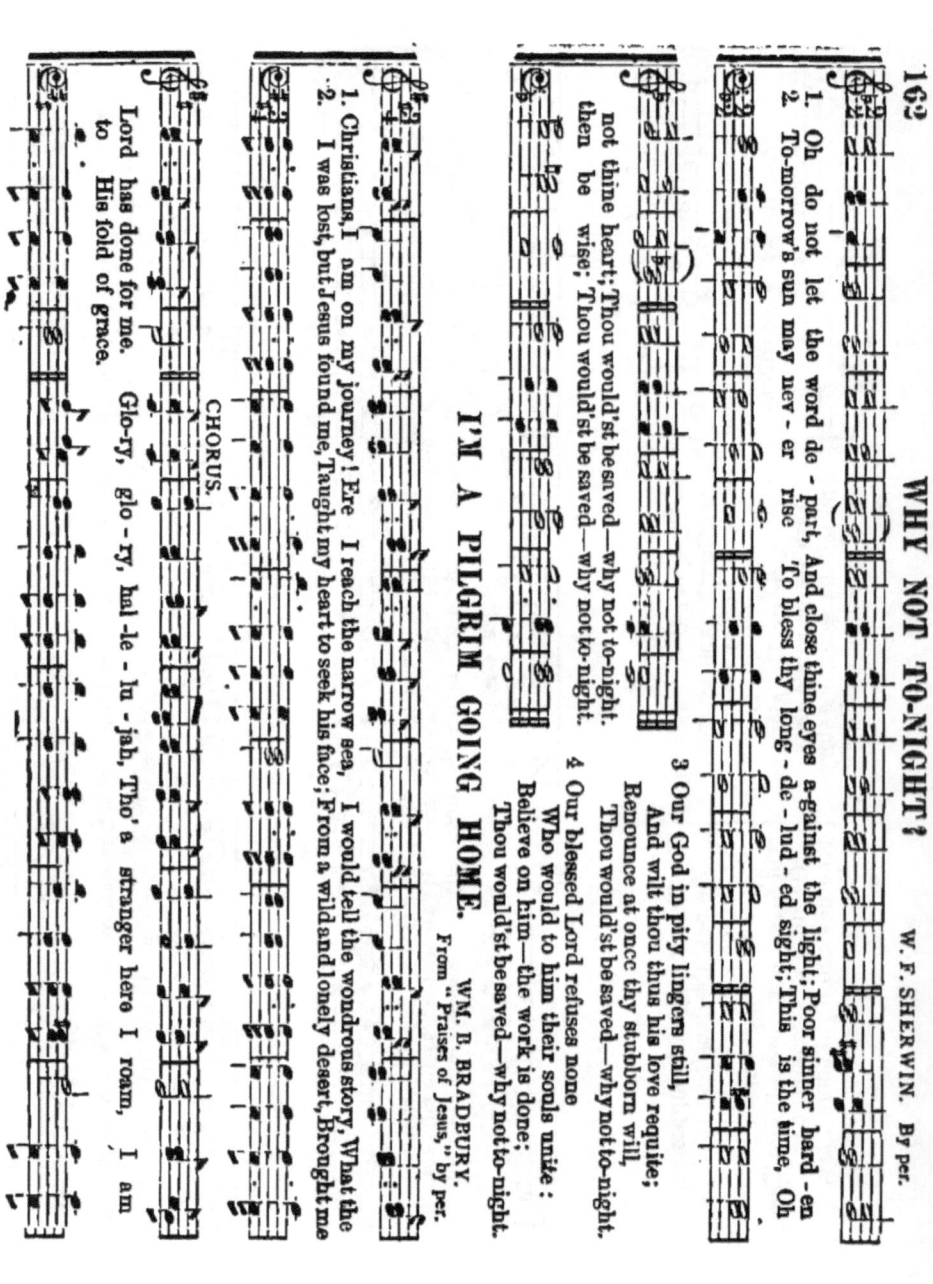

I'M A PILGRIM GOING HOME. Concluded.

on my way to Zi-on, I'm a pil-grim go-ing home.

3 Now my soul with rapture glowing,
Sings aloud His pard'ning love;
Looks beyond a world of sorrow,
To the pilgrim's home above.—*Cho.*

4 I shall yet behold my Saviour,
When the day of life is o'er,
I shall cast my crown before Him,
I shall praise Him evermore.—*Cho.*

VARINA. C. M. Double.

From RINK.

1. { There is a glorious world of light, A-bove the star-ry sky; }
  { Where saints departed, cloth'd in white, Adore the Lord most high. } And hark! a-mid the sacred songs Those heavenly voi-ces raise, Ten thousand, thousand in-fant tongues U-nite in per-fect praise.

2 Those are the hymns that we shall know
If Jesus we obey;
That is the place where we shall go
If found in wisdom's way;
This is the joy we ought to seek
And make our chief concern;
For this we come, from week to week,
To read and hear and learn.

3 Soon will our earthly race be run,
Our mortal frame decay,
Children and teachers, one by one,
Must pass from earth away.
Great God, impress this serious thought
This day on every breast,
That both the teachers and the taught,
May enter to thy rest.

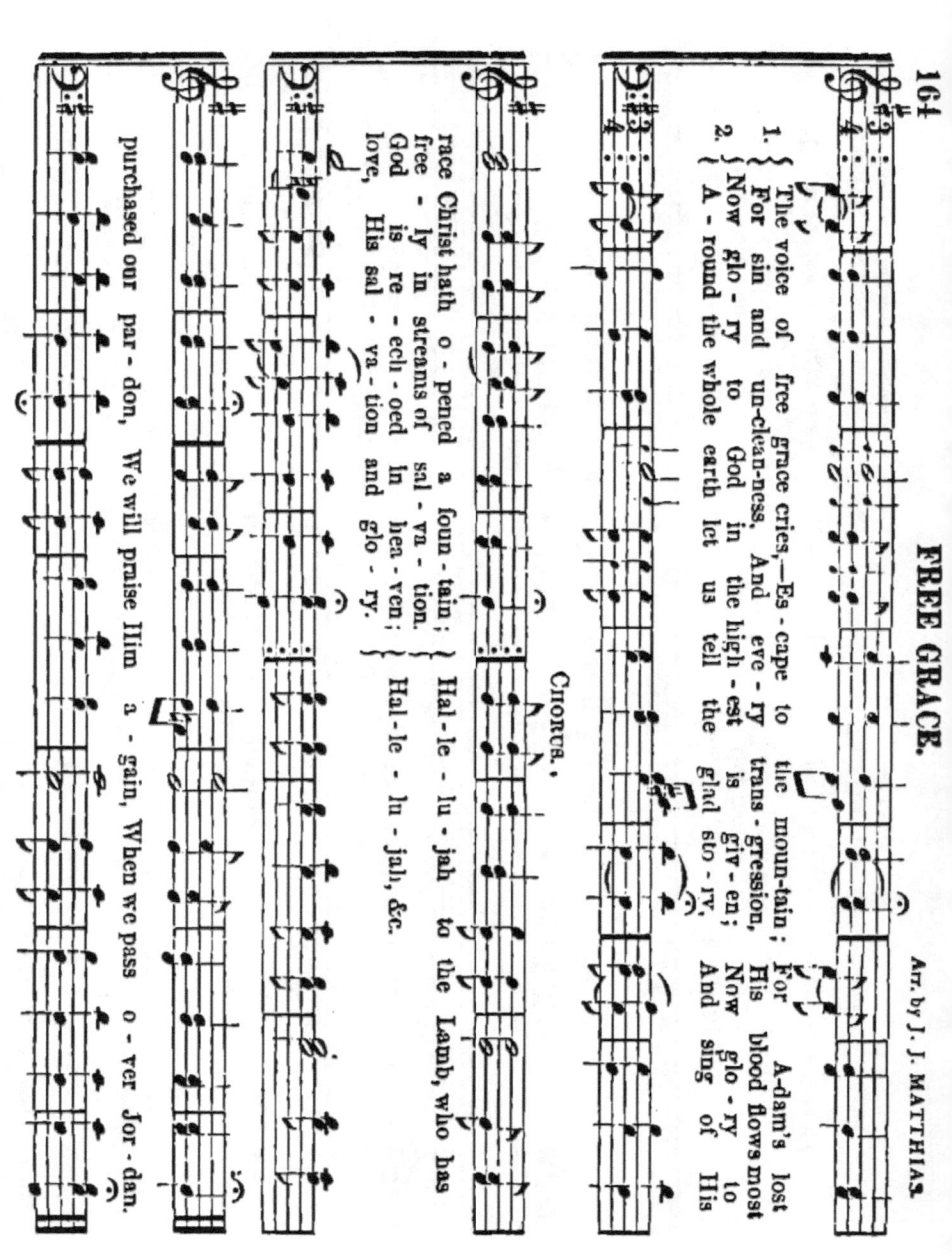

FREE GRACE. Concluded.

3 O Jesus, ride on,—
Thy kingdom is glorious;
O'er sin, death, and hell,
Thou wilt make us victorious:
Thy name shall be praised
In the great congregation,
And saints shall ascribe
Unto thee their salvation.

4 When on Zion we stand,
Having gain'd the blest shore,
With our harps in our hands,
We will praise ever more:
We'll range the blest fields
On the banks of the river,
And sing of redemption
For ever and ever.

DEAR JESUS, HEAR ME. (Child's Prayer.)

Words by F. J. C.

Wm. B. BRADBURY.
From "Bright Jewels," by per.

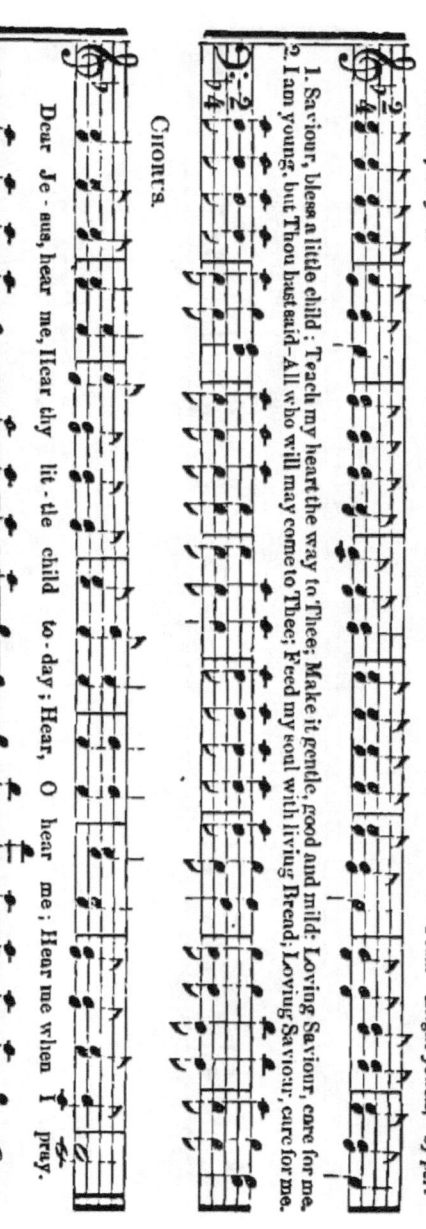

Dear Je-sus, hear me, Hear thy lit-tle child to-day; Hear, O hear me; Hear me when I pray.

1. Saviour, bless a little child; Teach my heart the way to Thee; Make it gentle, good and mild; Loving Saviour, care for me.
2. I am young, but Thou hast said—All who will may come to Thee; Feed my soul with living Bread; Loving Saviour, care for me.

CHORUS.

3 Jesus, help me, I am weak;
Let me put my trust in Thee;
Teach me how, and what to speak;
Loving Saviour, care for me.—Cho.

4 I would never go astray,
Never turn aside from Thee;
Keep me in the heavenly way;
Loving Saviour, care for me.—Cho.

165

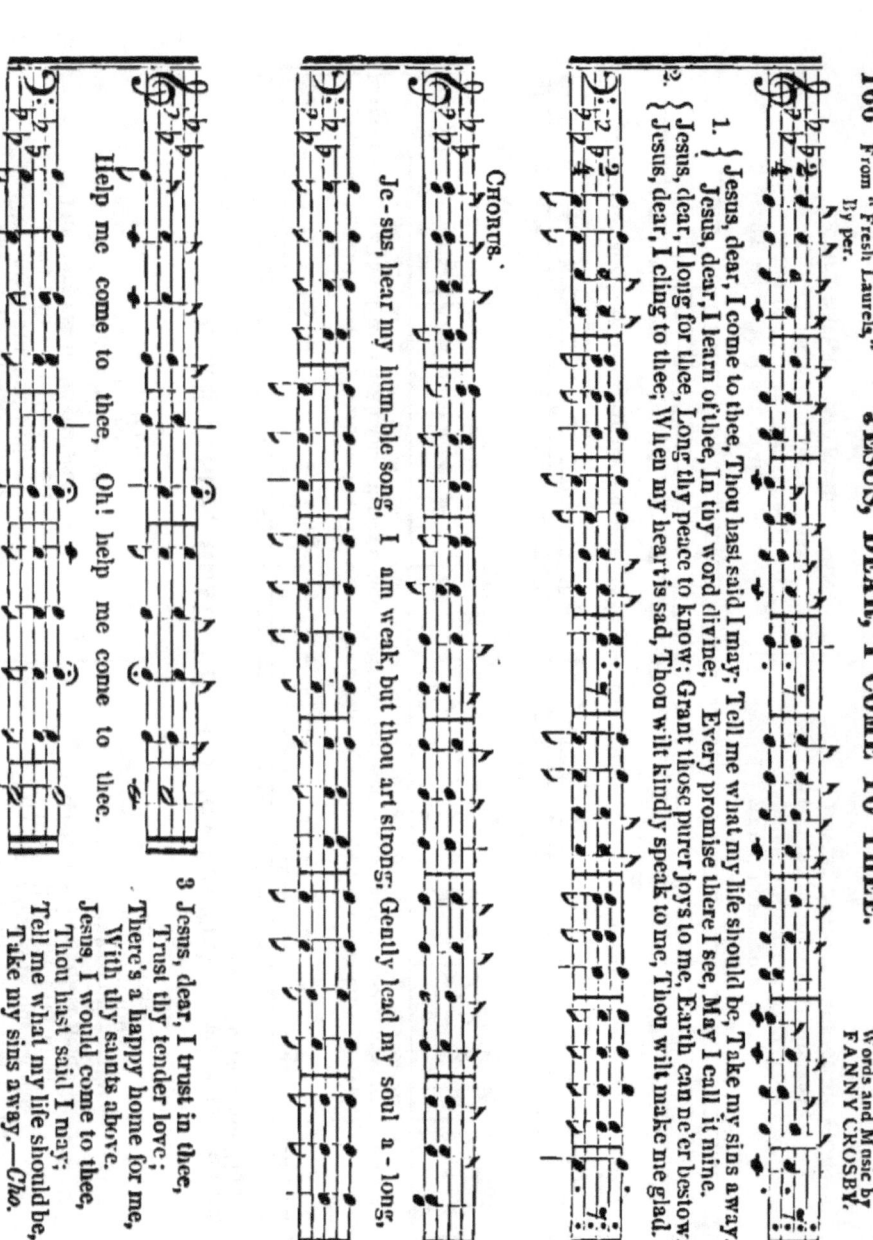

ONWARD, CHRISTIAN SOLDIERS.

Arr. from J. HAYDN.

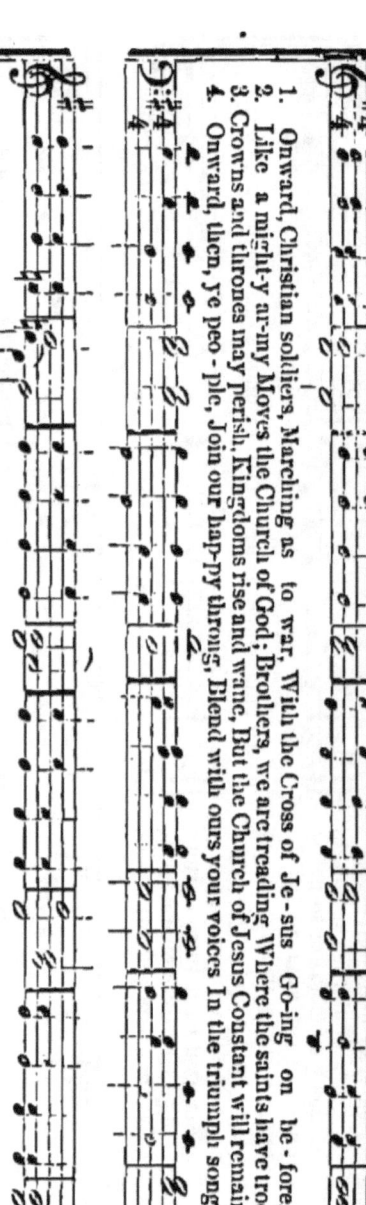

1. Onward, Christian soldiers, Marching as to war, With the Cross of Jesus Going on before.
2. Like a mighty army Moves the Church of God; Brothers, we are treading Where the saints have trod;
3. Crowns and thrones may perish, Kingdoms rise and wane, But the Church of Jesus Constant will remain;
4. Onward, then, ye people, Join our happy throng, Blend with ours your voices In the triumph song;

Christ the Royal Master Leads against the foe, Forward into battle, See, His banners go.
We are not divided, All one body we, One in hope, and doctrine, One in charity.
Gates of hell can never 'Gainst that Church prevail; We have Christ's own promise, And that cannot fail.
Glory, laud, and honor, Unto Christ the King, This thro' countless ages Men and Angels sing.

Onward, Christian soldiers, Marching as to war, With the Cross of Jesus Going on before.

THY WAY, NOT MINE, O LORD.

HUBERT P. MAIN. By per.

1. Thy way, not mine, O Lord, Howe-er dark it be; Lead me by thine own hand; Choose out the path for me.
2. The kingdom that I seek Is thine: so let the way That leads to it be thine, Else I must sure-ly stray.
3. Choose thou for me my friends, My sickness or my health, Choose thou my cares for me, My poverty or wealth.

I dare not choose my lot; I would not, if I might; Choose thou for me, my God, So shall I walk a-right.
Take thou my cup, and it With joy or sor-row fill. As best to thee may seem, Choose thou my good and ill.
Not mine, not mine the choice, In things or great or small; Be thou my Guide, my Strength, My Wisdom, and my All.

GUIDE US TO THEE.

W. F. SHERWIN. By per.

1. Father, Thou art great and holy, Hear us when we bend the knee; Make us humble, meek, and lowly, Guide us to Thee.
2. Saints and angels fall before Thee, Where the soul is ev-er free; Humbly still we would adore Thee, Guide us to Thee.
3. By Thy love and pow'r defended, May we ev - er faith-ful be, And when life's short day is ended, Guide us to Thee.

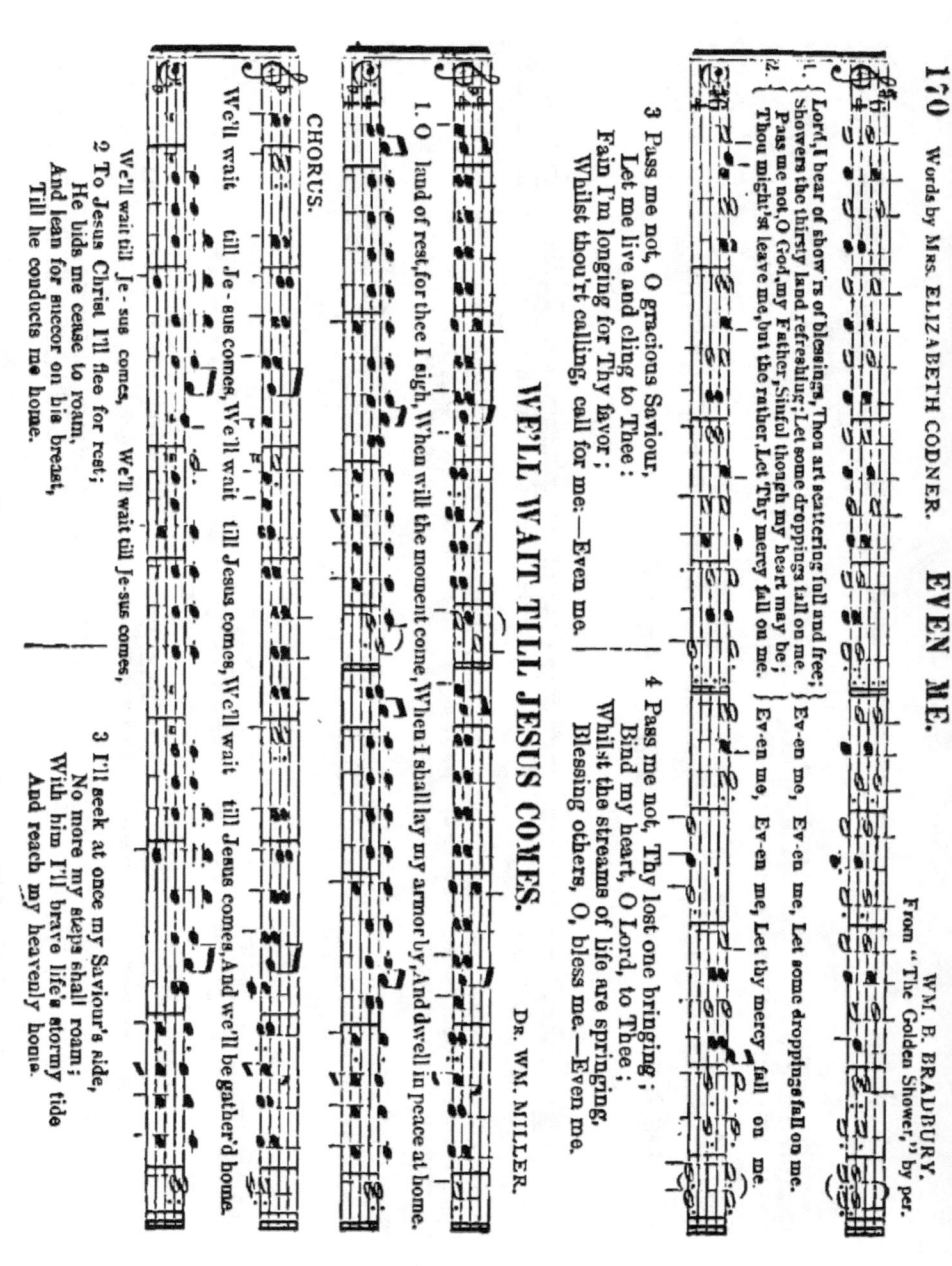

SUN OF MY SOUL.

WM. F. SHERWIN.
By per.

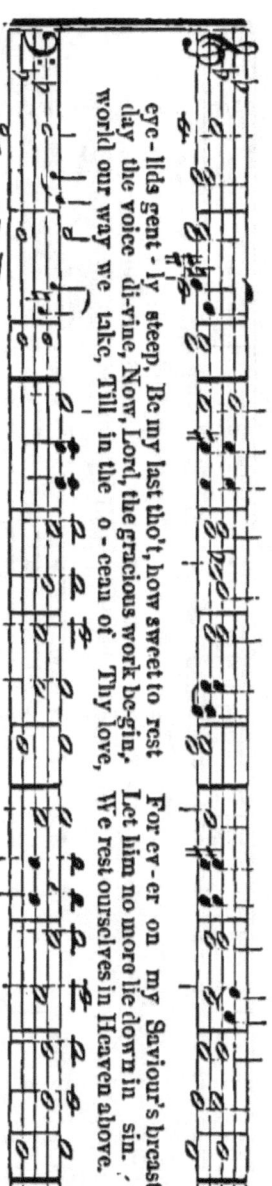
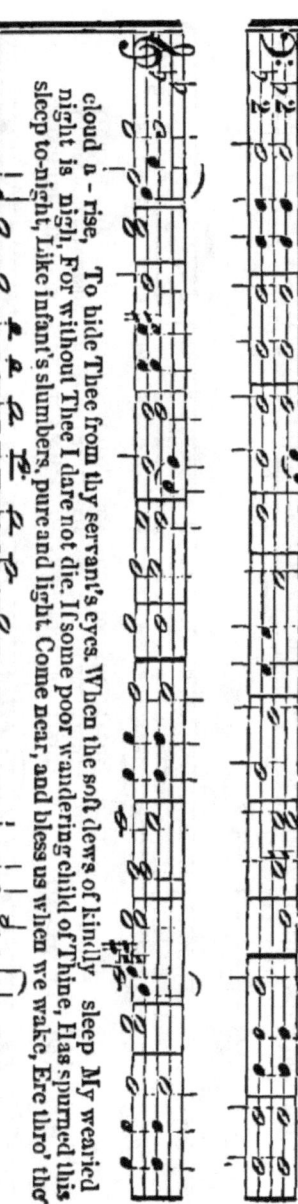
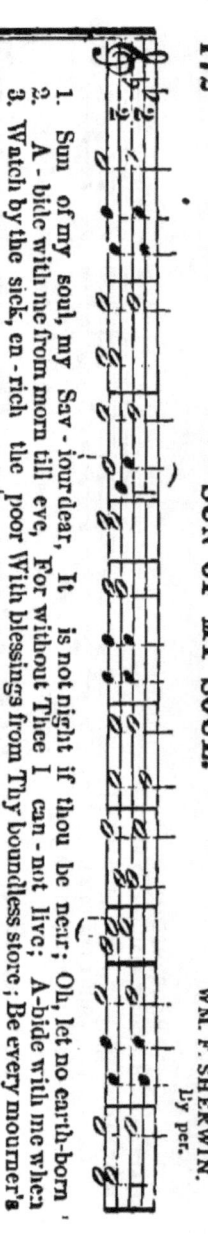

1. Sun of my soul, my Saviour dear, It is not night if thou be near; Oh, let no earth-born cloud arise, To hide Thee from thy servant's eyes. When the soft dews of kindly sleep My wearied eye-lids gently steep, Be my last tho't, how sweet to rest For ev-er on my Saviour's breast.

2. A-bide with me from morn till eve, For without Thee I can-not live; A-bide with me when night is nigh, For without Thee I dare not die. If some poor wandering child of Thine, Has spurned this day the voice di-vine, Now, Lord, the gracious work be-gin, Let him no more lie down in sin.

3. Watch by the sick, en-rich the poor With blessings from Thy boundless store; Be every mourner's sleep to-night, Like infant's slumbers, pure and light. Come near, and bless us when we wake, Ere thro' the world our way we take, Till in the o-cean of Thy love, We rest ourselves in Heaven above.

COME, YE SINNERS.

J. INGALLS.

1. Come, ye sinners, poor and needy, Weak and wounded, sick and sore, Jesus ready stands to save you, Full of pity, love and power. Turn to the Lord and seek salvation, Sound the praise of his dear name.
2. Let not conscience make you linger, Nor of fitness fondly dream; All the fitness he requireth, Is to feel your need of Him.
3. Come, ye weary, heavy laden, Bruised and mangled by the fall; If you tarry till you're better, You will never come at all.

CHORUS.

Glory, honor, and salvation, Christ the Lord is come to reign.

SECOND HYMN.

1 Now the Saviour standeth pleading
   At the sinner's bolted heart;
Now in heaven He's interceding,
   Taking there the sinner's part.

2 Sinner! can you hate this Saviour?
   Will you thrust Him from your arms?
Once He died through your behavior,
   Now He calls you by His charms.

3 Now He's waiting to be gracious,
   Now He stands and looks on thee;
See what kindness, love, and pity;
   Shine around on you and me.

4 Come, for all things now are ready,
   Yet there's room for many more;
O ye blind, ye lame and needy,
   Come to wisdom's boundless store?

174 SAVIOUR CARE FOR ME.

Words by F. J. CROSBY.
CHESTER G. ALLEN, by per.

1. Leave me not, O bless-ed Sav - iour, Hold my trembling hand; Cheer me on my jour-ney home-ward To the bet-ter land. Seek-ing Thy di-vine pro-tec-tion, So I come to Thee; O, I thirst for liv-ing wa-ter; Sav-iour care for me.

2. May Thy spir-it full of com-fort Like a gen-tle dove, Hov - er o'er my soul and keep me In Thy ten-der love. Trust-ing on - ly in Thy mer - cy, Let me cling to Thee; At Thy cross de-vout-ly kneel-ing, Sav-iour care for me.

3. By Thy heav'n-ly grace de-fend me From the tempt-er's power; Give me strength for ev-ery tri - al, Save me ev-ery hour. Leave me not, O bless-ed Sav - iour, Let me rest in Thee; I be-lieve, for Thou hast prom-ised Thou wilt care for me.

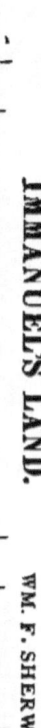

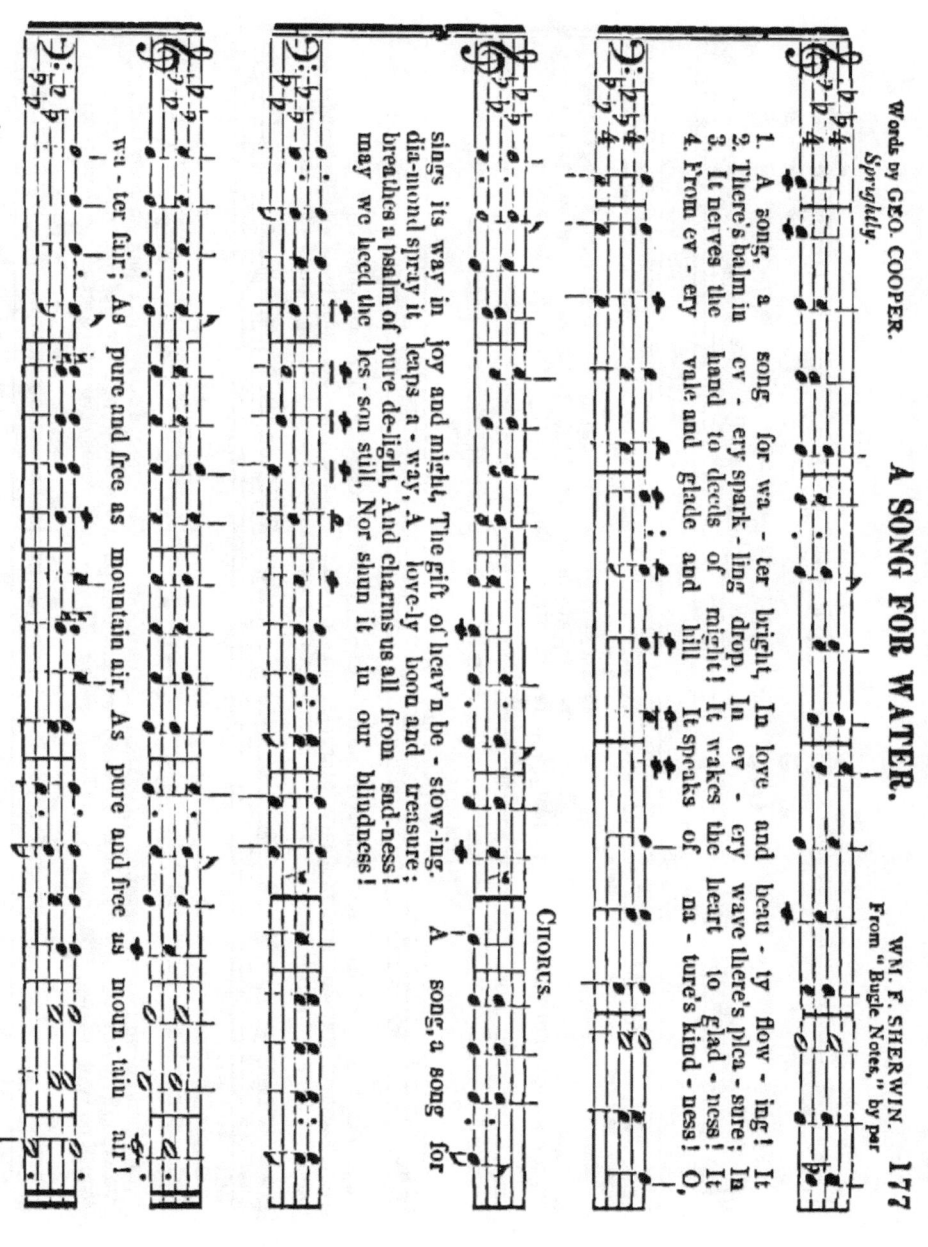

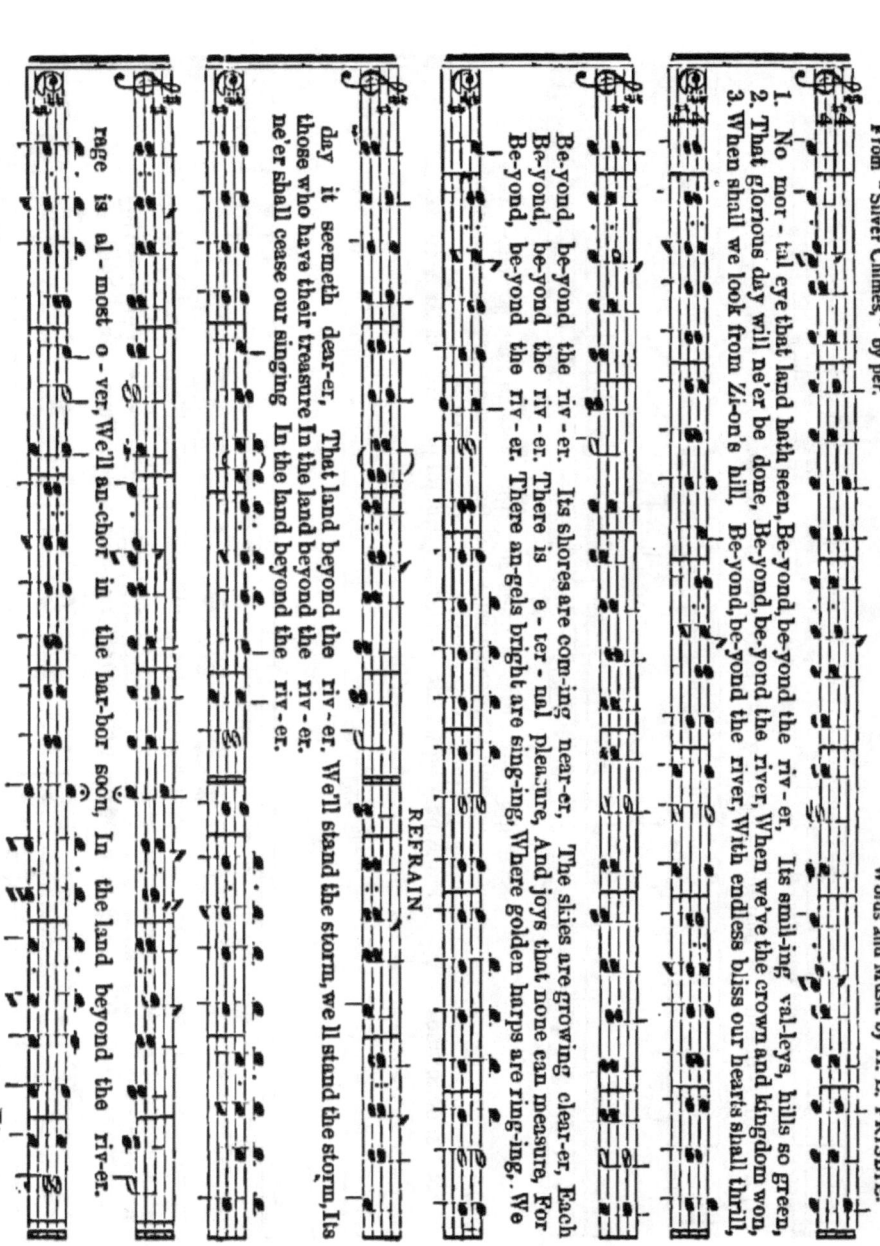

JESUS, MY ALL.

Words by FANNY CROSBY.

Scotch Air.

"I will appear in the cloud upon the mercy-seat." Lev. 16:2.

1. Lord, at Thy mercy seat, Humbly I fall; Pleading Thy promise sweet, Lord, hear my call; Now let Thy work begin, Oh, make me pure within, Cleanse me from every sin, Jesus my all.

2. Tears of repentant grief
Silently fall;
Help Thou my unbelief,
Hear thou my call;
Oh, how I pine for thee!
'Tis all my hope, my plea:
Jesus has died for me,
Jesus, my all.

3. Hark! how the words of love
Tenderly fall;
Ere to the realms above,
Heard is my call;
Now every doubt has flown,
Broken my heart of stone,
Lord, I am Thine alone,
Jesus, my all.

4. Still at Thy mercy-seat
Humbly I fall;
Pleading Thy promise sweet,
Heard is my call;
Faith wings my soul to thee;
This all my hope shall be,
Jesus has died for me,
Jesus, my all.

BLUMENTHAL.

Andante.

1. Depth of mer-cy, can there be Mer-cy still reserved for me? Can my God His wrath forbear?
2. Kin-dled, His re-lent-ings are; Me, He now de-lights to spare; Cries, how shall I give thee up?—

Me, the chief of sin-ners, spare? I have long withstood His grace, Long provoked Him to His face,
Lets the lifted thunder drop. There for me the Saviour stands; Shows His wounds, and spreads His hands;

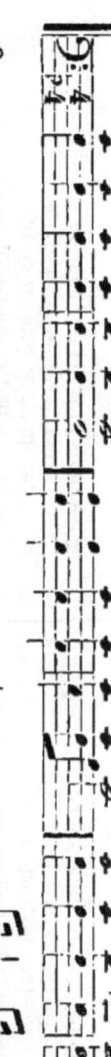

Would not hearken to His calls, Grieved Him by a thousand falls.
God is love! I know, I feel; Jesus weeps and loves me still.

2 While I am a pilgrim here,
Let Thy love my spirit cheer;
As my guide, my guard, my friend,
Lead me to my journey's end.

SECOND HYMN.

1 Come, my soul, thy suit prepare:
Jesus loves to answer prayer;
He Himself invites thee near,
Bids thee ask Him, waits to hear.

Lord, I come to Thee for rest;
Take possession of my breast;
There Thy blood-bought right maintain,
And without a rival reign.

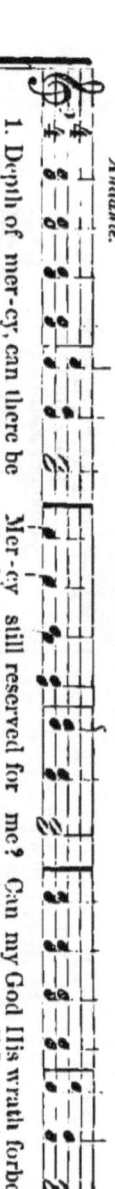

Show me what I have to do;
Every hour my strength renew;
Let me live a life of faith,—
Let me die Thy people's death.

ALL TO CHRIST I OWE.

Words by Mrs. E. M. HALL.
John T. Grape, by per.

1. I hear the Saviour say, Thy strength indeed is small; O child of weakness, pray, I am thine All in All.

CHORUS.

Jesus paid it all; All to Him I owe! Sin had left a crimson stain; He wash'd it white as snow.

2.
Lord, now indeed I find
Thy faith, and thine alone,
Can change the leper's spots,
And melt the heart of stone.—*Cho.*

3.
For nothing good have I,
Whereby thy grace to claim—
I'll wash me in the blood,
The blood of Calvary's Lamb.—*Cho.*

4.
When from my dying bed,
My ransomed soul shall rise,
Then "Jesus paid it all,"
Shall rend the vaulted skies.—*Cho.*

5.
And when before the throne,
I stand in Him complete,
I'll lay my trophies down,
All down, at Jesus' feet.—*Cho.*

COME LET US SING OF JESUS.

ITALIAN.

1. Come let us sing of Jesus, While hearts and accents blend; Come let us sing of Jesus,
2. We love to sing of Jesus, Who wept our path along; We love to sing of Jesus,
3. We love to sing of Jesus, Who died our souls to save; We love to sing of Jesus,

The sinners' only friend. His holy soul rejoices, Amid the choirs above,
The tempted and the strong. None who besought his healing, He passed unheeded by;
Triumphant o'er the grave. And in our hour of danger, We'll trust His love along,

To hear our grateful voices, Exulting in His love.
None now to Him appealing, For help will He deny,
Who once slept in a manger, And now sits on the throne.

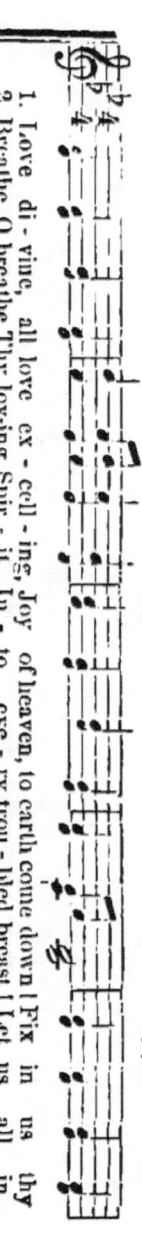

From "Golden Chain," by per.

SAVIOUR EVER NEAR.

WM. B. BRADBURY.

1. Dear Saviour! ev - er at my side, How lov - ing must Thou be, To leave Thy home in heaven to guard A lit-tle child like me. Thy beau-ti-ful and shining face I see not, tho' so near;
2. I can - not feel Thee touch my hand, With pressure light and mild, To check me, as my mother did When I was but a child. But I have felt Thee in my thoughts Fighting with sin for me;

The sweetness of thy soft, low voice I am too deaf to hear.
And when my heart loves God, I know Thee sweetness is from Thee.

3. And when, dear Saviour! I kneel down,
   Each morn and night in prayer,
   Something there is within my heart,
   Which tells me Thou art there.
   Yes! when I pray, Thou prayest too—
   Thy prayer is all for me;
   But when I sleep, Thou sleepest not,
   But watchest patiently.

SECOND HYMN. C. M.

1 APPROACH, my soul! the mercy-seat,
  Where Jesus answers prayer;
  There humbly fall before His feet,
  For none can perish there.
  Thy promise is my only plea,
  With this I venture nigh;
  Thou callest burdened souls to Thee,
  And such, O Lord! am I.

2 Be Thou my shield and hiding-place,
  That, sheltered near Thy side,
  I may my fierce accuser face,
  And tell Him—"Thou hast died."
  Oh! wondrous Love—to bleed and die,
  To bear the cross and shame,
  That guilty sinners, such as I,
  Might plead Thy gracious name.

LAMB OF GOD, I LOOK TO THEE.

L. SPOHR.

1. Lamb of God, I look to Thee; Thou shalt my ex-am-ple be:
2. Fain I would be as Thou art; Give me Thy o-be-dient heart!

Thou art gen-tle, meek and mild: Thou wast once a lit-tle child.
Thou art pit-i-ful and kind; Let me have Thy lov-ing mind. A-men.

3.
Let me above all fulfil
God my Heavenly Father's will;
Never His good Spirit grieve;
Only to His glory live!

4.
Loving Jesus, Gentle Lamb,
In Thy gracious hands I am:
Make me, Saviour, what Thou art!
Live Thyself within my heart.

SAVIOUR, BLESSED SAVIOUR.

JOS. P. HOLBROOK.
By per.

1. Saviour, Blessed Saviour, Listen whilst we sing, Hearts and voices rais-ings, Praises to our King;
2. Nearer, ev-er near-er, Christ, we draw to Thee, Deep in ad-o-ra-tion Bending low the knee:

All we have to of-fer; All we hope to be, Bod-y, soul, and spir-it,
Thou for our redemption Cam'st on earth to die; Thou, that we might follow, Hast gone up on high,

All we yield to Thee,

Bod-y, soul, and spirit, All we yield to Thee,
Thou, that we might follow, Hast gone up on high.

3.
Onward, ever onward, Journeying o'er the road
Worn by saints before us, Journeying on to God:
Leaving all behind us, May we hasten on,
Backward never looking, Till the prize is won.

4.
Brighter still and brighter Glows the western sun,
Shedding all its gladness O'er our work that's done;
Time will soon be over, Toil and sorrow past,
May we, Blessed Saviour, Find a rest at last.

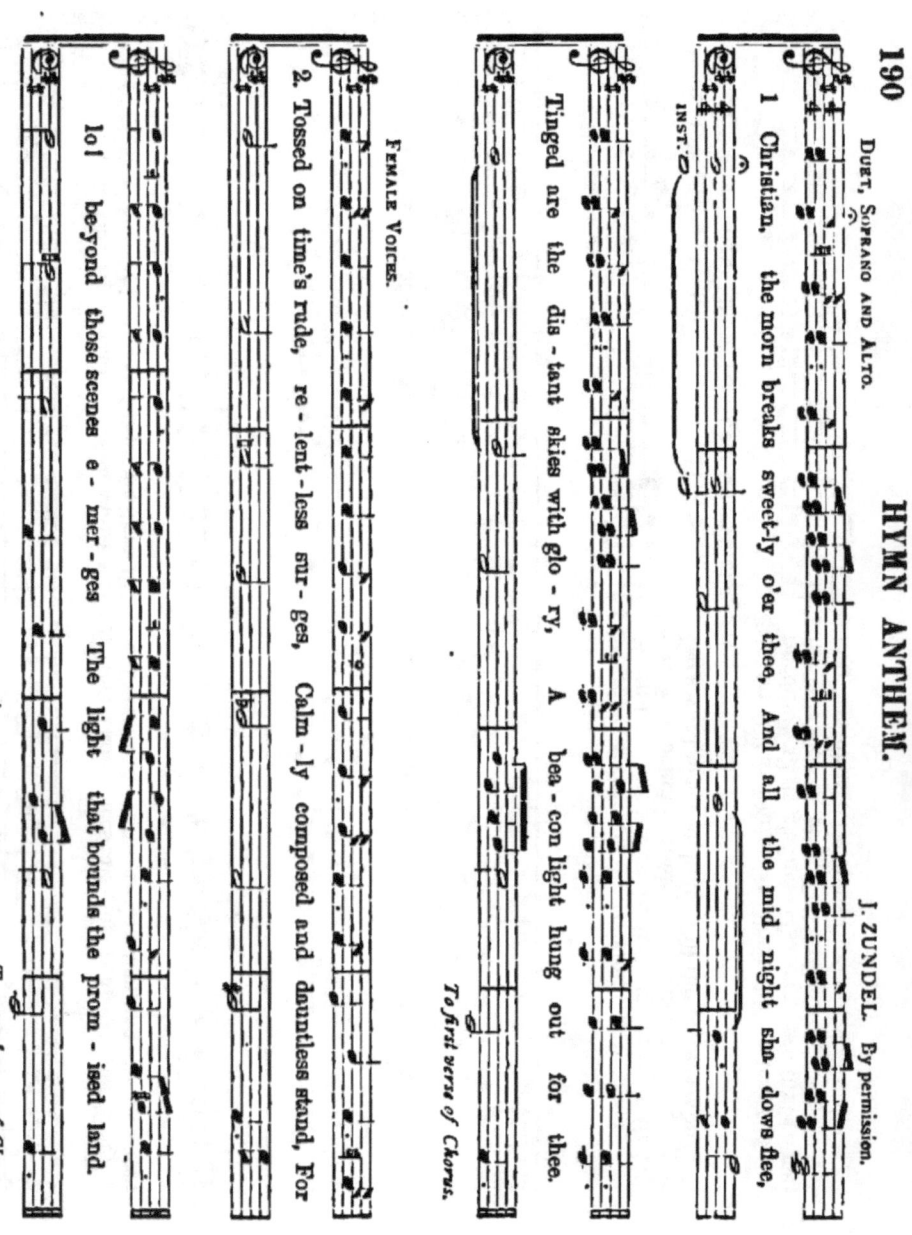

HYMN ANTHEM. Concluded.

f M LE VOICES. *dolce.*

3. Cheer up! cheer up! the day breaks o'er thee, Bright as the summer's noon-tide ray; The star-gem'd crowns and realms of glo-ry In-vite thy hap-py soul a-way.

To third verse of Chorus.

CHORUS.

1st Cho. A - rise, a - rise! the light breaks o'er thee, Thy name is graven on the throne; Thy home is in the world of glo - ry, Where thy Re-deem-er reigns a - lone, Where thy Re-deem-er reigns a - lone.

2d Cho. Be-hold, be-hold, the land is nearing, Where the wild sea-storm's rage is o'er; Hark! how the heav'nly host are cheering. See in what throngs they range the shore! See in what throngs they range the shore.

3d Cho. A - way, a - way! leave all for glo - ry, Thy name is graven on the throne; Thy home is in that world of glo - ry, Where thy Re-deem-er reigns a - lone, Where thy Re-deem-er reigns a - lone.

AVISON.

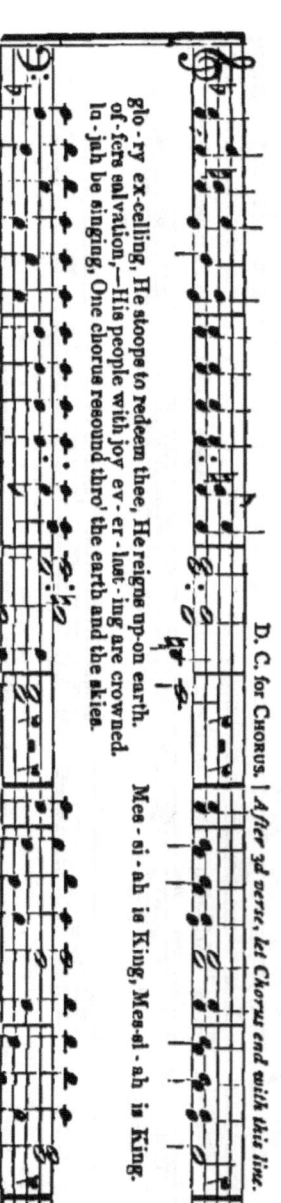

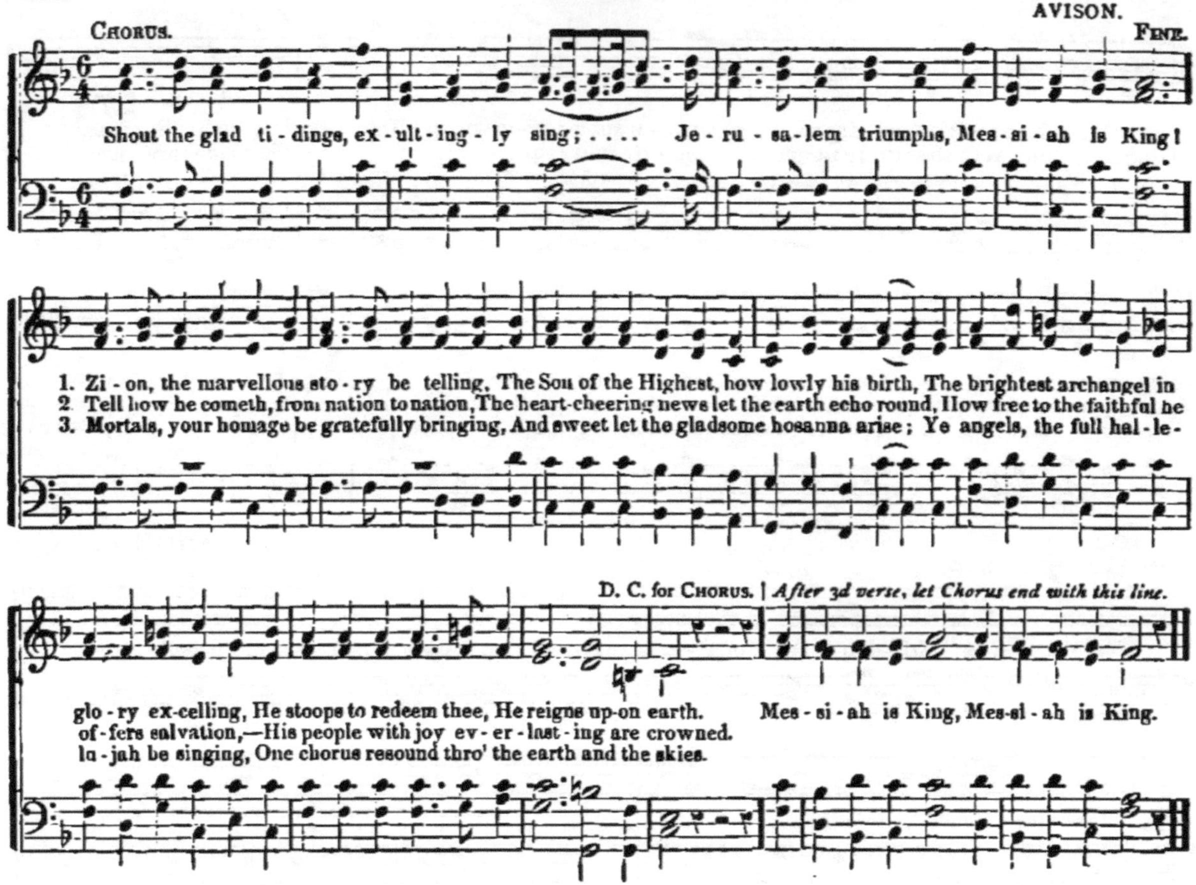
AVISON.
Chorus.
Fine.
Shout the glad ti - dings, ex - ult - ing - ly sing; . . . . Je - ru - sa - lem triumphs, Mes - si - ah is King!
1. Zi - on, the marvellous sto - ry be telling, The Son of the Highest, how lowly his birth, The brightest archangel in
2. Tell how he cometh, from nation to nation, The heart-cheering news let the earth echo round, How free to the faithful he
3. Mortals, your homage be gratefully bringing, And sweet let the gladsome hosanna arise; Ye angels, the full hal - le -
D. C. for Chorus. | After 3d verse, let Chorus end with this line.
glo - ry ex-celling, He stoops to redeem thee, He reigns up-on earth.
of - fers salvation,—His people with joy ev - er - last - ing are crowned.
lu - jah be singing, One chorus resound thro' the earth and the skies.
Mes - si - ah is King, Mes - si - ah is King.

PRAISE THE LORD. Chant No. 1.

NORRIS.

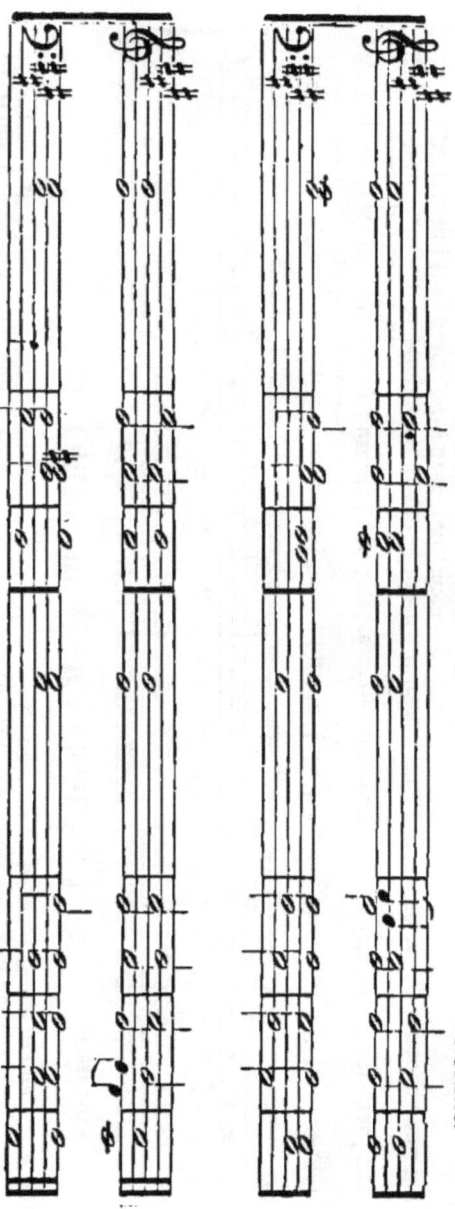

1. Praise the Lord, | O my | soul, | and all that is within me, | praise his | ho-ly | name.
2. Praise the Lord, | O my | soul, | and for- | get not | all his | benefits;
3. Who forgiveth | all thy | sin, | and | healeth | all thine | infirmities;
4. Who saveth thy | life .. from de- | struction, | and crowneth thee with | mercy and | loving | kindness.
5. O praise the Lord, ye Angels of his, ye that ex- | cel in | strength; | ye that fulfil his commandment, and hearken unto the | voice of | his — | word.
6. O praise the Lord, all | ye his | hosts; | ye servants of | his that | do his | pleasure.
7. Glory be to the Father, | and .. to the | Son, | and | to the | Holy | Ghost;
8. As it was in the beginning, is now, and | ever shall | be, | world without | end.— | A- | men.

193

194   COME UNTO ME. Chant No. 2.   WM. B. BRADBURY.

1 With tearful eyes I look around,
  Life seems a dark and | stormy | sea:
  Yet, 'midst the gloom I hear a sound,
  A heavenly | whisper, | Come to | me.

2 It tells me of a place of rest—
  It tells me where my | soul may | flee;
  Oh! to the weary, faint, oppressed,
  How sweet the | bidding, | Come to | me.

3 When nature shudders, loth to part
  From all I love, en- | joy, and | see,
  When a faint chill steals o'er my heart,
  A sweet voice | utters, | Come to | me.

4 Come for all else must fail and die,
  Earth is no resting | place for | thee;
  Heavenward direct thy weeping eye,
  I am thy | portion, | Come to | me.

5 O voice of mercy! voice of love!
  In conflict, grief, and | ago- | ny,
  Support me, cheer me from above!
  And gently | whisper, | Come to | me.

THE LORD'S PRAYER. Chant No. 3.   GREGORIAN.

1. Our Father, who art in heaven, | hallowed | be thy | name; | thy kingdom come, thy will be done on | earth,. .as it | is in | heaven;
2. Give us this | day our | daily | bread; | and forgive us our trespasses, as we forgive | them that | tres- pass. .a- | gainst us.
3. And lead us not into temptation, but de- | liv-er | us from | evil; | for thine is the kingdom, and the power, and the | glory, for- | ever. A- | men.

GLORIA IN EXCELSIS. Chant No. 4.

GLORIA IN EXCELSIS.

To the First Part of the Chant.

1. Glory be to | God on | high, | and on earth | peace, good | will towards | men.
2. We praise thee, we bless thee, we | worship thee, | we glorify thee, we give thanks to | thee for | thy great | glory.

To the Second Part.

3. O Lord God, | Heavenly | King, | God the | Father | Al- — | mighty!
4. O Lord, the only-begotten Son | Jesus | Christ, | O Lord God, Lamb of God, | Son..of the | Fa- — | ther!

To the Third Part.

5. That takest away the | sins..of the | world, | have mercy up- | on — | us.
6. Thou that takest away the | sins..of the | world, | have mercy up- | on — | us.
7. Thou that takest away the | sins..of the | world, | re- | ceive our | prayer.
8. Thou that sittest at the right hand of | God the | Father, | have mercy up- | on — | us.

To the First Part.

9. For Thou only | art — | holy, | Thou | only | art the | Lord.
10. Thou only, O Christ, with the | Holy | Ghost, | art most high in the | glory..of | God the | Father, | A-|men

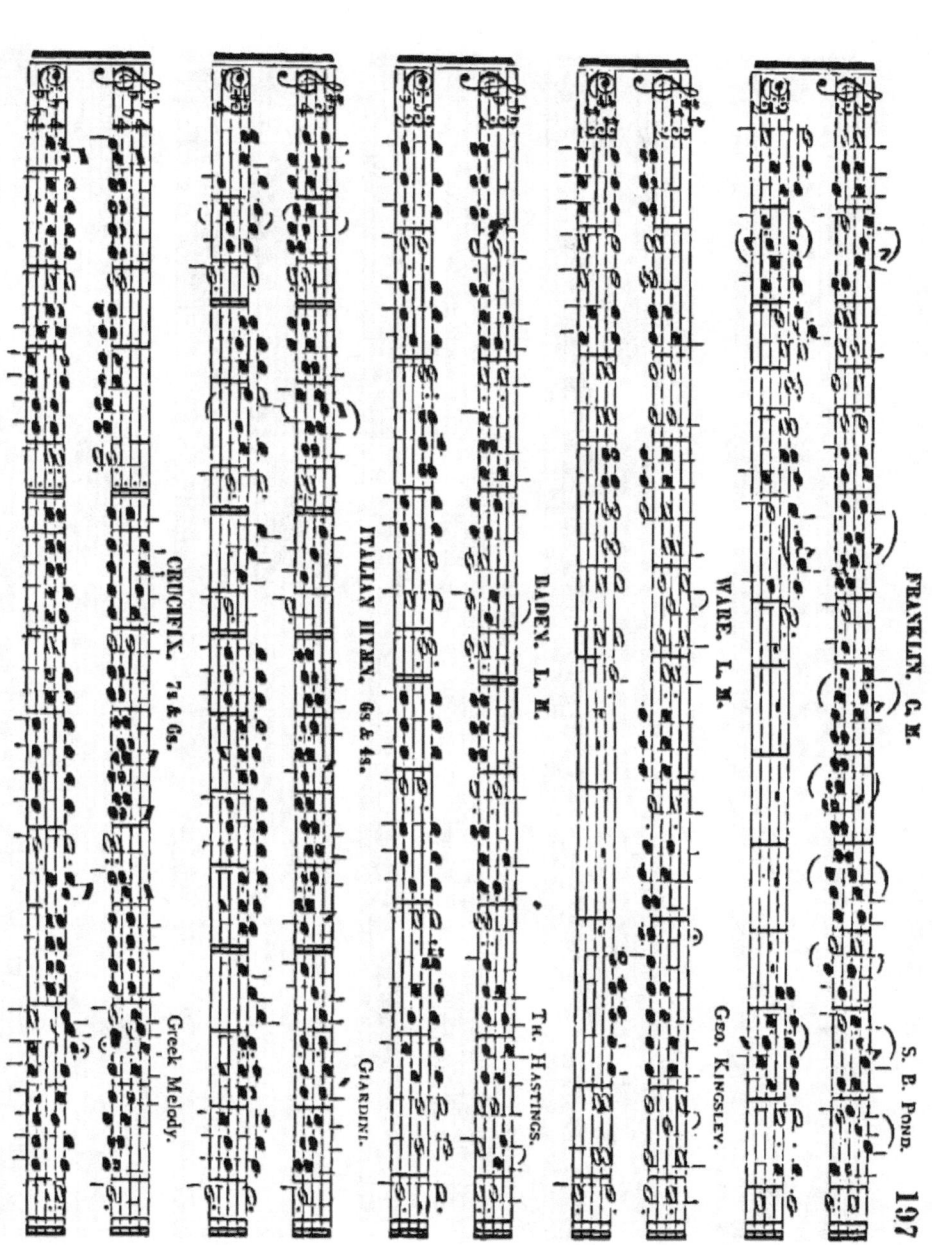

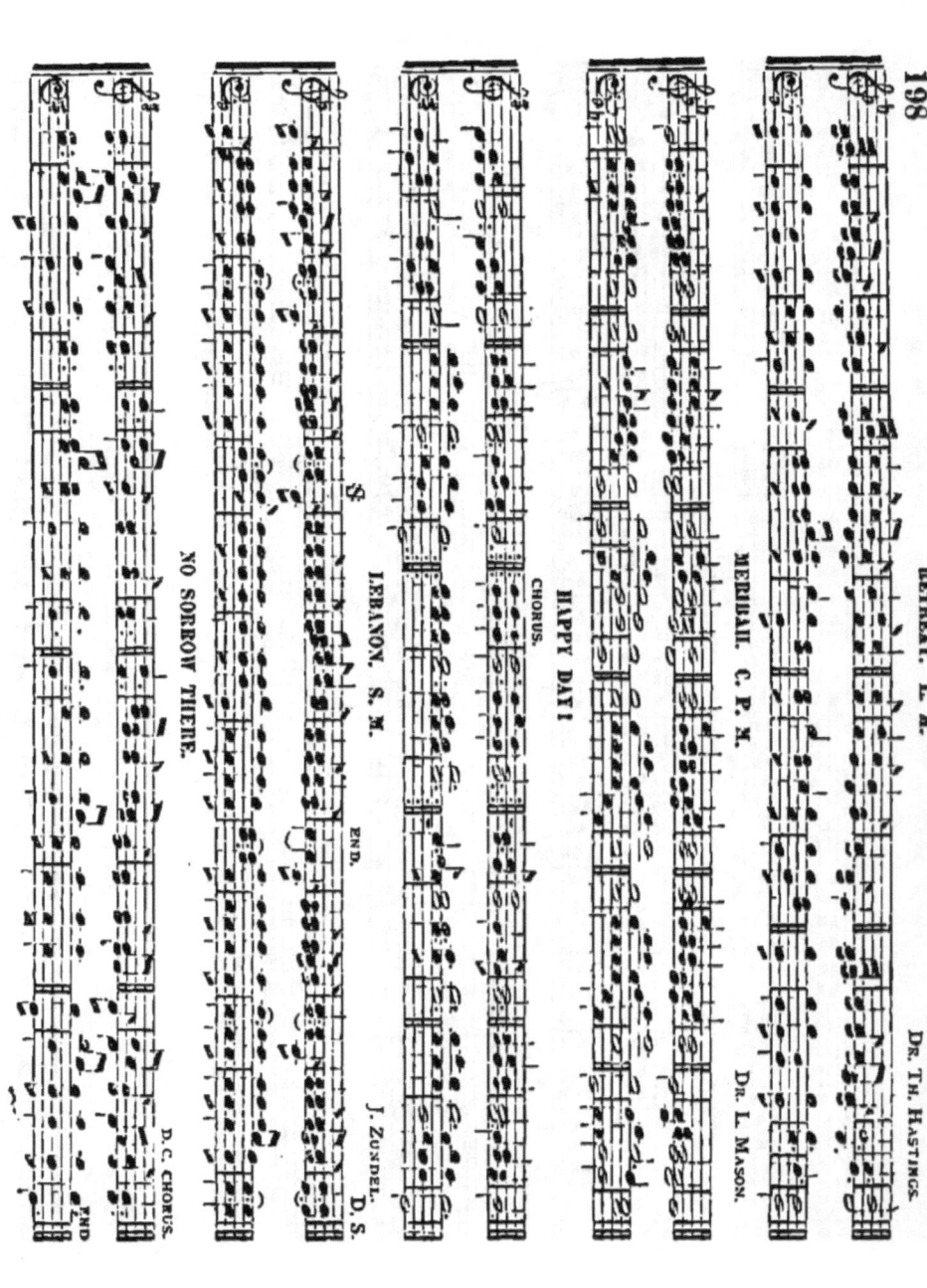

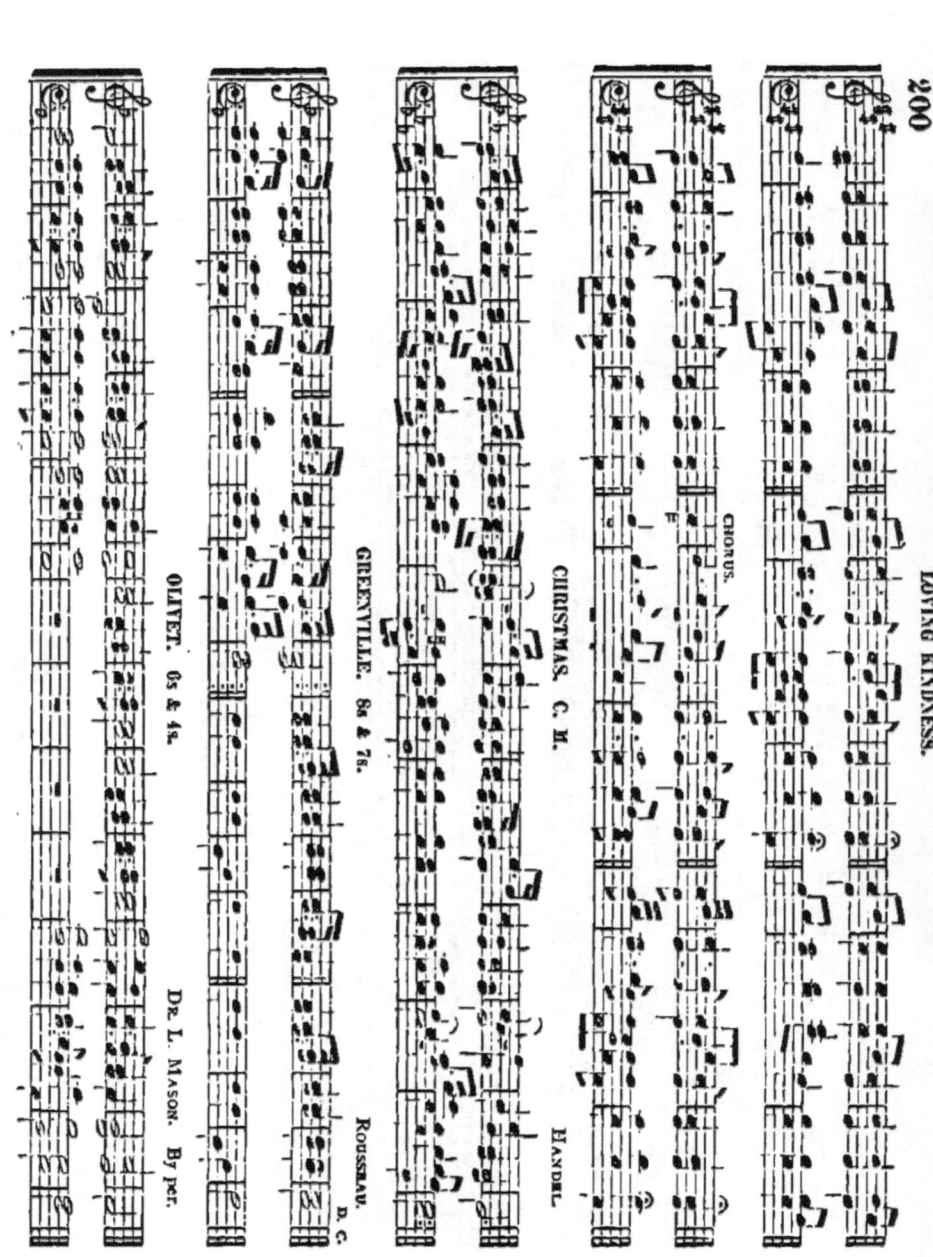

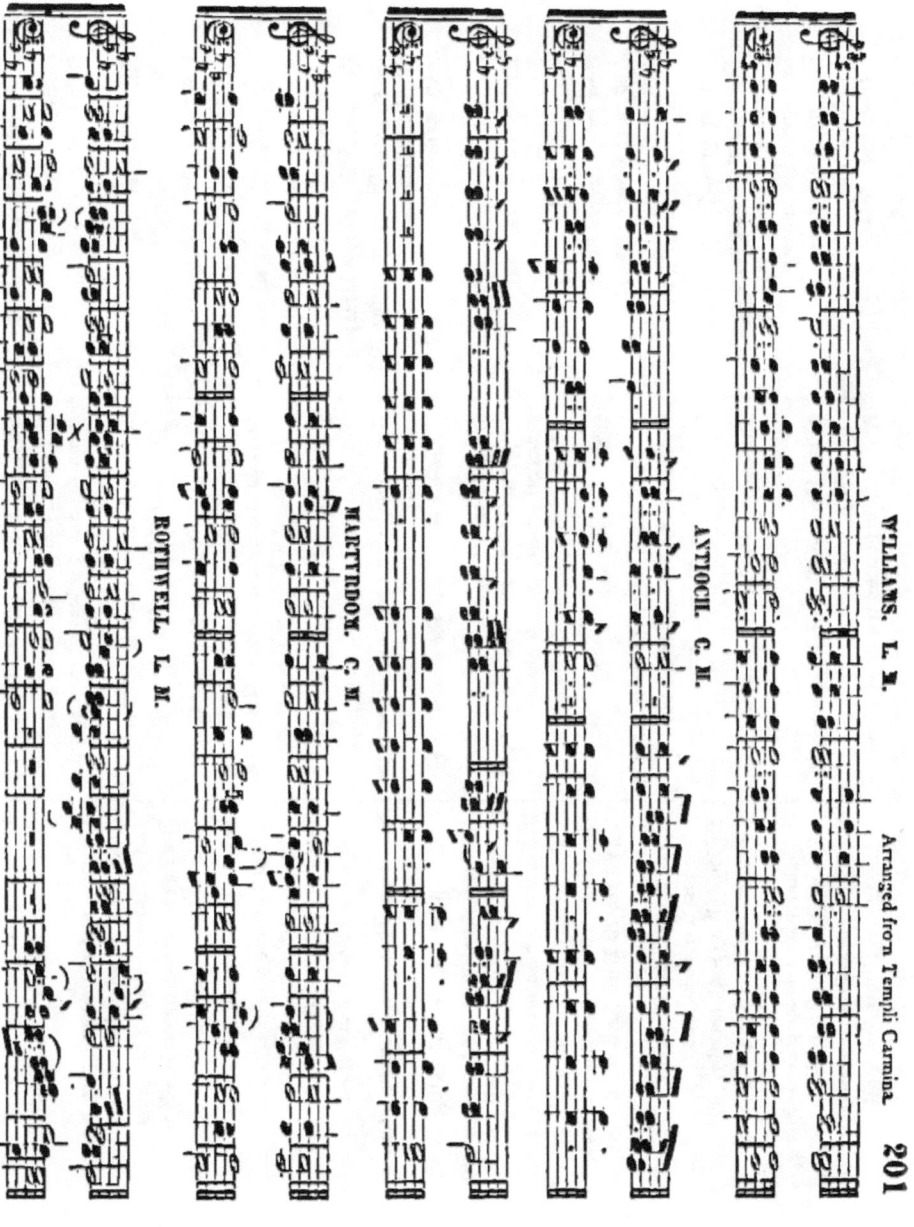

CHRISTIAN SONGS.

220. [*Italian Hymn*, page 197.]

1. Come, thou almighty King,
Help us Thy name to sing,
Help us to praise!
Father all glorious,
O'er all victorious,
Come and reign over us,
Ancient of days.

2. Come, thou incarnate Word
Gird on Thy mighty sword;
Our prayer attend;
Come, and Thy people bless;
Come, give Thy word success;
Spirit of holiness,
On us descend.

3. Come, holy Comforter,
Thy sacred witness bear,
In this glad hour;
Thou, who almighty art,
Now rule in every heart,
And ne'er from us depart,
Spirit of power.

4. To thee, great One in Three,
The highest praises be,
Hence evermore;
Thy sovereign majesty
May we in glory see,
And to eternity
Love and adore.

221. [*Old Hundred*, 101 *Trio.*]

1. Lord hallelujahs to the Lord,
From distant worlds where creatures dwell,
Let heav'n begin the solemn word,
And sound it dreadful down to hell.

2. Wide as His vast dominion lies,
Make the Creator's name be known;
Loud as His thunder, shout His praise,
And sound it lofty as His throne.

3. Jehovah—'tis a glorious word!
O, may it dwell on every tongue!
But saints, who best have known the Lord,
Are bound to raise the noblest song.

4. Speak of the wonders of that love
Which Gabriel plays on every chord;
From all below, and all above,
Loud hallelujahs to the Lord.

222. [*Ware*, page 197.]

1. Jesus shall reign where'er the sun
Doth his successive journeys run;
His kingdom spread from shore to shore,
Till moons shall wax and wane no more.

2. To Him shall endless prayer be made,
And endless praises crown His head;
His Name like sweet perfume shall rise
With every morning sacrifice.

3. People and realms of every tongue
Dwell on His love with sweetest song,
And infant voices shall proclaim
Their early blessings on His Name.

223. [*Coronation*, 179 *Trio.*]

1. All hail the power of Jesus' name,
Let angels prostrate fall;
Bring forth the royal diadem,
And crown Him Lord of all.

2. Crown Him, ye morning stars of light,
Who fix'd this floating ball;
Now hail the strength of Israel's might,
And crown Him Lord of all.

3. Sinners, whose love can ne'er forget
The wormwood and the gall;
Go, spread your trophies at his feet,
And crown Him Lord of all.

4. Let every kindred, every tribe,
On this terrestrial ball,
To Him all majesty ascribe,
And crown Him Lord of all.

5. O that with yonder sacred throng,
We at His feet may fall!
We'll join the everlasting song,
And crown Him Lord of all.

CHRISTIAN SONGS.

224. [*Bothwell*, 201.]

1. HE lives, the great Redeemer lives,
What joy the blest assurance gives;
And now, before His Father, God,
Pleads the full merit of His blood.

2. Repeated crimes awake our fears,
And justice, armed with frowns, appears;
But in the Saviour's lovely face,
Sweet mercy smiles, and all is peace.

3. Hence, then, ye black, despairing thoughts;
Above our fears, above our faults,
His powerful intercessions rise,
And guilt recedes, and terror dies.

4. Great Advocate, Almighty Friend!
On Him our humble hopes depend;
Our cause can never, never fail,
For Jesus pleads, and must prevail.

225. [*Franklin*, 197.]

1. THE head that once was crowned with thorns
Is crowned with glory now;
A royal diadem adorns
The mighty Victor's brow.

2. The highest place that heaven affords,
Is His by sovereign right;
The King of kings, and Lord of lords,
He reigns in glory bright,—

3. The joy of all who dwell above,
The joy of all below,
To whom He manifests His love,
And grants His name to know.

4. To them, the cross, with all its shame,
With all its grace is given;
Their name, an everlasting name,
Their joy—the joy of heaven.

226. [*Palerma*, 123 Trio.]

1. JESUS, the very thought of Thee,
With sweetness fills my breast;
But sweeter far Thy face to see,
And in Thy presence rest.

2. Nor voice can sing, nor heart can frame,
Nor can the memory find,
A sweeter sound than Thy blest name,
O Saviour of mankind!

3. O hope of every contrite heart!
O joy of all the meek!
To those who fall how kind Thou art!
How good to those who seek!

4. But what to those who find? Ah!
this,
Nor tongue, nor pen can show,
The love of Jesus, what it is,
None but his loved ones know.

227. [*Martyrdom*, 201.]

1. I'M not ashamed to own my Lord,
Nor to defend his cause;
Maintain the honor of His word,
The glory of His cross.

2. Jesus, my God! I know His name;
His name is all my trust;
Nor will He put my soul to shame,
Nor let my hope be lost.

3. Firm, as His throne, His promise stands,
And He can well secure
What I've committed to His hands,
Till the decisive hour.

4. Then will He own my worthless name,
Before His Father's face;
And in the New Jerusalem
Appoint my soul a place.

228. [*Antioch*, page 201.]

1. JOY to the world, the Lord is come!
Let earth receive her King;
Let every heart prepare Him room,
And heav'n and nature sing.

2. Joy to the world, the Saviour reigns,
Let men their songs employ;
While fields and floods, rocks hills and plains,
Repeat the sounding joy.

3. He rules the world with truth and grace,
And makes the nations prove
The glories of His righteousness,
And wonders of His love.

229. [*Tune Williams, page 201.*]

1. WHEN I survey the wondrous cross,
On which the Prince of glory died,
My richest gain I count but loss,
And pour contempt on all my pride.

2. Forbid it, Lord, that I should boast,
Save in the death of Christ, my God;
All the vain things that charm me most,
I sacrifice them to His blood.

3. See, from His head, His hands, His feet,
Sorrow and love flow mingled down:
Did e'er such love and sorrow meet,
Or thorns compose so rich a crown!

4. Were the whole realm of nature mine,
That were a present far too small;
Love so amazing, so divine,
Demands my soul, my life, my all.

230. [*Crucifix, page 197.*]

1. O SACRED Head now wounded,
With grief and shame weigh'd down,
Now scornfully surrounded,
With thorns Thy only crown;
O sacred Head, what glory,
What bliss till now was Thine;
Yet though despised and gory,
I joy to call Thee mine.

2. What language shall I borrow,
To thank Thee, dearest Friend,
For this Thy dying sorrow,
Thy pity without end!
O make me Thine forever,
And should I fainting be,
Lord, let me never, never
Outlive my love to Thee.

3. If I, a wretch, should leave Thee,
O Jesus, leave not me;
In faith may I receive Thee,
When death shall set me free.
When strength and comfort languish,
And I must hence depart,
Release me then from anguish,
By Thine own wounded heart.

4. Be near, when I am dying,
O, show Thy cross to me!
And for my succor flying,
Come, Lord, to set me free.
These eyes, new faith receiving,
From Jesus shall not move;
For he who dies believing,
Dies safely—through Thy love.

231. [*Martyn, 14 Trio.*]

1. JESUS, lover of my soul,
Let me to Thy bosom fly;
While the billows near me roll,
While the tempest still is high.
Hide me, O my Saviour, hide,
Till the storm of life be past,
Safe into the haven guide,
O receive my soul at last.

2. Other refuge have I none—
Hangs my helpless soul on Thee;
Leave, ah! leave me not alone,
Still support and comfort me;
All my trust on Thee is stayed,
All my help from Thee I bring—
Cover my defenceless head
With the shadow of Thy wing.

3. Thou, O Christ, art all I want,
More than all in Thee I find,
Raise the fallen, cheer the faint,
Heal the sick, and lead the blind.

4. Plenteous grace with Thee is found—
Grace to pardon all my sin;
Let the healing streams abound,
Make and keep me pure within;
Thou of life the fountain art,
Freely let me take of Thee;
Spring Thou up within my heart,
Rise to all eternity.

232. [*Dennis, 225 Trio.*]

1. THE Lord my Shepherd is;
I shall be well supplied;
Since He is mine, and I am His
What can I want beside?

2. He leads me to the place
Where heavenly pasture grows,
Where living waters gently pass,
And full salvation flows.

3. If e'er I go astray,
He doth my soul reclaim,
And guides me in His own right way
For His most holy name.

4. In sight of all my foes,
Thou dost my table spread:
My cup with blessings overflows,
And joy exalts my head.

5. The bounties of Thy love
Shall crown my future days;
Nor from Thy house will I remove,
Nor cease to speak Thy praise.

Just and holy is Thy name,
I am all unrighteousness;
Vile and full of sin I am—
Thou art full of truth and grace.

CHRISTIAN SONGS.

233. [*Loving Kindness,* 200.]

1. AWAKE, my soul, to joyful lays,
And sing the great Redeemer's praise;
He justly claims a song from me,
His loving kindness, Oh! how free!

2. He saw me ruined in the fall,
Yet loved me notwithstanding all:
He saved me from my lost estate,
His loving kindness, Oh! how great!

3. Though numerous hosts of mighty foes,
Though earth and hell my way oppose,
He safely leads my soul along,
His loving kindness, Oh! how strong!

4. Often I feel my sinful heart,
Prone from my Jesus to depart;
But, though I have Him oft forgot,
His loving kindness changes not.

234. [*Duke St.,* 7 *Trio.*]

1. OH! the sweet wonders of that cross,
Where God, the Saviour, loved and died;
Her noblest life my spirit draws
From His dear wounds, and bleeding side.

2. I would for ever speak His name,
It sounds to mortal ears unknown,
With angels join to praise the Lamb,
And worship at His Father's throne.

3. All hail! Thou great Immanuel, hail!
Ten thousand blessings on Thy name!
While thus Thy wondrous love we tell,
Our bosoms feel the sacred flame.

4. Come, quickly come, Immortal King!
On earth Thy regal honors raise;
The full salvation promised bring,
Then every tongue shall sing Thy praise!

235. [*Martyrdom,* 201.]

1. ALAS! and did my Saviour bleed?
And did my Sovereign die?
Would He devote that sacred head
For such a worm as I?

2. Was it for crimes that I had done
He groaned upon the tree?
Amazing pity! grace unknown!
And love beyond degree!

3. Well might the sun in darkness hide,
And shut his glories in,
When Christ, the Lord of glory,
died
For man the creature's sin.

4. Thus might I hide my blushing face
While his dear cross appears,
Dissolve my heart in thankfulness,
And melt mine eyes to tears.

5. But drops of grief can ne'er repay
The debt of love I owe:
Here, Lord, I give myself away;
'Tis all that I can do.

236. [*Ortonville,* 82 *Trio.*]

1. MAJESTIC sweetness sits enthroned
Upon the Saviour's brow;
His head with radiant glories crown'd,
His lips with grace o'erflow.

2. He saw me plunged in deep distress,
And flew to my relief;
For me He bore the shameful cross,
And carried all my grief.

3. To Him I owe my life and breath,
And all the joys I have,
He makes me triumph over death,
And saves me from the grave.

4. Since from Thy bounty I receive
Such proofs of love divine,
Had I a thousand hearts to give,
Lord, they should all be Thine.

237. [*Martyrdom,* 201.]

1. DEAR Refuge of my weary soul,
On Thee, when sorrows rise—
On Thee, when waves of trouble roll,
My fainting hope relies.

2. To Thee I tell each rising grief,
For Thou alone canst heal;
Thy word can bring a sweet relief
For every pain I feel.

3. But O! when gloomy doubts prevail,
I fear to call Thee mine;
The springs of comfort seem to fail,
And all my hopes decline.

4. Yet, gracious God, where shall I flee?
Thou art my only trust;
And still my soul would cleave to Thee,
Though prostrate in the dust.

CHRISTIAN SONGS.

238. [St. Thomas, 24 Trio.]

1. Awake, and sing the song
Of Moses and the Lamb;
Wake, every heart, and every tongue,
To praise the Saviour's name.

2. Sing of His dying love,
Sing of His rising power;
Sing on how He intercedes above,
For those whose sins He bore.

3. Sing on your heavenly way,
Ye ransomed sinners, sing;
Sing on, rejoicing, every day,
In Christ, the exalted King.

4. Soon shall your raptured tongue
His endless praise proclaim;
And sweeter voices tune the song
Of Moses and the Lamb.

239. [State Street, 71 Trio.]

1. Jesus, who knows full well,
The heart of every saint,
Invites us all our griefs to tell,
To pray, and never faint.

2. He bows His gracious ear;
We never plead in vain;
Yet we must wait till He appear,
And pray, and pray again.

3. Jesus, the Lord will hear
His chosen when they cry;
Yes, though He may a while forbear,
He'll help them from on high.

4. Then let us earnest be,
And never faint in prayer;
He loves our importunity,
And makes our cause His care.

240. [Ortonville, 82 Trio.]

1. How sweet the name of Jesus sounds
In a believer's ear!
It soothes his sorrows, heals his wounds,
And drives away his fear.

2. It makes the wounded spirit whole,
And calms the troubled breast;
'Tis manna to the hungry soul,
And for the weary, rest.

3. By Thee my prayers acceptance gain,
Although with sin defiled;
Satan accuses me in vain,
And I am owned a child.

4. Jesus! my Shepherd, Guardian, Friend,
My Prophet, Priest, and King:
My Lord, my Life, my way, my End,
Accept the praise I bring.

241. [Baden, 197.]

1. Though all the world my choice deride,
Yet Jesus shall my portion be;
For I am pleased with none beside;
The fairest of the fair is He.

2. Sweet is the vision of Thy face,
And kindness o'er Thy lips is shed;
Lovely art Thou, and full of grace,
And glory beams around Thy head.

3. Thy sufferings I embrace with Thee,
Thy poverty and shameful cross;
The pleasures of the world I flee,
And deem its treasures only dross.

242. [Shining Shore, 83 Trio.]

1. My days are gliding swiftly by,
And I, a pilgrim stranger,
Would not detain them as they fly!
Those hours of toil and danger,

CHORUS.

For oh! we stand on Jordan's strand,
Our friends are passing over,
And just before, the shining shore,
We may almost discover.

2. We'll gird our loins, my brethren dear,
Our distant home discerning;
Our absent Lord has left us word,
Let every lamp be burning.
Cho.—For oh!

3. Should coming days be cold and dark,
We need not cease our singing;
That perfect rest nought can molest,
Where golden harps are ringing.
Cho.—For oh!

4. Let sorrow's rudest tempest blow,
Each chord on earth to sever,
Our King says, come, and there's our home,
For ever, oh! for ever!
Cho.—For oh!

CHRISTIAN SONGS.

213. [*Christmas, 200.*]

1. AWAKE, my soul, stretch every nerve,
And press with vigor on;
A heavenly race demands thy zeal,
And an immortal crown.

2. A cloud of witnesses around
Hold thee in full survey;
Forget the steps already trod,
And onward urge thy way.

3. 'Tis God's all animating voice,
That calls thee from on high;
'Tis His own hand presents the prize
To thine aspiring eye.

4. Blest Saviour, introduced by Thee,
Have I my race begun;
And, crowned with victory, at thy Feet
I'll lay my honors down.

214. [*Palermo, 127 Trio.*]

1. AMAZING grace; how sweet the sound
That saved a wretch like me!
I once was lost, but now am found—
Was blind, but now I see.

2. 'T was grace that taught my heart to fear,
And grace my fears relieved;
How precious did that grace appear,
The hour I first believed!

3. Through many dangers, toils, and snares,
I have already come;
'Tis grace has brought me safe thus far,
And grace will lead me home.

215. [*Uxbridge.*]

1. WHAT sinners value I resign;
Lord! 'tis enough that Thou art mine;
I shall behold Thy blissful face,
And stand complete in righteousness.

2. This life's a dream—an empty show;
But the bright world, to which I go,
Hath joys substantial and sincere;
When shall I wake and find me there?

3. Oh! glorious hour!—Oh! blest abode,
I shall be near, and like my God;
And flesh and sin no more control
The sacred pleasures of the soul.

4. My flesh shall slumber in the ground,
Till the last trumpet's joyful sound;
Then burst the chains with sweet surprise,
And in my Saviour's image rise.

216. [*L. M.*]

1. WE sing His love, who once was slain,
Who soon o'er death revived again,
That all His saints through Him might have
Eternal conquests o'er the grave.

CHORUS.

Soon shall the trumpet sound, and we
Shall rise to immortality.

2. The saints who now with Jesus sleep,
His own Almighty power shall keep,
Till dawns the bright illustrious day
When death itself shall die away.

3. When Jesus we in glory meet,
Our utmost joys shall be complete;

4. Hasten, dear Lord, the glorious day,
And this delightful scene display,
When all Thy saints from death shall rise,
Raptured in bliss beyond the skies!

217. [*Olivet, 200.*]

1. MY faith looks up to Thee,
Thou Lamb of Calvary,
Saviour divine!
Now hear me while I pray,
Take all my guilt away,
O let me from this day
Be wholly Thine.

2. May Thy rich grace impart
Strength to my fainting heart;
My zeal inspire:
As Thou hast died for me,
O may my love to Thee,
Pure, warm, and changeless be,
A living fire.

3. While life's dark maze I tread,
And griefs around me spread,
Be Thou my guide;
Bid darkness turn to day,
Wipe sorrow's tears away,
Nor let me ever stray,
From Thee aside.

4. When ends life's transient dream,
When death's cold sullen stream
Shall o'er me roll,
Blest Saviour, then in love,
Fear and distrust remove;
O bear me safe above,
A ransomed soul!

When landed on that heavenly shore,
Death and the curse will be no more.

248.
[*Joyfully.*]

1. JOYFULLY, joyfully onward I move,
Bound to the land of bright spirits above,
Angelic choristers, sing as I come—
Joyfully, joyfully haste to thy home!
Soon with my pilgrimage ended below,
Home to the land of bright spirits I go;
Pilgrim and stranger no more shall I roam,
Joyfully, joyfully resting at home!

2. Friends, fondly cherished, have passed on before;
Waiting, they watch me approaching the shore;
Singing to cheer me thro' death's chilling gloom;
Joyfully, joyfully, haste to thy home!
Sounds of sweet melody fall on my ear;
Harps of the blessed your voices I hear!
Rings with the harmony heaven's high dome—
Joyfully, joyfully haste to thy home.

3. Death, with thy weapons of war lay me low,
Strike, king of terrors! I fear not the blow;
Jesus hath broken the bars of the tomb!
Joyfully, joyfully will I go home.
Bright will the morn of eternity dawn,
Death shall be banished, his scepter be gone;
Joyfully, then, shall I witness his doom,
Joyfully, joyfully, safely at home.

249.
[*Portuguese Hymn, page 199.*]

1. How firm a foundation, ye saints of the Lord,
Is laid for your faith in His excellent word;
What more can He say than to you He hath said—
Who unto the Saviour for refuge have fled.

2. Fear not, I am with thee, oh! be not dismayed,
For I am thy God, and will still give thee aid:
I'll strengthen thee, help thee, and cause thee to stand,
Upheld by my righteous, omnipotent hand.

3. When through the deep waters I call thee to go,
The rivers of sorrow shall not overflow;
For I will be with thee thy trials to bless,
And sanctify to thee thy deepest distress.

4. When through fiery trials thy pathway shall lie,
My grace, all-sufficient, shall be thy supply;
The flame shall not hurt thee; I only design
Thy dross to consume, and thy gold to refine.

5. E'en down to old age all My people shall prove
My sovereign eternal, unchangeable love;
And then, when gray hairs shall their temples adorn,
Like lambs they shall still in my bosom be borne.

6. The soul that on Jesus hath leaned for repose,
I will not—I will not desert to His foes;
That soul—though all hell should endeavor to shake,
I'll never—no never—no never forsake!

250.
[*Expostulation, page 199.*]

1. O TURN ye, O turn ye, for why will ye die?
When God, in great mercy, is coming so nigh;
Now Jesus invites you, the Spirit says come,
And angels are waiting to welcome you home.

2. How vain the delusion, that while you delay,
Your hearts may grow better by staying away;
Come wretched, come starving, come just as you be,
While streams of salvation are flowing so free.

CHRISTIAN SONGS.

251.

[*Homeward Bound, page 199.*]

1. Out on an ocean all boundless we ride,
   We're homeward bound;
   Tossed on the waves of a rough, restless tide,
   We're homeward bound;
   Far from the safe, quiet harbor we rode,
   Seeking our Father's celestial abode,
   Promise of which on us each be bestowed,
   We're homeward bound.

2. Wildly the storm sweeps us on as it roars;
   We're homeward bound;
   Look! yonder lie the bright heavenly shores,
   We're homeward bound;
   Steady! O pilot! stand firm at the wheel,
   Steady, we soon shall outweather the gale,
   Oh! how we fly 'neath the loud-creaking sail,
   We're homeward bound.

3. We'll tell the world as we journey along,
   We're homeward bound;
   Try to persuade them to enter our throng,
   We're homeward bound;
   Come, trembling sinner, forlorn and oppressed,
   Join in our number, O come and be blest;
   Journey with us to the mansions of rest,
   We're homeward bound.

4. Into the harbor of heaven now we glide,
   We're home at last;
   Softly we drift on its bright silver tide,
   We're home at last;
   Glory to God! all our dangers are o'er;
   We stand secure on the glorified shore,
   Glory to God! we will shout evermore,
   We're home at last.

252.

[*Hail to the Brightness.*]

1. Hail to the brightness of Zion's glad morning!
   Joy to the lands that in darkness have lain;
   Hushed be the accents of sorrow and mourning,
   Zion in triumph begins her mild reign.

2. Hail to the brightness of Zion's glad morning,
   Long by the prophets of Israel foretold;
   Hail to the millions from bondage returning,
   Gentiles and Jews the blest vision behold.

3. Lo! in the desert rich flowers are springing,
   Streams ever copious are gliding along,
   Loud from the mountain-tops, echoes are ringing,
   Wastes rise in verdure, and mingle in song.

4. See, from all lands—from the isles of the ocean,
   Praise to Jehovah ascending on high,
   Fallen are the engines of war and commotion,
   Shouts of salvation are rending the sky.

---

3. And now Christ is ready your souls to receive,
   O how can you question, if you will believe?
   If sin is your burden, why will you not come?
   'Tis you He bids welcome; He bids you come home.

4. Come, give us your hand, and the Saviour your heart,
   And trusting in Heaven, we never shall part;
   O how can we leave you? why will you not come?
   We'll journey together, and soon be at home.

253. [Weld, 104 Tri.]

1. We bring no glittering treasures,
No gems from earth's deep mine;
We come with simple measures,
To chant Thy love divine.
We all, Thy favors sharing,
Our voice of thanks would raise;
Father, accept our offering,
Our song of grateful praise.

2. The dearest gift of Heaven,
Love's precious word of Truth,
To sinners thou hast given,
To guide their steps in youth;
To tell the wondrous story,
The tale of Calvary;
To tell of homes in glory,
From sin and sorrow free.

3. Redeemer, grant Thy blessing;
Oh, teach us how to pray!
That we, Thy love possessing,
May tread life's devious way;
Till where the pure are dwelling
By grace we meet again,
And, sweeter numbers swelling,
Forever praise Thy name.

254. [Amsterdam, page 199.]

1. Rise, my soul, and stretch thy wings,
Thy better portion trace;
Rise, from transitory things,
Toward heaven, thy native place:
Sun, and moon, and stars decay,
Time shall soon this earth remove;
Rise, my soul, and haste away
To seats prepared above.

2. Rivers to the ocean run,
Nor stay in all their course;
Fire descending, seeks the sun,
Both speed them to their source;
So a soul that's born of God,
Pants to see His glorious face,
Upward tends to His abode,
To rest in His embrace.

3. Cease, ye pilgrims, cease to mourn,
Press onward to the prize;
Soon our Saviour will return
Triumphant in the skies;
There we'll join the heavenly train,
Welcomed to partake the bliss;
Fly from sorrow and from pain,
To realms of endless peace.

255. [Bethany, 77 Trio.]

1. Nearer, my God, to Thee,
Nearer to Thee!
Even though it be a cross
That raiseth me;
Still all my song shall be—
Nearer my God, to Thee,
Nearer to Thee!

2. Though, like the wanderer,
The sun gone down,
Darkness be over me,
My rest a stone;
Yet in my dreams I'd be
Nearer, my God, to Thee—
Nearer to Thee!

3. There let the way appear,
Steps unto heaven;
All that Thou sendest me,
In mercy given;
Angels to beckon me,
Nearer, my God, to Thee—
Nearer to Thee!

4. Then with my waking thoughts,
Bright with Thy praise,
Out of my stony griefs,
Bethel I'll raise;
So by my woes to be
Nearer, my God, to Thee!
Nearer to Thee!

5. Or if on joyful wing,
Cleaving the sky,
Sun, moon, and stars forgot,
Upward I fly;
Still all my song shall be—
Nearer, my God, to Thee!
Nearer to Thee!

CHRISTIAN SONGS. 211

256. [*Violet, 73 Tris.*]

1. JESUS, I my cross have taken,
All to leave and follow Thee;
Naked, poor, despised, forsaken,
Thou, from hence, my all shalt be.
Perish every fond ambition,
All I've sought, or hoped, or known;
Yet how rich is my condition!
God and heaven are still my own.

2. Let the world despise and leave me,
They have left my Saviour, too;
Human hearts and looks deceive me,
Thou art not like them untrue;
And whilst Thou shalt smile upon me,
God of wisdom, love, and might,
Foes may hate, and friends may scorn me;
Show Thy face, and all is bright.

3. Man may trouble and distress me,
'Twill but drive me to Thy breast;
Life with trials hard may press me,
Heaven will bring me sweeter rest.
Oh! 'tis not in grief to harm me,
While Thy love is left to me;
Oh! 'twere not in joy to charm me,
Were that joy unmixed with Thee.

4. Soul, then know thy full salvation,
Rise o'er sin, and fear, and care;
Joy to find in every station,
Something still to do or bear.
Think what Spirit dwells within thee;
Think what Father's smiles are thine;
Think that Jesus died to win thee;
Child of heaven, can'st thou repine!

5. Haste thee on from grace to glory,
Armed by faith, and winged by prayer;
Heaven's eternal day's before thee,
God's own hand shall guide thee there.
Soon shall close thy earthly mission,
Soon shall pass thy pilgrim days;
Hope shall change to glad fruition,
Faith to sight, and prayer to praise.

257. [*Christmas, page 200.*]

1. AM I a soldier of the cross—
A follower of the Lamb—
And shall I fear to own His cause,
Or blush to speak His name!

2. Must I be carried to the skies
On flowery beds of ease,
While others fought to win the prize,
And sailed through bloody seas!

3. Are there no foes for me to face?
Must I not stem the flood?
Is this vile world a friend to grace?
To help me on to God?

4. Since I must fight if I would reign,
Increase my courage, Lord;
I'll bear the toil, endure the pain,
Supported by Thy word.

258. [*Meribah, page 193.*]

1. OFT when the waves of passion rise,
And storms of life conceal the skies,
And o'er the ocean sweep,
Toss'd in the long tempestuous night,
We feel no ray of heavenly light,
To cheer the lonely deep.

2. But lo! in our extremity,
The Saviour walking on the sea!
E'en now He passes by!
He silences our clamorous fear,
And mildly says, "Be of good cheer,
Be not afraid, 'tis I."

3. Ah, Lord! if it be Thou indeed,
So near us in our time of need,
So good, so strong to save—
Speak the kind word of power to me,
Bid me believe, and come to Thee,
Swift-walking on the wave.

4. He bids me come! His voice I know,
And boldly on the waters go,
And brave the tempest's shock;
O'er rude temptations now I bound,
The billows yield a solid ground,
The wave is firm as rock!

5. Come in, come in, Thou Prince of peace!
And all the storms of sin shall cease,
And fall, no more to rise;
O, if Thy Spirit still remain,
Our rest on distant shores we gain,
Our haven in the skies!

259. [L. M.]

1. When marshalled on the nightly plain,
The glittering host bestud the sky,
One star alone, of all the train,
Can fix the sinner's wandering eye.

2. Hark! hark! to God the chorus breaks,
From every host, from every gem;
But One alone, the Saviour speaks—
It is the Star of Bethlehem.

3. Once on the raging seas I rode,
The storm was loud, the night was dark;
The ocean yawned, and rudely blowed
The wind that tossed my foundering bark.

4. Deep horror then my vitals froze,
Death-struck, I ceased the tide to stem;
When suddenly a Star arose—
It was the Star of Bethlehem.

5. It was my guide, my light, my all;
It bade my dark forebodings cease;
And through the storm, and danger's thrall,
It led me to the port of peace.

6. Now safely moored—my perils o'er,
I'll sing, first, in night's diadem,
For ever, and for evermore,
The Star—the Star of Bethlehem!

260. [Dundee.]

1. Prostrate, dear Jesus! at Thy feet
A guilty rebel lies;
And upward to the mercy-seat
Presumes to lift his eyes.

2. If tears of sorrow would suffice
To pay the debt I owe,
Tears should from both my weeping eyes
In ceaseless torrents flow.

3. But no such sacrifice I plead
To expiate my guilt;
No tears, but those which Thou hast shed—
No blood, but Thou hast spilt.

4. Think of Thy sorrows, dearest Lord!
And all my sins forgive;
Justice will well approve the word
That bids the sinner live.

261. [To-Day, 8 Trio.]

1. To-day the Saviour calls:
Ye wanderers, come!
O ye benighted souls,
Why longer roam?

2. To-day the Saviour calls;
For refuge fly:
The storm of vengeance falls,
Ruin is nigh.

3. To-day the Saviour calls;
Oh, listen now!
Within these sacred walls
To Jesus bow.

4. The Spirit calls to-day:
Yield to his power;
Oh, grieve him not away!
'Tis mercy's hour.

262. [Meribah, page 198.]

1. When Thou, my righteous Judge, shalt come,
To take Thy ransomed people home,
Shall I among them stand?
Who sometimes am afraid to die,
Be found at Thy right hand?

2 I love to meet Thy people now,
Before Thy feet with them to bow,
Though vilest of them all;
But—can I bear the piercing thought!—
What if my name should be left out,
When Thou for them shalt call?

3. O Lord, prevent it by Thy grace—
Be Thou my only hiding-place,
In this the accepted day;
Thy pardoning voice, O let me hear,
Nor let me fall, I pray.

263. [Woodworth, 139 Trio.]

1. Just as I am—without one plea,
But that Thy blood was shed for me,
And that Thou bid'st me come to Thee,
O Lamb of God, I come, I come.

2. Just as I am—and waiting not
To rid my soul of one dark blot,
To Thee whose blood can cleanse each spot,
O Lamb of God, I come! I come!

CHRISTIAN SONGS. 213

3. Just as I am—though tossed about
With many a conflict, many a doubt,
"Fightings within, and fears without,"
O Lamb of God, I come! I come!

4. Just as I am—poor, wretched, blind;
Sight, riches, healing of the mind,
Yea, all I need, in Thee to find,
O Lamb of God, I come! I come!

5. Just as I am—Thou wilt receive;
Wilt welcome, pardon, cleanse, relieve;
Because Thy promise I believe,
O Lamb of God, I come! I come!

6. Just as I am—Thy love unknown
Has broken every barrier down;
Now, to be Thine, yea, Thine alone,
O Lamb of God, I come! I come!

264. [349 *Trio.*]

1. THERE is a fountain filled with blood,
Drawn from Immanuel's veins;
And sinners plunged beneath that flood
Lose all their guilty stains.

2. The dying thief rejoiced to see
That fountain in his day;
And there may I, tho' vile as he,
Wash all my sins away.

3. Dear, dying Lamb, Thy precious blood
Shall never lose its power
Till all the ransomed church of God
Be saved to sin no more.

4. E'er since, by faith, I saw the stream
Thy flowing wounds supply,
Redeeming love has been my theme,
And shall be, till I die.

5. Then in a nobler, sweeter song,
I'll sing Thy power to save,
When this poor, lisping, stammering tongue
Lies silent in the grave.

265. [*State Street*, 71 *Trio.*]

1. BLEST be the tie that binds
Our hearts in Christian love;
The fellowship of kindred minds
Is like to that above.

2. Before our Father's throne,
We pour our ardent prayers;
Our fears, our hopes, our aims are one—
Our comforts and our cares.

3. We share our mutual woes;
Our mutual burdens bear;
And often for each other flows
The sympathizing tear.

4. When we asunder part,
It gives us inward pain;
But we shall still be join'd in heart,
And hope to meet again.

5. This glorious hope revives
Our courage by the way;
While each in expectation lives,
And longs to see the day.

266. [*Martyrdom, page* 201.]

1. O COULD I find from day to day,
A nearness to my God,
Then would my hours glide sweet away,
While leaning on His word.

2. Lord, I desire with Thee to live
Anew from day to day,
In joys the world can never give,
Nor ever take away.

3. Blest Jesus, come, and rule my heart,
And make me wholly Thine,
That I may never more depart,
Nor grieve Thy love divine.

267. [*Happy Day, page* 198.]

1. O HAPPY day that fix'd my choice
On Thee, my Saviour and my God!
Well may this glowing heart rejoice,
And tell its raptures all abroad.

2. O happy bond, that seals my vows
To Him who merits all my love;
Let cheerful anthems fill His house,
While to the sacred shrine I move.

3. 'Tis done, the great transaction's done,
I am my Lord's, and He is mine;
He drew me, and I follow'd on,
Charm'd to confess the voice divine.

4. Now rest, my long-divided heart;
Fix'd on this blissful centre, rest;
Nor ever from Thy Lord depart;
With Him of every good possess'd.

268. [*Jesus Paid it All.*]

1. NOTHING, either great or small
Remains for me to do;
Jesus died, and paid it all—
Yes, all the debt I owe.
CHO.—Jesus paid it all;
All the debt I owe.
Sin had left a crimson stain,
He washed it white as snow.

2. When He from His lofty throne,
Stoop'd down to bleed and die,
Every thing was fully done;
"'Tis finished!" was His cry.
CHO.—Jesus paid it all, etc.

3. Weary, working, plodding one,
Oh, wherefore toil you so?
Cease your doing,—all was done;
By Jesus, long ago.
CHO.—Jesus paid it all, etc.

269. [*Lebanon, page 198.*]

1. I WAS a wandering sheep,
I did not love the fold;
I did not love my Shepherd's voice,
I would not be controll'd;
I was a wayward child,
I did not love my home,
I did not love my Father's voice,
I loved afar to roam.

2. The Shepherd sought His sheep,
The Father sought His child;
They followed me o'er vale and hill,
O'er deserts waste and wild;
They found me nigh to death,
Famish'd, and faint, and lone;
They bound me in the bands of love,
They saved the wandering one.

3. Jesus my Shepherd is,
'Twas He that loved my soul,
'Twas He that wash'd me in His blood
'Twas He that made me whole;
'Twas He that sought the lost,
That found the wandering sheep,
'Twas He that brought me to the fold—
'Tis He that still doth keep.

270. [*Cross and Crown, 85 Trio.*]

1. MUST Jesus bear the cross alone,
And all the world go free?
No: there's a cross for every one,
And there's a cross for me.

2. How happy are the saints above,
Who once went sorrowing here;
But now they taste unmingled love,
And joy without a tear.

3. The consecrated cross I'll bear,
Till death shall set me free,
And then go home my crown to wear—
For there's a crown for me.

271. [*Martyrdom, 201.*]

1. O THOU, whose tender mercy hears
Contrition's humble sigh;
Whose hand, indulgent, wipes the tears
From sorrow's weeping eye,—

2. See, low before Thy throne of grace,
A wretched wanderer mourn;
Hast Thou not bid me seek Thy face?
Hast Thou not said—"Return?"

3. And shall my guilty fears prevail?
To drive me from Thy feet?
O let not this dear refuge fail,
This only safe retreat.

4. O shine on this benighted heart,
With beams of mercy shine!
And let Thy healing voice impart
A taste of joys divine.

272. [*Dennis, 225 Trio.*]

1. How gentle God's commands!
How kind His precepts are!
Come, cast your burdens on the Lord,
And trust His constant care.

2. Beneath His watchful eye,
His saints securely dwell;
That hand that bears all nature up,
Shall guard His children well.

3. Why should this anxious load
Press down your weary mind?
Haste to your heavenly Father's throne,
And sweet refreshment find.

CHRISTIAN SONGS.

273. [*Dover.*]

1. GIVE to the winds thy fears;
Hope, and be undismay'd;
God hears thy sighs, and counts thy tears,
God shall lift up thy head.

2. Through waves, through clouds, and storms,
He gently clears thy way;
Wait thou His time: so shall this night
Soon end in joyous day.

3. Still heavy is thy heart!
Still sink thy spirits down!
Cast off the weight, let fear depart!
Bid every care be gone.

4. Far, far above thy thought
His counsel shall appear,
When fully He the work hath wrought,
That caused thy needless fear.

5. What, though Thou rulest not!
Yet heaven, and earth, and hell
Proclaim God sitteth on the throne,
And ruleth all things well!

274. [*Will You Go?* Gl *Trio.*]

1. We're trav'ling home to heav'n above,
Will you go? will you go?
To sing the Saviour's dying love,
Will you go? will you go?
Millions have reach'd that blest abode,
Anointed kings and priests to God,
And millions now are on the road,
Will you go? will you go?

2. We're going to see the bleeding Lamb,
Will you go? will you go?
In rapturous strains to praise His name,
Will you go? will you go?
The crown of life we there shall wear,
The conqueror's palms our hands shall bear,
And all the joys of heaven we'll share;
Will you go? will you go?

3. Ye weary, heavy-laden, come,
Will you go? will you go?
In the blest house there still is room,
Will you go? will you go?
The Lord is waiting to receive,
If thou wilt on Him now believe,
He'll give thy troubled conscience ease,
Will you go? will you go?

275. [*No Sorrow There, p. 198.*]

1. FAR from these scenes of night
Unbounded glories rise,
And realms of joy and pure delight
Unknown to mortal eyes.
Cho.—There'll be no sorrow there,
There'll be no sorrow there,
In heaven above, where all is love,
There'll be no sorrow there.

2. Fair land!—could mortal eyes
But half its charms explore,
How would our spirits long to rise,
And dwell on earth no more.
Cho.—There'll be no sorrow there.

3. No cloud those regions know—
Realms ever bright and fair;
For sin, the source of mortal woe,
Can never enter there.
Cho.—There'll be no sorrow there.

4. O may the prospect fire
Our breasts with ardent love,
Till wings of faith and strong desire,
Bear every thought above.
Cho.—There'll be no sorrow there.

276. [*Woodland, page 196.*]

1. THERE is an hour of peaceful rest,
To mourning wanderers given;
There is a joy for souls distress'd,
A balm for every wounded breast,—
'Tis found above in heaven.

2. There faith lifts up the tearless eye,
To brighter prospects given;
And views the tempest passing by,
The evening shadows quickly fly,
And all serene in heaven.

3. There fragrant flowers immortal bloom,
And joys supreme are given;
There rays divine disperse the gloom;
Beyond the confines of the tomb
Appears the dawn of heaven.

CHRISTIAN SONGS.

277. [*Work, for the Night is Coming.* 194 Trio.]

1. Work, for the night is coming,
Work thro' the morning hours;
Work, while the dew is sparkling,
Work, 'mid springing flowers;
Work when the day grows brighter,
Work in the glowing sun;
Work, for the night is coming,
When man's work is done.

2. Work, for the night is coming;
Work through the sunny noon;
Fill brightest hours with labor,
Rest comes sure and soon.
Give every flying minute
Something to keep in store;
Work, for the night is coming;
When man works no more.

3. Work, for the night is coming,
Under the sunset skies;
While their bright tints are glowing,
Work, for daylight flies,
Work till the last beam fadeth,
Fadeth to shine no more;
Work, while the night is dark'ning,
When man's work is o'er.

278. [*Rothwell, page 201.*]

1. Stand up, my soul, shake off thy fears,
And gird the gospel armor on;
March to the gates of endless joy,
Where Jesus, thy great Captain's gone.

2. Hell and thy sins resist thy course;
But hell and sin are vanquished foes,
Thy Saviour nailed them to the cross,
And sung the triumph when He rose.

3. Then let my soul march boldly on,—
Press forward to the heavenly gate;
There peace and joy eternal reign,
And glittering robes for conquerors wait.

4. There shall I wear a starry crown,
And triumph in almighty grace,
While all the armies of the skies
Join in my glorious Leader's praise.

279. [*Laban, 61 Trio.*]

1. My soul, be on thy guard,
Ten thousand foes arise;
And hosts of sin are pressing hard
To draw thee from the skies.

2. O! watch, and fight, and pray;
The battle ne'er give o'er;
Renew it boldly every day,
And help divine implore.

3. Ne'er think the vict'ry won,
Nor lay thine armor down;
Thine arduous work will not be done,
Till thou obtain thy crown.

4. Fight on, my soul, till death
Shall bring thee to thy God;
He'll take thee at thy parting breath
To His divine abode.

280. [*Retreat, page 198.*]

1. From every stormy wind that blows,
From every swelling tide of woes,
There is a calm, a sure retreat,
'Tis found beneath the mercy-seat.

2. There is a place where Jesus sheds
The oil of gladness on our heads;
A place than all besides more sweet,
It is the blood-bought mercy-seat.

3. There is a scene where spirits blend,
Where friend holds fellowship with friend,
Though sundered far, by faith they meet
Around one common mercy-seat.

281. [*Ward, 61 Trio.*]

1. Behold a Stranger at the door!
He gently knocks, has knocked before;
Has waited long—is waiting still:
You treat no other friend so ill.

2. Oh! lovely attitude—He stands
With melting heart and loaded hands:
Oh! matchless kindness—and He shows
This matchless kindness to his foes!

3. But will He prove a friend indeed?
He will—the very Friend you need;
The Friend of sinners—yes, 'tis He,
With garments dyed on Calvary.

4. Admit Him ere His anger burn,
His feet, departed, ne'er return;
Admit Him, or, the Lord's at hand,
You'll at his door rejected stand.

CHRISTIAN SONGS. 217

282. [*Metropolis*, 196.]

1. JERUSALEM, my happy home,
Name ever dear to me,
When shall my labors have an end,
In joy and peace and Thee?

2. When shall these eyes Thy heaven-built walls
And pearly gates behold?
Thy bulwarks with salvation strong,
And streets of shining gold?

3. There happier bowers than Eden bloom,
Nor sin nor sorrow know;
Blest seats, through rude and stormy scenes
I onward press to you.

4. Jerusalem, my happy home,
My soul still pants for Thee;
Then shall my labors have an end
When I Thy joys shall see.

283. [*Happy Land.*]

1. THERE is a happy land,
Far, far away,
Where saints in glory stand,
Bright, bright as day.
Oh, how they sweetly sing,
Worthy is our Saviour King,
Loud let His praises ring,
Praise, praise for aye!

2. Come to that happy land,
Come, come away;
Why will ye doubting stand?
Why still delay?
Oh, we shall happy be,
When, from sin and sorrow free,
Lord, we shall live with thee,
Blest, blest for aye!

3. Bright, in that happy land,
Beams every eye;
Kept by a Father's hand,
Love cannot die.
Oh, then to glory run,
Be a crown and Kingdom won;
And bright above the sun,
We reign for aye.

284. [*Ives.*]

1. WHO are these in bright array,
This innumerable throng,
Round the altar night and day,
Hymning one triumphant song?
"Worthy is the Lamb once slain,
Blessing, honor, glory, power,
Wisdom, riches to obtain;
New dominion every hour."

2. These through fiery trials trod;
These from great afflictions came;
Now before the throne of God,
Sealed with His almighty name,
Clad in raiment pure and white,
Victor palms in every hand,
Through their dear Redeemer's might,
More than conquerors they stand.

3. Hunger, thirst, disease unknown,
On immortal fruits they feed;
Them, the Lamb amid the throne,
Shall to living fountains lead;
Joy and gladness banish sighs;
Perfect love dispels all fears,
And for ever from their eyes
God shall wipe away the tears.

285. [*Heaven is my Home.*]

1. I'M but a stranger here,
Heaven is my home;
Earth is a desert drear,
Heaven is my home;
Dangers and sorrows stand
Round me on every hand,
Heaven is my Fatherland,
Heaven is my home.

2. What though the tempest rage,
Heaven is my home;
Short is my pilgrimage;
Heaven is my home;
And time's wild, wintry blast
Soon will be over past,
I shall reach home at last;
Heaven is my home.

3. Therefore I murmur not,
Heaven is my home;
Whate'er my earthly lot,
Heaven is my home;
And I shall surely stand
There at my Lord's right hand,
Heaven is my Fatherland,
Heaven is my home.

286. [Around the Throne.]

1. AROUND the throne of God in heaven,
Thousands of children stand;
Children whose sins are all forgiven,
A holy, happy band;
Singing, Glory, Glory, Glory be to
God on high.

2. In flowing robes of spotless white,
See every one arrayed;
Dwelling in everlasting light,
And joys that never fade,
Singing, Glory, Glory, etc.

3. What brought them to that world
above—
That heaven so bright and fair,
Where all is peace, and joy, and love,
How came those children there.
Singing, Glory, Glory, etc.

4. Because the Saviour shed His blood
To wash away their sin;
Bathed in that pure and precious flood,
Behold them white and clean,
Singing, Glory, Glory, etc.

5. On earth they sought the Saviour's
grace,
On earth they loved His name;
So now they see His blessed face,
And stand before the Lamb,
Singing, Glory, Glory, etc.

287. [Evening Song, 10 Fresh Laurels.]

1. "Tis sweet to think, as nighteomes on,
Dark and drear,
Ere "stars come twinkling one by one,"
Earth to cheer

There is a world where comes no night,
It needs no sun or moon to light,
For Jesus' presence makes it bright—
No night there.

2. 'Tis sweet to think when round us lie,
Grief and care,
Our Jesus hears the softest sigh,
Breath'd in pray'r;
And if we love Him, we shall see,
That "land from sin and sorrow free,"
And oh! we know that there will be—
No tears there.

288. [Tune Return.]

1. RETURN, O wand'rer, to thy home,
Thy Father calls for thee;
No longer now an exile roam,
In guilt and misery;
Return, return!

2. Return, O wand'rer, to thy home,
'Tis Jesus calls for thee;
The Spirit and the Bride say—come;
Oh! now for refuge flee.

3. Return, O wand'rer, to thy home,
'Tis madness to delay;
There are no pardons in the tomb,
And brief is mercy's day.

289. [For Ever with the Lord.]

1. "FOR ever with the Lord!"
Amen, so let it be!
Life from the dead is in that word,
'Tis immortality.
CHO.—Here in the body pent,
Absent from Him I roam;

Yet nightly pitch my moving tent
A day's march nearer home;
Nearer home, nearer home,
A day's march nearer home.

2. My Father's house on high.
Home of my soul, how near
At times, to faith's foreseeing eye
Thy golden gates appear.
CHO.—Here in the body pent, etc.

3. "For ever with the Lord!"
—Father, if 'tis Thy will.
The promise of that faithful word,
Even here to me fulfill.
CHO.—Here in the body pent, etc.

290. [1C5 Trio.]

1. ASLEEP in Jesus! blessed sleep,
From which none ever wakes to weep;
A calm and undisturbed repose,
Unbroken by the last of foes.

2. Asleep in Jesus! oh, how sweet,
To be for such a slumber meet!
With holy confidence to sing
That death has lost its cruel sting.

3. Asleep in Jesus! peaceful rest,
Whose waking is supremely blest;
No fear, no woe, shall dim the hour
That manifests the Saviour's power.

4. Asleep in Jesus! oh, for me
May such a blissful refuge be;
Securely shall my ashes lie,
Waiting the summons from on high.

CHRISTIAN SONGS.

291. *[Bradbury Trio, 100.]*

1. From Greenland's icy mountains,
From India's coral strand,
Where Afric's sunny fountains
Roll down the golden sand—
From many an ancient river,
From many a palmy plain,
They call us to deliver
Their land from error's chain.

2. What though the spicy breezes
Blow soft o'er Ceylon's isle;
Though every prospect pleases,
And only man is vile:
In vain with lavish kindness
The gifts of God are strewn;
The heathen, in his blindness,
Bows down to wood and stone.

3. Shall we, whose souls are lighted
With wisdom from on high,
Shall we to men benighted
The lamp of life deny?
Salvation, O salvation!
The joyful sound proclaim,
Till each remotest nation
Has learned Messiah's name.

4. Waft, waft, ye winds, his story,
And you, ye waters, roll,
Till, like a sea of glory,
It spreads from pole to pole—
Till o'er our ransomed nature
The Lamb for sinners slain,
Redeemer, King, Creator,
In bliss returns to reign.

292. *[Bradbury Trio, 104.]*

1. The morning light is breaking,
The darkness disappears;
The sons of earth are waking
To penitential tears;
Each breeze that sweeps the ocean
Brings tidings from afar,
Of nations in commotion
Prepared for Zion's war.

2. Rich dews of grace come o'er us,
In many a gentle shower,
And brighter scenes before us
Are opening every hour:
Each cry to heaven going
Abundant answer brings,
And heavenly gales are blowing
With peace upon their wings.

3. See heathen nations bending
Before the God of love,
And thousand hearts ascending
In gratitude above:
While sinners now confessing,
The gospel's call obey,
And seek a Saviour's blessing,
A nation in a day.

4. Blest river of salvation,
Pursue thy onward way;
Flow thou to every nation,
Nor in thy richness stay;
Stay not till all the lowly
Triumphant reach their home,
Stay not till all the holy
Proclaim the Lord is come.

293. *[Tune Zion.]*

1. On the mountain's top appearing,
Lo! the sacred herald stands,
Welcome news to Zion bearing,
Zion long in hostile lands.
Mourning captive,
God himself shall loose thy bands.

2. Has thy night been long and mournful?
Have thy friends unfaithful proved?
Have thy foes been proud and scornful?
By thy sighs and tears unmoved?
Cease thy mourning;
Zion still is well beloved.

3. God, thy God, will now restore thee;
He Himself appears thy Friend;
All thy foes shall flee before thee;
Here their boasts and triumphs end;
Great deliverance
Zion's King will surely send.

4. Peace and joy shall now attend thee;
All thy warfare now is past;
God thy Saviour will defend thee;
Victory is thine at last;
All thy conflicts
End in everlasting rest.

294. [Sabbath.]

1. SAFELY thro' another week,
   God has brought us on our way;
   Let us now a blessing seek,
   Waiting in His courts to-day;
   Day of all the week the best,
   Emblem of eternal rest.

2. While we seek supplies of grace,
   Thro' the dear Redeemer's name,
   Show Thy reconciling face—
   Take away our sin and shame;
   From our worldly cares set free—
   May we rest this day in Thee.

3. Here we come Thy name to praise;
   Let us feel Thy presence near;
   May Thy glories meet our eyes,
   While we in Thy house appear;
   Here afford us, Lord, a taste
   Of our everlasting rest.

4. May the Gospel's joyful sound
   Wake our minds to raptures new;
   Let Thy victories abound—
   Unrepenting evils subdue;
   Thus let all our Sabbaths prove,
   Till we rest in Thee above.

295. [Beauteous Day, page 84.]

1. BLESSED Saviour, watch us, guard us,
   As we leave our "Sabbath home;"
   Guide, and keep us from all danger,
   Till again to thee we come.

2. Though we very often wander
   In the paths of vice and sin,
   Yet we pray t'ant T' ou wouldst hear us,
   Cleanse and make us pure within.

3. Make each spirit meek and lowly,
   Make us leave the ways of strife,
   Lead us in the path of duty,
   Lead us to the "better life."

4. Thus we'll serve Thee, blessed Saviour,
   Till we've crossed life's stormy sea,
   And with each loved friend and teacher,
   All are gathered home to thee.

296. [9 Trio or Greenville.]

1. LORD, dismiss us with Thy blessing,
   Fill our hearts with joy and peace;
   Let us each 'Thy love possessing,
   Triumph in Redeeming grace;
      Oh! refresh us,
   Travelling through this wilderness!

2. Thanks we give, and adoration,
   For Thy Gospel's joyful sound;
   May the fruits of Thy salvation
   In our hearts and lives abound!
      May Thy presence
   With us evermore be found.

3. So, whene'er the signal's given,
   Us from earth to call away;
   Borne on angel's wings to heaven,
   Glad to leave our cumbrous clay,
      May we, ready,
   Rise and reign in endless day!

297. [Milwaukee, page 151.]

1. SAVIOUR! breathe an evening blessing,
   Ere repose our eyelids seal;
   Sin and want we come confessing,
   Thou canst save, and Thou canst heal.

2. Though destruction walk around us,
   Though the arrows past us fly,
   Angel-guards from Thee surround us—
   We are safe, if Thou art nigh.

3. Though the night be dark and dreary,
   Darkness cannot hide from Thee;
   Thou art He who, never weary,
   Watcheth where Thy people be.

4. Should swift death this night o'ertake us,
   And our couch become our tomb,
   May the morn in heaven awake us,
   Clad in bright and deathless bloom.

298. [Evening Hymn, 29] Trio.]

1. GLORY to Thee, my God, this night,
   For all the blessings of the light;
   Keep me, O keep me, King of kings,
   Beneath the shadow of Thy wings.

2. Forgive me, Lord, for Thy dear Son,
   The ill which I this day have done;
   That with the world, myself, and Thee,
   I, ere I sleep, at peace may be.

3. Teach me to live, that I may dread
   The grave as little as my bed;
   Teach me to die, that so I may
   Rise glorious at the judgment-day.

4. O let my soul on Thee repose,
   And may sweet sleep mine eyelids close;
   Sleep, which shall me more vig'rous make,
   To serve my God, when I awake.

INDEX.

Titles in CAPS. First Lines in Roman.

A BEAUTIFUL land by faith	135
Abide with me! fast falls	49
Above the waves of earthly strife	124
A LAND WITHOUT A STORM	137
Alas! and did my Saviour bleed	205
A LIGHT IN THE WINDOW	52
All hail, the power of Jesus' name	202
All night long, till break of day	90
ALL TO CHRIST I OWE	182
Almost anchored, life's rough journey	115
ALMOST HOME	115
Amazing grace, how sweet the sound	207
AM I a Soldier of the Cross	211
AMSTERDAM	199
Another fleeting day is gone	153
ANTIOCH	201
Approach, my soul! the mercy seat	187
Around the throne of God	218
As Jesus Prayed	71
Asleep in Jesus! blessed sleep	218
A SONG FOR WATER	17
AUTUMN	184
AVISON	192
Awake, and sing the song	206
Awake, my soul, stretch every nerve	207
Awake, my soul, to joyful lays	205
BADEN	
BALMY DEW	197
BATTLE SONG	114
BEAUTIFUL EDEN	98
BEAUTIFUL RIVER	34
BEAUTIFUL ZION	20
BEECHER	87
Behold a stranger at the door	185
Behold me standing at the door	106
Behold ye a fountain that springs	4
HE JOYFUL IN GOD	47
Beyond the smiling and the weeping	51
Blessed Saviour, watch us, guard us	220
Blest be the tie that binds	213
BLUMENTHAL	181
Breaking through the clouds that gather	21
BRIGHT HOME ABOVE	102
BRIGHTLY GLEAMS OUR BANNER	29
By faith I view my Saviour dying	86
CAN my soul find rest	150
CHANTS	191, 194, 195
CHILDREN'S PRAYER	33
CHILD'S PRAYER	140
Christians, I am on my journey	162
Christian, the morn	190
CHRISTMAS	200
CHRISTMAS ANTHEM	128
CHRISTMAS CAROL	35
Christ, the Lord, is risen to-day	101, 110
CLOSER TO ME	81
Come, and join the glorious army	10
Come, burdened souls, with all	63
COME, CHILDREN, JOIN AND SING	134
Come, come to Jesus	131
COME LET US BE JOYFUL TO-DAY	31
COME LET US SING OF JESUS	183
COME LITTLE SOLDIERS	196
Come, my soul, thy suit prepare	181
COME, SING WITH HOLY GLADNESS	146
Come, Thou Almighty King	202
COME, THOU FOUNT	149
Come to Jesus, erring one	82
COME UNTO ME, (Chant)	194
COME, YE SINNERS	173
Come, ye thankful people	65
COMING TO JESUS	150
CROWN HIM WITH MANY CROWNS	79
Crown His head with endless blessings	77
CRUCIFIX	197
DARE TO DO RIGHT	54
DEAR JESUS NEAR ME	165
Dear Refuge of my weary soul	205
Dear Saviour, ever at my side	187
Depth of mercy, can there be	181
EARLY SEEKING	140
EASTER ANTHEM	110
ESSEX	85
EVEN ME	170
EVENTIDE	49
EVER TO THE RIGHT	171
EXPOSTULATION	199
FAR from these scenes of night	215
Far out on the desolate billow	126
Father above, Thou God of love	140
Father Thou art great and holy	163
FLEMMING	116
Forever with the Lord	218
FRANKLIN	197
FREE GRACE	164
From every stormy wind that blows	216
From Greenland's Icy Mountains	219
GENTLE Saviour, God of love	33
Give to the winds thy fears	215
GLORIA IN EXCELSIS, (Chant)	195
Glory be to God on high, (Chant)	195
GLORY, GLORY TO THE LAMB	104

INDEX.

Glory to Thee, my God, this night	220
Go and tell Jesus	53
God of mercy throned on high	117
Gone to the grave is our loved one	100
Go to Jesus with thy sorrow	138
Go work while you may	37
Greenville	200
Guidance	122
Guide me, O Thou great Jehovah	186
Guide us to Thee	169

HAIL to the brightness	209
Happy Day	198
Hark! hark, my soul	14, 38
Hark! the herald angels sing	77
Hark! the sweetest notes of angels	104
Hark! the voice of Jesus	108
Hark! what mean those holy voices	16
He leadeth me	148
He lives, the great Redeemer lives	203
Herald Angels	77
Here we throng to praise the Saviour	145
He shall reign forever	10
He will guide thee	138
Holly	119
Holy Father, thou hast taught me	184
Holy! holy! Lord God Almighty	141
Homeward Bound	199
Hosanna to the living Lord	25
How can I keep from singing	7
How firm a foundation	208
How gentle God's commands	214
How sweet the name of Jesus sounds	206
How sweet will be the welcome home	147
How we love to sing	92
Hymn Anthem	190
Hymns of grateful love	103

I AM waiting by the river	83
I heard the voice of Jesus say	159
I hear the Saviour say	182
I know that my Redeemer lives	114
I love to tell the story	127
I'm a Pilgrim	157
I'm a Pilgrim going home	162

I'm but a stranger here	217
I'm not ashamed to own my Lord	203
Immanuel's Land	175
In heavenly love abiding	61
In the rifted rock I'm resting	161
In the west the beams of day	67
In Zion's sacred gates	3
Is there one for me	186
I stood outside the gate	107
Italian Hymn	197
I think when I read that sweet	88
I was a wandering sheep	214

JACOB'S Prayer	90
Jerusalem, my happy home	217
Jerusalem the Golden	64
Jesus, dear, I come to Thee	166
Jesus, holy, undefiled	59
Jesus, I my cross have taken	211
Jesus is all	69
Jesus is our loving Saviour	121
Jesus, lover of my soul	204
Jesus loves a little child	166
Jesus, my all	75
Jesus, Saviour! I bear my call	179
Jesus shall reign where'er the sun	19
Jesus, tender Saviour	202
Jesus, the very thought of Thee	93
Jesus, the water of life will give	106
Jesus, to thy dear arms I flee	42
Jesus, we Thy lambs would be	43
Jesus who knows full well	125
Jewett	132
Joyfully, joyfully onward I move	208
Joyful the message of gospel grace	30
Joy to the world, the Lord is come	203
Just as I am without one plea	212

KEEP praying as you go	63
Keep Thou my way, O Lord	5
Kittredge	159

LAMB of God, I look to Thee	188
Land ahead! its fruits are waving	56

Latter Day	76
Leave me not, O blessed Saviour	174
Lebanon	198
Let Heaven with music ring	35
Let the words of my mouth	155
Life has many a pleasant hour	111
Lo! descending, the heavens rending	128
Looking at the Cross	66
Lord, abide with me	19
Lord, at Thy mercy seat	179
Lord, dismiss us with Thy blessing	220
Lord, do not leave me	144
Lord, I hear of showers of blessings	170
Lord's Day	101
Loud hallelujahs to the Lord	201
Loud swell in choral numbers	99
Love at Home	120
Love divine, all love excelling	185
Loving Kindness	200
Lubila	93
Lyman	3

MAJESTIC sweetness sits enthroned	205
Mansions are prepared above	186
Marching along	94
Marching on	130
Martyrdom	201
May I come in	106
Meet me in that lovely land	89
Mercy, O Thou Son of David	149
Mercy's Free	86
Meribah	198
Metropolis	196
'Mid scenes of confusion	154
Milwaukee	151
More love to Thee, O Christ	41
Morning Red	156
Mountain of the Lord	70
Mt. Blanc	9
Must Jesus bear the cross alone	214
My country, 'tis of thee	126
My days are gliding swiftly by	4
My faith looks up to Thee	207
My home is there	206
My Jesus, as Thou wilt	132

INDEX.

My life flows on in endless song	7
My Sabbath Home	20
My Sabbath Song	50
My Shepherd	144
My soul be on thy guard	216
My soul to Christ I bring	69
NEARER, my God, to Thee	210
Never alone	226
Never be afraid	8
No mortal eye that land hath seen	178
No sorrow there	198
Not dreary the world we inhabit	129
Nothing either great or small	214
Now I lay me down to sleep	67
Now the Saviour standeth pleading	173
OFT when the waves of passion rise	211
Oh a goodly thing is the cooling	139
Oh could I find from day to day	213
Oh do not be discouraged	79
Oh do not let the word depart	162
Oh happy day that fixed my choice	213
Oh heavenly Guest, Thy call I hear	106
Oh holy Saviour, Friend unseen	116
Oh how happy are they	24
Oh how He loves	160
Oh, if my house is built upon a rock	68
Oh Lamb of God, come in	106
Oh land of rest for thee I sigh	170
Oh Paradise!	72
Oh sacred Head, now wounded	204
Oh! the happy time is coming	17
Oh! the sweet wonders of that cross	205
Oh Thou whose tender mercy hears	214
Oh turn ye, oh turn ye	208
Oh what can you tell little pebble	142
Oh! what shall I do to be saved	143
Oliver	200
One more day's work for Jesus	78
One there is above all others	160
On the mountain's top appearing	219
Onward, Christian Soldiers	168
Onward, Christian, though the region	76
Onward! Onward!	39
One by one the sands are flowing	176
Our Father, who art in Heaven (Chant)	194
Our Saviour is risen	18
Our Shepherd	152
Our weary days will soon be over	88
Out on an ocean all boundless	209
PASS me not, O gentle Saviour	27
Peacefully rest	153
Peaceful shore	74
Peace on earth	109
Pilgrim Band	196
Portuguese Hymn	199
Praise the Lord	118
Praise the Lord (Chant)	193
Praise ye the Father!	116
Press close, my child, to me	81
Prostrate, dear Jesus at Thy feet	212
RETREAT	198
Return O wanderer, to thy home	218
Rise, my soul, and stretch thy wings	210
Revive us again	23
Rock of Ages	158
Rothwell	201
SABBATH Welcome	96
Safe in the arms of Jesus	13
Safely through another week	220
Safe within the vail	56
Saviour bless a little child	165
Saviour, blessed Saviour	189
Saviour, breathe an evening blessing	220
Saviour care for me	174
Saviour, ever near	152
Saviour, like a Shepherd	152
Saviour, listen to our prayer	150
Saviour, Thou art ever dear	140
Saviour, Thy dying love	11
Saviour, who died for me	156
Saviour, who Thy flock art feeding	151
See, and the winter's snow	167
See Jesus standing at the door	82
Seeking Jesus	45
Shall hymns of grateful love	103
Shall we anchor	55
Shall we gather at the river	20
Shall we meet beyond the river	74
Shall we sing in heaven	105
Shout aloud for joy	94
Shout the glad tidings	192
Sing always	48
Sing with a tuneful spirit	48
Softly now the light of day	119
Something for Jesus	11
Something to do in heaven	44
Sometimes a light surprises	16
Songs of praise the angels sang	85
Sound the battle cry	62
Sterling	176
St. George	65
Stand up, my soul, shake off thy fears	216
Still pressing on	129
Still, still with Thee	26
Strains of music often greet me	50
Strike, strike for victory	28
Strike the harp of Zion	12
Submission	82
Sunday School Volunteer Song	40
Sun of my soul	172
Sweet home	154
Sweet hour of prayer	59
Sweet Sabbath School, more dear to me	6
Sweet Story	86
Sweet the moments	180
TAKE thy staff and journey onward	15
Tell me the old, old story	80
Thalberg	161
That beautiful land	135
The beauteous day	84
The better land	113
The Bridegroom comes	21
The bright forever	24
The children are gathering	94
The children's Saviour	121
The chorus of praise	142
The cooling spring	139
The dear ones all at home	51
Tree of life	98
The God who spanned the heavens	98

223

INDEX.

The Golden Shore	112
The Good Old Way	22
The Happy Time	17
The Head that once was crowned	203
The House upon a Rock	68
The Joyful Message	30
The Land Beyond the River	178
The Land to which we go	111
The Little Wanderer	43
The Lord my Shepherd is	204
The Lord, our God, is faithful	93
The Lord's Prayer (*Chant*)	194
The mansions of the blest	123
The morning light is breaking	219
The Old, Old Story	80
The Penitent	150
The Praise of Jesus' Name	99
There is a fountain filled with blood	213
There is a glorious world of light	163
There is a happy land	217
There is an hour of peaceful rest	215
There is beauty all around	120
There is Life for a Look	60
There is work to do for Jesus	32
There'll be something in heaven	44
There's a Home weary Pilgrim	15
There's a gentle voice within calls away	58
There's a light in the window	52
There's a Room and a Welcome for all	4
The Rifted Rock	61
The Saints' Sweet Home	123
The sands of time are sinking	175
The Saviour's Praise	145
The Sweetest Name	36
The voice of free grace	164
The Water of Life	42
The Welcome Home	147
They are going down the valley	100
Thine, Lord, Forever	88
Thou art my Shepherd	117
Though all the world my choice	144
Through the world we daily roam	206
Thy way, not mine, O Lord	45
'Tis sweet to think as night comes on	169
To-day the Saviour calls	218
To Jesus I will go	212
To Thee, our God and Saviour	58
Traveller, whither art thou going	161
Trust in God	137
Turn to the Lord and live	93
"Twill not be long	95
	97

V

Varina	163

W

Waiting Saviour	82
Walbridge	95
Ware	197
We are but little children weak	26
We are coming, Blessed Saviour	91
We are going forth with our staff	22
We are going, we are going	102
We are living, we are dwelling	76
We are marching on with shield	40
We are on our journey home	9
We are out on an ocean sailing	112
We are watching, we are waiting	84
We bring no glittering treasures	210
We'll wait till Jesus comes	170
We praise Thee, O God	23
We're going home	88
We're travelling home to heaven above	215
We shall meet	133
We sing His love, who once was slain	207
We speak of the realms of the blest	73
We welcome this beautiful Sabbath	96
What are these soul reviving strains	136
What shall I do to be there	73
What shall I do to be saved	143
What sinners value I resign	207
When I survey the wondrous cross	204
When marshalled on the nightly plain	212
When mourning o'er my sense of guilt	66
When Thou, my righteous Judge	212
Whither, pilgrims, are you going	113
Who are these in bright array	167
Why not to-night	162
Why weepest thou	57
With Gladsome Feet we press	201
Williams	119
With tearful eyes I look (*Chant*)	194
Woodland	196
Work for the night is coming	216
Work to do for Jesus	32

Y

Yes! a brighter morn is breaking	70
Ye valiant soldiers of the cross	49

Z

Zion's Hill	136

www.ingramcontent.com/pod-product-compliance
Lightning Source LLC
Chambersburg PA
CBHW020813230426
43666CB00007B/996